Moving On

Moving On

New Perspectives on the Women's Movement

edited by
Tayo Andreasen, Anette Borchorst, Drude Dahlerup,
Eva Lous, Hanne Rimmen Nielsen

ACTA JUTLANDICA LXVII:1
Humanities Series 66

AARHUS UNIVERSITY PRESS

Copyright: Aarhus University Press, 1991
Printed in Denmark by Phønix a /s, Aarhus
ISBN 87 7288 368 5
ISSN 0065 1354 (Acta Jutlandica)
ISSN 0106 0556 (Humanities Series)

AARHUS UNIVERSITY PRESS
Building 170, Aarhus University
DK-8000 Aarhus C, Denmark

Cover:
Henrik B. Andersen,
Farvel til P-klassicisme
(Goodbye to P-Classicism), 1990.

Photo credits:
Photo archive of the Tampere City Museums (Finland): 39, 41, 45, 47
Women's History Archive, Aarhus (Denmark): 70, 74
Local History Archive, Aarhus (Denmark): 95, 98, 103, 106, 109, 117
P.E. Blume: 130, 131
University Library, Trondheim (Norway): 146, 149
Jesper Vig: 166
Liisa Alatalo: 210

Preface

1990 was a special year for the Danish Women's Movement and for Women's Studies in Denmark. 1990 was the 75th anniversary of women's suffrage in Denmark. It was 20 years since the start of the core organization of the new Women's Movement, the Redstockings. And we could celebrate the 15th anniversary of the official acknowledgement of the word "Kvindeforskning" ("Women's Studies") as part of the Danish language.

So it was the right year to organize the conference: "New Theoretical Perspectives on the Study of the Women's Movements", which was held at Sostrup Castle in Denmark, October 28—November 1, 1990.

The articles in this book are all but one revised editions of the papers presented at the Sostrup Castle Conference.

The participants of the Conference were scholars who are engaged in research on the Women's Movement. Mostly they were historians, sociologists, political scientists and anthropologists.

The book is edited and published by the Danish *"Women's Movement Project"*, which also organized the Conference. This project is an interdisciplinary coalition of scholars doing research on the Women's Movement. The domicile of the project is the University of Aarhus and the State Library in Aarhus, which contains the *Women's History Archive*.

The women involved in the "Women's Movement Project" are listed at the end of the book together with notes on the contributors to this anthology.

We want to thank the authors for their part in making the conference a success and for their readiness to revise their papers for this book. We also want to thank Anette Riber, who typed and edited the manuscripts. Ida Warburg read the proofs of the book and Kirsten Busck Mellor who translated the articles by Ann-Dorte Christensen and Hanne Rimmen Nielsen, and part of the article by Karin Lützen and served as language editor of the book.

The Learned Society of Aarhus has supported the publication of the book.

Aarhus, October 1991

Tayo Andreasen

Contents

Introduction

Tayo Andreasen, Anette Borchorst, Drude Dahlerup,
Eva Lous, Hanne Rimmen Nielsen

There has always been a Women's Movement this century—this is the title of a book about the English Women's Movement, written by Dale Spender, herself a long time feminist activist (Spender, 1983).

This expression could also have been the title of this book: It focuses on the idea that the history of the Women's Movement is characterized more by continuity than discontinuity, even though the movement has different historical faces.

The Women's Movement should be regarded as a broad and heterogeneous movement—although always based on some kind of protest against the subjection of women and on the solidarity between women.

This anthology puts forth some empirical and theoretical results of research that deal with the Women's Movement. Much more empirical research is needed to excavate the history of the Women's Movement all over the world. This book will tell the story of women's hard work for new forms of life in some countries in Western Europe and the USA. However, the primary aim of the book is to contribute to the theoretical debate on *how* to study the Women's Movements. The articles discuss and demonstrate several new theoretical and methodological approaches to the study of the Women's Movements.

We shall start this introduction with a discussion of the crucial question: What is the Women's Movement and what is feminism? After that we will discuss different approaches to the study of the Women's Movement.

What Is the Women's Movement—What Is Feminism?

Should we choose a broad or a narrow definition of the Women's Movement? Lately this has been the subject of a lively debate; see, e.g., Offen, 1988; Dubois et al., 1989).

In the Women's Movement itself, there have been constant debates about who was to be considered part of the Movement? The women's organizations that considered themselves part of the Women's Movement have been numerous in some historical periods, scarce in others.

A broad or a narrow definition of the Women's Movement is of consequence not only for the subject of women's studies, but also for the approaches and the research strategies.

By choosing a narrow definition of the Women's Movement, we risk enforcing a contemporary, i.e. anachronistic, political attitude on women's activities and organizations in earlier historical periods. This means that "we" decide beforehand where to find the emancipatory potentials and the correct political direction. In other words, "we" identify the "real" Women's Movement. Besides, this cuts off obvious areas of research from the general research in the Women's Movement, and leaves them to scholars with other concerns.

If we choose a broad definition, then the Women's Movement consists of different historical and contemporary expressions of women's activities, social needs, and efforts in feminism and in policies concerning women. The study of the Women's Movement must encompass a wide variety of organizations and networks, such as women's trade unions, women's political organizations within and outside the political parties, charities and religious associations, Women's Co-operative Guilds and Women's Institutes, the "grand old" women's rights organizations, local and social associations and communities and the variety of organizational efforts of the "new" Women's Movement. The articles included in this anthology deal with a broad variety of women's organizations, old and new, in the United States and Western and Northern European countries.

Should, however, all the women's organizations and groups mentioned above be considered part of the Women's Movement? One could also argue for a narrower definition of the Women's Movement, only including those that are *feminist*. At any rate, "the women's movement" and "feminism" are not synonymous, since the word feminism connotes an *ideology* (like liberalism or socialism), whereas the women's movement signifies an *activity*. A narrow definition of the Women's Movement limits the phenomenon to those activities that express feminist ideas. The next question is of course how to define feminism.

In recent years, the concept of feminism and the construction of a typology of different feminist traditions have been subject to much debate. *Richard Evans'* definition of feminism (Evans, 1977: 39) as "the doctrine of equal rights for women, based on the theory of the equality of the sexes" takes us no further, because what is "equality of the sexes"? *Olive Banks* understands the feminist movement as "any groups that have tried to change the position of women, or the ideas about women" (1981: 3). This broad definition, however, does not exclude anti-feminists, and this is a problem. *Nancy Cott* has three components in her interesting working definition of feminism: first feminism represents an opposition to the sex hierarchy, second the belief that women's condition is socially constructed—and not predestined by Nature or God—and third the perception that women constitute a social grouping, an identification with the group "women" (Cott, 1987, see also Cott, 1989).

In our opinion—and contrary to Cott's viewpoint—this definition seems useful and applicable for 20th as well as 19th century feminism and for American as well as European feminism.

Only a few of the women's organizations and Women's Movements in history will be able to live up to such a decisive definition. But that does not mean that these organizations and movements did not have any feminist potential. We wish to suggest that the women's movements are placed in a continuum according to the persuasiveness of the feminist impulses in the individual movement at different historical periods. This means that the discussion will not hinge on the validity of characterizing the individual organizations as clearly feminist or not, but rather on the strength and character of the feminist and emancipatory elements in the organization and the movement as such at a given point in history.

A Plurality of Approaches

The nature of the Women's Movement in a way demands research by many different academic disciplines. As all other social movements, the Women's Movement embraces more than its organizational expressions. It is a *movement* in society. *Social movement theory* makes the important distinction between a movement and its organizations and centres. Seen this way, the Women's Movement represents conscious, collective activities to change women's position, often including a challenge to male dominance and the values and norms that oppress women (Dahlerup, 1986: 2).

Defined in this way, feminist writers, feminist literary circles, feminist theater groups as well as feminist summer camps and new ways of living are also part of the Women's Movement. It is exactly this characteristically broad spectrum of activities of the Women's Movement throughout history that makes research on the Women's Movement so open to and appropriate for interdisciplinary studies.

Therefore, it is important not to limit the study of the Women's Movement to organizations, although these are important parts of the Movement's history. A broader *cultural approach* is useful in the study of the Women's Movement. If the starting point is a broad definition of the Women's Movement, then it becomes even more important to include studies of women's networks in their everyday lives and local communities of women. Research that starts with women's everyday lives will give an idea of women's potential resources for changing their situation.

The articles in this book demonstrate different approaches to the study of the Women's Movement. In the following we shall give a short presentation of these approaches: new ways of looking at the public/private dichotomy, studies of women's culture, studies of the ideologies of different groups of women, and structural analyses comparing the movement in different historical periods in one country, or cross-national comparative analyses.

Let us just mention a couple of other approaches to the study of the Women's Movement that are being discussed today.

Whereas studies of the ideologies, strategies and activities of women's movements are well-known in research in this field, studies of the *impact* of the movements have been given little attention. Maybe, because this approach raises some very difficult methodological questions: How can we separate the effect of the movement from the effect of those social forces which gave rise to the movement?

The dramatic change of the "new" Women's Movement since the beginning of the 1970s has encouraged studies of the Movement's own transformation and its impact in the short as well as in the long run. Impact on what?

Because of the broad agenda of the Women's Movement, many aspects are important: the Movement's impact on the discourse about women, on the political agenda, and on those who participated in the movement. And what about the impact on women in general, who, in fact, make up the main target group of the new Women's Movement in most countries? According to Jane Jenson, the main importance of the new Women's Movement was that it created a new collective identity among women and changed the political discourse about women (Jenson, 1985).

The discussion about movement impact is inspired by the fact that the core organizations of the "new" Women's Movement have declined, while feminism is still alive. The same questions of movement impact are, however, also relevant for the studies of the Women's Movement in other historical periods. We could also start asking other simple questions, which require complex approaches, like this one: what was the impact of women's suffrage—not only for the party system, but also for women and their daughters?

The rise of the new Women's Movement has put studies in the Women's Movement on the agenda in a new way. The "new" Women's Movement has now grown so old (approximately 20 years) that we see an increasing interest in the study of the Movement as a historical phenomenon and in a scholarly context. This interest puts the study of the "old" Women's Movement into a new perspective. For instance, the question of continuity and disruption in the history of the Women's Movement is highly relevant here. To which degree do the old and the new Women's Movements represent comparable or totally different efforts and ideas? The personal experiences of scholars researching the Women's Movement make *a generational perspective* obvious when it comes to the history of the Women's Movement. Will the generational perspective provide an access to the understanding of the waves that have characterized the history of the Women's Movement. Does the interest in the generations of the Women's Movement together with the renaissance of the biographical genre reflect our own need to understand the subjective and psychological motivations for women's engagement in the women's struggle then and now? (For studies based on a generational approach, see Ware, 1981; Banks, 1986).

This book is written by scholars representing different academic disciplines. Literary historians and psychologists are, however, not represented in this book, although their contributions are also important for the interdisciplinary endeavour to analyse the Women's Movement from many different points of view.

Reading the articles in this book, it is not always possible to guess the academic background of the specific authors. Perhaps it is a characteristic of the study of the Women's Movement that the widespread and challenging nature of its activities attract scholars from many different disciplines and leads us to explore the borders of our own long established disciplines.

The Public-Private Dichotomy

Jane Rendall's article "Nineteenth Century Feminism and the Separation of Spheres" surveys the ways in which Women's Studies uses this important terminology. She describes the development of various approaches to women's history: At first, women's history emphasized the rediscovery of the private worlds of women, the women's cultures, then the efforts concerned an examination of the relations between the two spheres. In the 1980s, two approaches have prevailed: on the one hand, the poststructuralist attempt to dissolve the distinction, to see it as an ever changing construction. On the other hand, feminist historians have tried to reinstall the dichotomy with a focus on the public sphere and the meaning of gender herein. The question now is what these new approaches will mean to the research on the Women's Movement, especially the Women's Movement of the eighteenth and nineteenth centuries. Jane Rendall suggests three different ways in which to reread the history of feminism in England, focusing on: 1) the complex relationship between liberalism and feminism, 2) the involvement of working-class women in the local community and in the public arena, and 3) the relationship between British feminism and British nationalism and imperialism.

Aino Saarinen's article "Patronesses, Gentlewomen, Feminists—and Common Wives" examines the structures which at one and the same time presented obstacles to and opened up opportunities for the political activities of upper-class women in Tampere, Finland during the latter half of the nineteenth century. The distinction between public and private—which Jane Rendall discusses in terms of theory—is debated here on the basis of empirical data.

The article examines how upper-class women came up with political demands which served to engage them on the political arena (the content aspect). Furthermore, the article examines the way in which they exerted their influence (the form aspect). In this local context, the connections between gender, class and nationality appear evident and complex at the same time.

Women's Culture

Several of the articles in this anthology study the phenomenon of women's culture in the Women's Movement and in the lives of women. However, the semantics of the term "women's culture" vary significantly.

In their article "Women's Culture and the Continuity of the Women's Movement", *Leila Rupp* and *Verta Taylor* opt for a narrow definition of women's culture as a specifically feminist culture in the Movement. The function of the women's culture was and is to create a collective identity among the participants, and this happens first and foremost through the values, rituals, personal relations between the women, and through separate organizations in which women participate. This type of women's culture plays a particularly important role in the survival of the Movement in so-called abeyance phases.

Rupp and Taylor discuss three cases: 1) the international Women's Movement in the first half of this century, 2) the American Women's Rights Movement in the 1940s and 1950s, and 3) contemporary lesbian feminism. In all three historical situations women's culture has helped the Movement to survive in spite of a hostile environment. At the same time, however, the women's culture has encouraged internal conflicts in the Movement, conflicts about identity, i.e. nationality, the character of the organization, class, race, and sexuality.

Hanne Rimmen Nielsen has a broader definition of women's culture in her article "Christian and Competent Schoolmistresses". The article is an empirical analysis of the women's culture at a christian teacher training college for women in the Danish provincial town of Aarhus. Her aim is to provide a perspective of cultural totality for a group of women in their everyday lives and their activities in the Women's Movement in the local context. The analysis is based on a definition of women's culture which embraces four dimensions: the space of the women's culture, the ideas of the women's culture, its interaction with the general culture, and the dynamics in the women's culture. Hanne Rimmen Nielsen shows how this women's culture contributed to a collective identity among the women teachers and students at the beginning of the century. Later, in the 1930s and 1940s, the women's culture gradually dissolved because of external resistance and internal dynamics. The young generation of women teachers came to see the women's culture as an anachronistic solution to the problems of modern femininity.

In her article "Spinsters and Families" *Karin Lützen* examines the sexual aspect of the women's culture. To be sure, she does not use the term women's culture, but she does place herself solidly within a broad cultural approach to the history of the Women's Movement. She analyses the communities and "homes" that unmarried, philantropical women established in Copenhagen around the turn of the century, especially with a view to "saving" young, "fallen" working-class women. The unmarried, philantropical women, who often lived as couples, i.e. two women together in a relationship which lasted a life-time, nonetheless aimed at socializing young women to live in heterosexual, nuclear families. Hereby Karin Lützen describes the construction of heterosexuality, as it is—paradoxically—promoted by women who themselves lived in homosocial relationships. At the same time Karin Lützen's article, like the one before it, points to factors that encouraged the dissolution of the women's culture from within, the internal dynamics in the women's culture.

The Ideas of the Women's Movement

The article "Women's Ideology: Difference, Equality or a New Femininity" by *Kari Melby* renews the examination of the concepts of Equality/Difference. On the basis of an empirical study of the organizations of women teachers and nurses, she identifies some characteristic differences in the professional strategies of the two groups. Both groups employed arguments of difference *and* equality, but in characteristically different ways. While the women teachers argued that their femininity was a resource, the nurses modelled themselves on the male version of professionalism. She shows, how the differences depended on the different social and cultural contexts, in which the two groups were placed. Kari Melby sees a close connection between the discussion of women's ideologies and the discussion of who the feminists were. But her discussion proves just how difficult it is to reach a clearcut definition of the concept of feminism without leaving out large and important women's organizations.

In her article "Women in the New Peace Movement in Denmark" *Ann-Dorte Christensen* deals with an important part of the new Women's Movement that has appeared in the 1980s. She identifies different groups and generations of women in her empirical study of women's peace movement in the provincial town of Aalborg. She argues that the ideological differences between the groups are determined by differences in the everyday lives of the women, their experiences in the labor force and their family background. The political identities of the women are based on and divided into the three classical goals: equal worth, equal rights and liberation. It is, however, remarkable that the ideological differences have not in practice resulted in conflict among the women in the peace movement. Instead the different goals have made possible the recruitment of different groups of women and their experience of empowerment and political identity.

Joyce Outshoorn's article "A Distaste of Dirty Hands: Gender and Politics in Second-Wave Feminism" discusses the concept of politics in relation to the new Women's Movement. She takes as her point of departure a specific case, viz. the Dutch feminist conference in 1982 "Feminism and Political Power". In the article she takes a closer look at the papers of the conference, the disagreements among the women and the new tendencies signalled by the conference. Her analysis of one of the important papers, with "Struggle in the Public Sphere: Necessary, but no Fun" clearly shows the disinclination to engage in a political task in the public sphere, to learn the necessary "masculine" skills. This also indicates how old concepts of femininity and women's politics have survived in the new Women's Movement. Old and new ideas of politics exist side by side in the Movement, but nonetheless the ambivalence signalled the entry of women into the traditional political institutions.

Social Structure and Women's Movement

In her article "The Gender System" *Yvonne Hirdmann* argues that there is a growing conflict between the sexes. She uses the concept "gender system" to characterize different historical periods of sexual contracts in Sweden. The period from 1930 to 1960 was dominated by a housewife contract, the period from 1965 to 1975 by a contract of equality, and from 1975 to 1989 by an equal status contract. In all these periods women have been defined as the problem, and they have been forced into an ideological dilemma, viz. that of women's sameness versus their difference. The household has played an important political role, and the democratic development as well as the economy has been crucial for the power relations of the sexes.

Solveig Bergman's article "Researching the Women's Movement" discusses a series of methodological problems in research concerning the new Women's Movement. Her starting point is her own comparative study of the new Women's Movement in Finland and Western Germany she argues that comparative studies will enable us to find out how each country's specific socio-structural conditions have shaped the social movements in general and the feminist movement in particular. Comparative studies will also make it easier to distinguish the effects of the Women's Movement from the effects of more general social change. Solveig Bergman advocates a broad definition of feminism, so as not to make invisible large sections of the Movement, which in countries like Finland have been channelled through the political parties and the established Women's Movement. In an account of the empirical results of her research she shows that the new Finnish and German Women's Movements have been each other's opposites. The great differences between the two national movements are accounted for in structural terms, for instance variations in the women's political participation and their relation to the labor market, and in the political culture and in the position of the New Left. Recent development is characterized, however, by a certain converging of the two systems.

This collection of articles demonstrates the scope, the openness to new approaches, and the interdisciplinary dialogue of contemporary research in the Women's Movement. We hope that the anthology will provide inspiration for further scholarship, and we expect that many fascinating efforts will see the light of day in the years to come—hopefully in a more global context than the one that we have been able to provide in this anthology.

16

References

Banks, Olive (1981), *Faces of Feminism. A Study of Feminism as a Social Movement*, Oxford: Martin Robertson.

Banks, Olive (1986), *Becoming a Feminist. The Social Origins of "First Wave" Feminism*, Brighton: Wheatsheaf Books.

Cott, Nancy F. (1987), *The Grounding of Modern Feminism*, New Haven & London: Yale University Press.

Cott, Nancy F. (1989), "What's in a Name? The Limits of "Social Feminism" or, Expanding the Vocabulary of Women's History", *The Journal of American History*, vol. 76, no. 3.

Dahlerup, Drude (1986), *The New Women's Movement, Feminism and Political Power in Europe and the USA*, London: Sage Publications.

DuBois, Ellen C. & Nancy F. Cott (1989), "Comments on Karen Offen's "Defining Feminism: A Comparative Historical Approach", *Signs*, vol. 15, no. 1.

Evans, Richard (1977), *The Feminists*, London: Croom Helm.

Jenson, Jane (1985), "Struggling for Identity: The Women's Movement and the State in Western Europe", *West European Politics*, vol. 8, no. 4.

Offen, Karen (1988), "Defining Feminism: A Comparative Historical Approach", *Signs*, vol. 14, no. 1.

Spender, Dale (1983), *There's Always Been a Women's Movement This Century*, London: Pandora Press.

Ware, Susan (1981), *Beyond Suffrage. Women in the New Deal*, Cambridge, Mass. & London: Harvard University Press.

Nineteenth Century Feminism
and the Separation of Spheres:
Reflections on the Public/Private Dichotomy

Jane Rendall

Beyond Public and Private

The notion of 'separate spheres' represents, it seems to me, one very specific—middle-class, western, and nineteenth century—variant of the public-private dichotomy. In that period, it is easy to find uses of this circular metaphor, both dualistic and confining. I take some international examples at random. Anna Barbauld, writing of women's education, spoke of the "uniform tenor and confined circle" of their lives (Barbauld, 1826). In its decree outlawing women's clubs in November 1793, the French National Convention ordained that:

Each sex is called to the kind of occupation which is fitting for it; its action is circumscribed within this circle which it cannot break through, because nature, which has imposed these limits on man, commands imperiously and receives no law. (Quoted from Levy et al., 1979: 215).

In 1835, Alexis de Tocqueville wrote of that 'narrow circle of domestic interests and duties' to which public opinion confined the married woman, in his *Democracy in America* (Kerber, 1988: 10).

Here I want to concentrate less on the confining, restrictive aspects of that metaphor: but to talk rather about the theme of separation, and about what has been happening to this binary view of women's history and the history of feminism. I shall be talking mainly about the nineteenth century: and I shall take the theme of separate spheres as one application—though a critical one in the history of western feminism—of the public/private distinction.

In an important essay written in 1983 Carole Pateman began by stating that "the dichotomy between the private and the public is central to almost two centuries of feminist writing and political struggle; it is ultimately what the feminist movement is about". Yet that public/private distinction has over the last ten years been substantially undermined by the variety of deconstructive techniques applied to it, not least by Pateman herself. If she is right, and that central core of writing and of struggle has been displaced—then we are all embarked on a difficult process of rethinking and restructuring. As she has shown, the distinction between public and private lives—which could be translated into the opposition between public and domestic worlds, and in the nineteenth century the notion of separate spheres—has become an increasingly slippery one.

The debate has taken place in different disciplines. Political philosophers, such as Pateman, looking particularly at liberal ideologies, have demonstrated how clearly the dichotomy familiar to us in the twentieth century was rooted in a particular form of liberal patriarchalism, recognizable from the seventeenth century onwards: one which was to mystify the realities of a growing western capitalist society, and obscure the actuality of dominance and subordination (Pateman, 1988). Twenty years ago, an influential anthropologist Michelle Rosaldo posited that that dichotomy might be of universal validity: ten years ago she expressed a scepticism of that earlier view (Rosaldo, 1974; 1980). But I am interested especially in the ways in which the terminology of public and private worlds has been used in a historical context. Here for the sake of clarity I suggest how different approaches to the problem in women's history have developed over time, simultaneously and in reaction to each other: I am not implying that each does not still contribute to our understanding of the past. I see four possible approaches dominating the picture.

First has been the challenging of the relative worth attached to public and private spheres in orthodox historical writing. The recovery of the private world of women in the past, of women's culture and women's relationships, proved an immensely rich and fertile area of writing. Through this we have begun to look at the networks that bound women together. These might be in the lesbian friendships that may be reconstructed, in the literate and letter-writing circles of early 19th century New England, or among the British aristocracy, or in the collective influence of the women of nineteenth century French rural communities, reconstructed through ethnographic evidence (Smith-Rosenberg, 1975; Cott, 1977; Segalen, 1983; Jalland, 1986). The study of "women's culture" could be linked to anthropology and to the study of symbolic forms and representations, in the innovative approaches of the new cultural history. Yet there have been notes of criticism too, most recently—satisfying though such reconstructions might be, did they not run the risk of ignoring the realities of power in each society, the violence and inequality that existed between the different worlds of women and men? (Dauphin et al., 1980).

Secondly, the stress on separation, on emphasizing the boundaries between public and private worlds has obscured and mystified the important relationships *between* those worlds. The personal has been charted as the politics of relationships, the political as incorporating the hierarchy of gender relations. In some sense this absorbed what was at its simplest level a unifying commitment of the feminism of the 1970s and 80s: that the personal was political. So in an important work which might be seen as coming out of the second stage I have illustrated, the historians of the nineteenth century English middle classes—Leonore Davidoff and Catherine Hall—carefully traced *not* the separation of spheres between women and men but the real interaction of public and private life: for them the growth of industrial capitalism, the formation of

Middle-class women in the private sphere: Drawing-room of a middle-class or upper middle-class home in the 1860s.

class and class consciousness were never merely events of the public sphere. For an integral part of the creation of that class was the construction of new patterns of gender difference (Davidoff et al., 1987). Here there are important shifts, in the writing not only of women's history, but the history of gender differences. Public and private spheres were shown to be integrally related: gender distinctions were not the biological distinctions of sex, but socially and culturally constructed, clearly rooted in time and place.

Such work, historically and theoretically rooted, moved the discussion to new levels. I see two paths developing in the late 1980s. In one, the very concept of the binary opposition, of dichotomous categories, an important but constraining inheritance from our past, was challenged (Pateman, 1989; Bock, 1991). These distinctions, between public and private, public and domestic, the natural and the cultural, were not only ideological constructions, the artefacts of a masculine culture, but also confining straitjackets. It seemed no longer enough simply to trace their historical origins, and to challenge the nature of the dichotomy. It had become important to find a way of writing historically which was both conscious of yet freer from assumptions derived from the orthodoxies of western culture and politics.

One important route to that end was of course outlined by Joan Scott, who in the search for a more fruitful kind of epistemology, deployed the insights of post-structuralism. In her writings, concepts—such as those of public and private—are not fixed, shared, held in common by all members of specific societies: but shifting, constantly in process, created by the acts of reader and of user. The way is open for a different kind of analysis of politics, as the arena in which new meanings—as of gender difference—are constructed, resisted, challenged. And the analysis of gender difference becomes one in which oppositions, of male/female, public/private, nature/culture—cannot be seen as rigid, but blurring, overlapping, concealing heterogeneity and difference (Scott, 1988: Introduction).

By the late 1980s, these questions were being addressed not only at a theoretical level but in concrete and important studies grounded in empirical material. The work of economic historians, Alice Kessler-Harris and others, has shown how far a dichotomous lens can distort understanding of the lives of women of different class, racial and ethnic backgrounds. Models of public and private which are rooted in a particular social and cultural pattern are applied by the feminist historian to the world of the wage-earning woman in the United States in the 20th century—in whose life the differences of ethnicity, race and class, might loom as large as gender differences. Indeed she points to a degree of romanticism in analyses relying on the common concerns of gender. Where gender differences are to be identified as *central* ones, then the binary vision is perpetuated as historical data is organized in that way. Important studies of the extension of domestic values into the world of work rest on the self-confirming assumptions of the historian: different paradigms may produce very different results. She suggests that what may be needed is to understand not "a single necessary dichotomy, but ... a set of intersecting circles of experience that together structure consciousness" (Kessler-Harris, 1990: 67; Turbin, 1989).

Yet this critique in itself has not gone unchallenged. In the second path taken in the late 1980s, the public/private dichotomy has been reinstated, in two important recent studies by Joan Landes (1988) and Mary Ryan (1990), works that focus unwaveringly on the public sphere, from the perspective of feminist historians. Ryan suggests that the obituaries are premature, that the strength and pervasiveness of the concepts in western culture still deserve our attention. Both are writing of the creation of a bourgeois public sphere in western Europe and in the US, drawing upon the work of Jürgen Habermas, locating the public sphere as "a realm of our social life in which something approaching public opinion can be formed" visualizing the possibility of a consensus as to the public good. In the public sphere, differences might be expressed yet reconciled. They call for a gendered interpretation of such a process, for to Ryan "only the public is big enough to accommodate the goals to which this feminist historian stubbornly aspires, gender justice and the equality of the sexes" (Ryan, 1990: 18).

Working-class women in the public sphere, 1870s. The streets were for many working-class women the place of work and social contact - for instance, flower sellers, newspaper sellers and, above all, second-hand dealers.

In the melting pots of nineteenth century American cities, as women entered public space, gender differences, as well as ethnic, religious and racial differences, became increasingly visible.

The Public/Private Dichotomy and the History of Feminism

The problem which I want to focus upon here is where these approaches have taken those of us whose interests lie in the history of eighteenth and nineteenth century feminism. If this dichotomy of public and private was one lying at the heart of their movement, central to all their writings and struggles, should the historian discard or recover it in rereading that movement? So much of the recovery of the activities of women in so-called first wave feminism across western societies has been written in these terms: it has been a history which has sought for origins and has traced the crossing of boundaries. It has benefited from the recovery of a culture which was rooted in the women's world of private life, and the informal networks that bound them together. Many recent historians have focused on these issues, as I myself did in a study of women's lives in Britain, France and the US in the late eighteenth and early nineteenth centuries, looking for the origins of modern feminism (Rendall, 1985).

Nancy Hewitt has summarized and offered a critique of the paradigm of change with which many of us have worked, in writing on nineteenth century feminism in western societies. In writing about the emergence of feminist movements we were describing the worlds of white, middle class women, for whom the contrast between public and private worlds had a meaning in their lives. In confronting the contradictions between the emergency of "true manhood" and women's entry into public activities, in, broadly, the same period, it was necessary to explain the "transformation of pious, pure, domestic, submissive and sororal women into social, and specifically feminist, activists, by 1848". So we did. And this was our explanation. Women's path to public life began at the family hearth. It led through religious revivalism, and benevolence, to the fight against vice, intemperance, and anti-slavery. Armed with this experience, they crossed over from the private world to purify the public, "confronting the masculine values of material progress with the feminine tenets of moral perfection", and claiming the rights of citizenship on these grounds (Hewitt, 1984: 17-20).

That was one route: but another form of explanation was to contrast the two models of "equal or different". Did 19th century feminists identify with the first path that used the language of separate spheres and the private world, or with the masculine values of equality in pursuing the goal of citizenship into public spaces? One recent historian has distinguished between the individualist feminists, claimants to equality, and the relational feminists, whose political challenge rested on an acceptance of sexual difference (Offen, 1988; DuBois and Cott, 1989). Such oppositions do of course equally reflect a binary vision from the historian: and we are increasingly warned of the dangers of such an approach, setting the two in an oppositional relationship, denying the possibility of equality in difference (Scott, 1988: "The Sears Case").

Nevertheless, the work of the last twenty years in the history of feminism in the west has been enormously fruitful. Linda Kerber pointed out how the notion of separate spheres, and the public/private dichotomy from the late 1960s enabled historical understanding, of women in private and women in public, and especially of feminist movements attempting to cross those boundaries, to move from the trivial, the anecdotal, the making of heroines, into ever more clearly structured analyses. Historians picked up, and deployed the metaphorical usages of earlier generations. They noted the kinds of worlds which women, sometimes but not always associated with feminist causes, might create for themselves, in what might be "independent communities". They found much evidence in the energy put into the maintenance of boundaries, in the world of antisuffragism or in the defence of the segregated world of women and of men at work. They asked new and fundamental questions. They imposed a form of order, created a historical narrative out of existing uncertainties (Kerber, 1988).

But, as Nancy Hewitt has written, that order was itself over-simplifying, culture-bound. It could create a distorting picture of sisterly relations, and common concerns, across ethnic, class and race divisions. A perspective which elevated sisterhood distorted differences: we needed to get "Beyond the Search for Sisterhood" (Hewitt, 1985; 1988). An alternative approach might yield a picture of common concerns and bonds within class or ethnic groups: and reveal hostility or conflict with the interests to other groups. Even in the promising setting of Rochester, New York, which Hewitt studied, three distinct groups of activists among white middle class women may be distinguished: and those three groups related in different ways to the free black and working class women of Rochester. Though each group was rooted in a pattern of domesticity, each, the benevolent women of the elite, evangelical women and radical Quakers all took their different paths into the public domain. A lens which insisted on simple oppositions was blind to different layers of loyalty.

And the implications are greater than this. The form of the public/private distinction is one rooted in western European culture since the Greek philosophers: though definitions of it have obviously shifted and are specific to time and place. Carole Pateman noted the centrality of the public/private distinction in feminist writing and action just as she has noted the common origins of feminism and liberalism in the west, in the emergence of a particular rhetoric of individualism. The metaphor of separate spheres is central to the liberal outlook: though that centrality is often concealed and mystified. It was as we have seen frequently employed in the United States and Europe by the late eighteenth century. Nineteenth century European feminists were drawn for the most part from that powerful liberal tradition of the nineteenth century middle classes. My meaning here is a simple one: we cannot escape the specific, class-related qualities of 19th century western feminism, and should not indeed try to do so. Rather we should tease out, as fully as we can, the nature of its complicated relationship to liberal politics and liberal ideology, and in doing so cast light on its intersections with differences both of class, and of race.

But are we bound by the limits of that so-called first wave feminism, which could be interpreted as gradually spreading out to the limits of the cultural imperialism of the west? Here of course comes the tricky question of definitions. We now know a little more about the history of the word itself, at least in English and in French (Offen, 1988): but the fact that the word was not used till the 1890s has not stopped many of us from using it for earlier periods. In just the same way as it has been used of the early nineteenth century in Europe, historians have written of a feminist consciousness within a nineteenth century Egyptian harem, though that term was not used in Egypt till 1923. It has been used very recently, of male feminists in 16th century China, as well as in 17th century France, and of the 17th century Mexican nun who raised questions about the injustice of denying women the right to think and learn for themselves (Sievers, 1989). It is a difficult choice to make: it is of course consistent to use that term only for the twentieth century itself, as Nancy Cott does in her *Grounding of Modern Feminism* (1987), and to argue that anything else is an anachronism.

We may well decide in the end that the term is just too useful to be sacrified on the grounds of authenticity. If we do that, we raise the possibility of a more flexible and perhaps a comparative and multi-cultural history of feminism. Karen Offen has called for a study of "the origins and growth of these ideas within a variety of cultural traditions", without the imposition of any single hegemonic model. Such a process may force a closer look at the variety of ways in which feminism has emerged from, conflicted with, and accommodated to, not only the politics of her liberalism but also those of socialism and nationalism in very different cultural and political contexts.

Bearing all this in mind, what are the possibilities of new approaches to the history of feminism? It does seem to me that the direction of contemporary critiques of the public/private distinction, especially those from the United States, open up some exciting possibilities for the historian of feminism. I welcome the deconstruction, the demystifying, of ideologies of gender, even of the concept of "woman": and the under-mining of dominant dichotomies. On the other hand the experiences of concrete historical women, their similarities and their many differences, also need to be studied: and the continuing meaning which the terminology of public and private may have held in their lives remains to be read. So I should like to spend much of the remainder of my time reflecting on possible rereadings of the history of feminism in Britain: though I hope that I shall be raising questions which may be relevant elsewhere. And I would suggest three possible lines of approach.

Multi-Faceted Approaches

The first would lie in a new reading—I would not personally claim a deconstruction, but at least a demystification—of *liberal* perspectives, one which goes beyond dichotomies and explores the overlapping circles that make up this most complex inheritance of the European middle classes. I would suggest that here in going beyond dualism we may tease out the intersecting circles of interest, identity and rhetoric, that bound together liberalism and feminism, from the late eighteenth century onwards. The language of an apparently universal, egalitarian and individualist liberal philosophy obscured the patriarchal nature of the relations between women and men, as Pateman pointed out. She has also pointed to the complexity of that language. Broadly speaking, at the centre of nineteenth century liberalism, one might see not a binary but a multi-faceted pattern: we should note the ground of division not just between public and private, but between the world of the state, government and public opinion, between that civil society in which private interests were pursued, and that social sphere in which the state and the philanthropist met, to investigate the "social conditions" of working class family life, and finally, that domestic haven, the circle of the family.

I suggest that it is no longer possible to pursue the theme of "Women in Public", to trace the crossing of boundaries from private to public, unless we define more carefully what that means in context. Mary Wolstonecraft, Barbara Bodichon, John Stuart Mill, Millicent Garrett Fawcett—to look at some of the luminaries of a liberal feminism—did *not* simply perceive their lives and works in dualistic terms, in a twentieth century version of the public and private split. They had different and sometimes inconsistent views of how the private world of the family should interact, with the private interests of civil society and the market-place, and with the public world of government. There is no necessary agreement to be found among them, but the differences may be both interesting and revealing. I would like to look at some ways in which these interactions may be or have been explored.

So, to take one possible rereading. Mary Wollstonecraft's *Vindication of the Rights of Woman* (1792) has frequently been analysed in terms of the relationship between her concept of private life—an almost Rousseauistic vision of domesticity—and the possibilities which she suggests of the reclamation of the public world. And this is quite convincing because she does use precisely that language. She writes of "private virtue becoming the cement of public happiness", of the transcendence of the old, corrupt, hierarchical, and privileged society by a new and more rational order. It seems to me feasible to argue however that within her vision of a different order lie overlapping possibilities, never quite distinguished. There is the vision of a new republic, a republic not far, in spite of all difference, from the Rousseauist conception, but one in which women, educated, recognized as rational creatures, and themselves educating new citizens for the future, play their part. Yet she does not look only to France and the idea of a republic, yet also to that founder of liberal political economy,

Adam Smith—who was also the author of a work on *The Theory of Moral Sentiments* (1759)—whose critique of the corruption of the rich she applied to the condition of the women she saw around her. In Smith's work may be found a grappling with new ways of ordering the social world, ways that no longer rested on an anachronistic republicanism, but on the free play of private interest in the market, achieved through the interiorization of rational goals, and the channelling of desire. To Wollstonecraft, clearly it will not be through the classic republican spheres of military and civic duties that women will achieve a new kind of existence. It may be through motherhood and the education of new citizens: or, she says:

How many women thus waste life away the prey of discontent, who might have practised as physicians, regulated a farm, managed a shop, and stood erect, supported by their own industry, instead of hanging their heads surcharged with the dew of sensibility ... (Rendall, 1987, Rendall, 1989).

Within her work, there are co-existing, different and significant variants on the private/public distinction.

I should like to pursue that further into the recesses of liberal feminism in the second half of the nineteenth century. I have myself been particularly interested in the work of a generation of middle class feminists who came to prominence in the 1850s and 1860s, who founded the first overtly feminist journal in England—*The English Woman's Journal*. The question of suffrage was not one of their initial interests. One outstanding theme was philanthropic endeavour, and their "sanitary mission" to the working classes. Another lay in the entry of women into the market-place, and most obviously the labour market: as middle class women sought for occupation, tried to earn a living and achieve the kind of independent productivity, they had to confront a dominant orthodoxy of their class—liberal political economy. There was no unity in their responses on this question: but its appearance in their language is striking. So the *English Woman's Journal* attempted to define the political economy of marriage. Parkes described the view of marriage prevalent among the English middle class as reflecting a "political economy which would throw the livelihood of all wives upon the earnings of all husbands", that is as having inbuilt a notion of total dependence. Or marriage could be seen as a working partnership to which each partner brought capital, the woman in the form of her dowry: this, though mercenary, was in many ways more effective than the view which "stressed" total dependence. Another view was that "the woman's power of household management is her natural capital" (Rendall, 1987; Rendall, 1989). There was indeed an overlap between the language of domesticity, and through philanthropy, of voluntary and even political activity: but so too was there overlap and intersection between civil society, the market, and perceptions of familial relationships.

In the question of female employment, the tensions were manifest. The *Journal* put it clearly: other factors besides the strictly economic influenced employers. Custom and prejudice operated among employers and among male workers: "In fact, custom and prejudice are at work to exclude us from earning a living". There were of course divisions. Some challenged the exclusive claims to authority made by the science of political economy. For Parkes, the operation of the scientific laws of political economy had to co-exist with Christian moral principles, centred in the personal relations of the domestic economy: so, she argued associations and co-operation offered a new kind of employment, which might challenge the harshness of the market. But others argued, like Emily Faithfull, that "every woman should be free to support herself by the use of whatever faculties God has given her", and were prepared to face the logical consequence of a free market in labour. If men and women were in competition, the advocates of women's employment should not accept the burden of suffering, but stake their own claims.

There is an overlap here with the dilemmas of John Stuart Mill, the precise contemporary of these women. The *Subjection of Women* (1869) was to be one of the best known feminist works of the mid-nineteenth century, because of its understanding of the cultural construction of womanhood, his denunciation of the tyrannical bonds of marriage and his support, in writing and in practice, for women's suffrage. Yet, although in his earlier *Principles of Political Economy* (1848) he called for "the opening of industrial occupations freely to both sexes" (Mill (1848), ed. Winch, 1970: 125f.), nevertheless one of the most striking omissions from the *Subjection of Women* is any consideration of a fundamental question most clearly engaging the contemporary women's movement: how were women of all classes to find and keep employment? He dismissed this issue in a few words only, suggesting that with all honourable employments freely open to women, the majority, while mothers of families, would not choose to contribute to the income of the family. And this is a piece of doublethink which many commentators have noted. His refusal even to contemplate the realities of the market place for women is startling, for a political economist whose conviction and commitment to this cause, should not be underestimated. The public sphere of citizenship for Mill, unlike the writers of the *English Woman's Journal* was not, fundamentally, the market place but the political arena, that arena in which the boundaries between the individual and the state may be defined. Within that section of the public sphere individuals, women and men might fulfil their own potential, might indeed reach towards a higher form of moral and political life. In Mill's stress on political equality he entirely fails to address himself to the question of the different situations of women in the labour market, a difference which the women's movement understood, for they did see how the structuring of the labour market derived from familial relationships and responsibilites: and they addressed themselves to immediate realities. Mill was more interested in the interrelationship of the equal and companionate marriage, freed from legal forms of patriarchy, with a political sphere in which both husband and wife may enjoy full citizenship.

One of the classic histories of the feminist movement in Britain, Ray Strachey's *The Cause* (1928)—still a valuable work and currently reprinted—is written from a standpoint which in many ways looks back to the liberalism of Mill. It offers a history of progressive reform, a celebration of the history and achievements of a progressive liberalism: in this feminist politics, it is the rational, moral and civilized individuals who stand out, who dominate the picture, who fight for their opportunities to be extended to others through an educated citizenship. Other definitions of politics—socialist feminism, pacifism, and sexual libertarianism—find little place here (Dodd, 1990).

There is a further facet, which remains to be explored. Women were by the mid-nineteenth century becoming both the objects of, and participators in, a newly constructed "social science". Denise Riley has written of the conceptualization of the "social sphere", the "blurred ground" between public and private, from the late eighteenth century, and of women participating both as objects in, and as investigators of, that "social sphere". Women may be seen as having a kind of affinity with that ground of "the social", dislocated from the high politics of government (Riley, 1988: chapter 3). From 1857, the National Association for the Promotion of Social Science offered a small number of women the opportunity to speak at its congresses and to address the "social" questions of the period.

The dilemmas of mid-nineteenth century feminism are not necessarily best represented by an undifferentiated version of public life: the meanings of that liberal public arena need to be uncovered. For some the language of domestic responsibility became that of social responsibility, expressed not only in voluntary labour but also to be extended eventually into the regulating powers of local and national government. For others, the contractarian model of the family might be extended into adherence to the free market, a market place in which women might be equipped to compete on equal terms. For others the model of a free and equal marriage might co-exist with an almost republican vision of a world in which through the exercise of civic duties and responsibilities, the individual woman and the individual man might equally achieve moral fulfilment. I caricature and oversimplify all these positions: but they *are* simultaneously held. We need of course not to look only at the texts of political theory, but at the practice of organizations. These themes need to be problematized and subjected to much clearer understanding: if we are to gain a clearer picture of the complexities of the feminist movement, and of its relationship with the dominant classes. The issues that I have seen as important here do of course relate specifically to Britain, and to its middle classes: it might be interesting to explore the relevance of similar questions in other contexts in which the balance between state and civil society differed.

What I have said so far is to suggest that there are aspects of the politics of class which have been overlooked. But there is I think a different direction in which too great a focus on the private/public dichotomy has obscured our understanding. Pateman wrote of the patriarchal nature of the liberal contract: we have only recently begun to understand the extent to which some nineteenth century feminists recognised the existence of that contract. Mary Maynard has pointed out that the focus of much historical work on nineteenth century feminism has been on campaigns and struggles, on action rather than thought (Maynard, 1989). She argues that underlying conflicting arguments for equality or for the representation of difference, arguments about the sexual division of labour, and the battle between advocates of protection and those of independence, it is possible to identify something rather different, an embryonic analysis of gender relations. Nineteenth century feminists did consistently and emphatically write of the attitudes of men, and male power and authority, at three levels: the level of individual behaviour, the social construction of masculinity, and the existence of a system of male power, institutionalized, entrenched and well-defended. Susan Kingsley Kent's recent work on *Sex and Suffrage* similarly suggested that the separation of personal and political was irrelevant to the political world of the nineteenth century: suffragists identified cultural constructions of femininity and female sexuality as at the heart of their exclusion from the political order (Kent, 1987). The campaign for the vote was a means of achieving a different kind of sexual order. There is room here for a much closer critique, for a careful reading of nineteenth century feminist ideas: as an analysis of gender oppression, but also as a diverse and varied pattern of objectives.

Rethinking the Political History of Working Class Women

The second line of approach that I want to discuss involves rethinking a different kind of politics, one for which the public/private distinction will not necessarily make sense. For so far I have been talking about one class in society alone: but we should consider the problems of writing the political history of working class women. Working class women did not necessarily share the masculine politics which centred on the propertied individual, the head of the household, and the assumptions which lay behind the separation of public and private worlds. Liberal assumptions of separate spheres might be irrelevant. Their lives might be to a greater degree oriented towards the collective life of the community, rural or urban, in which the notion of a separate domestic life, of privacy itself, might have relatively little meaning. Much would of course depend on the local economy, and "consequent" sexual division of labour, and on the stability and strength of communities, long-established or new. So in work on New York we may find illustrated women's role in their neighbourhoods, defined of course by class, by race and by ethnicity, but also by their common labour, for "labouring women made their lives as wives and mothers on the streets as much as by their hearthsides" (Stansell, 1986: 52).

Here a fruitful way forward would seem to be that reinterpretation of the study of public life which Ryan has indicated: at least, that might serve as a working hypothesis. There are a number of possibilities here. The historian Dorothy Thompson

English woman missionary with two mission school students in China, 1919.

some years ago asked why working class women in England ceased to be active in public life in the 1840s after the decline of the Chartist movement which had as its aim universal male suffrage though it attracted a very substantial female membership and organisation (Thompson, 1976; 1986). A variety of answers have been suggested, answers which centre on a process of retreat, a move backwards into a separate sphere of home and family in the second half of the nineteenth century. Those answers may well be right, yet we still know little about the lives of working class women in this quite complex and difficult period in the history of an industrializing society, from the 1840s to the 1880s. Perhaps a more detailed history of the public arena, broadly defined, may help to clarify the relationships between feminist activity, and the activity of women in public: and on the other hand between working class women and the politics of feminism. Such an arena, here viewed in an urban context, can be viewed in the widest social and cultural sense.

So, there is room for more study of the kind which has already been begun on both the representation of womanhood, and the participation of women in public ceremony. Much work has been done in tracing the female symbolism underlying the changing image of France, of its Republics and of Liberty, in the nineteenth century (Ryan, 1990; Hunt, 1984; Agulhon, 1981). In England the female figure plays a significant role in hostile and conservative representations of the French Revolution. A sense of sexual disorder is used to convey a quality of unrestrained savagery, and women's participation in the sans-culottes movement is one of the themes used to mark out so-called British liberty from so-called French licence.

In cartoons of the period, it is a monstrous and hideous woman who represents at the same time Liberty, and the French Republic: it is she who is the symbolic source of "Rapine, Murder, Famine, Atheism" (Anon. 28 February 1798; Cruikshank, Isaac, 10 February 1794). The point of such depictions here is that there is a marked continuity with representations of visible public ceremonies in political movements after the end of the Napoleonic wars: in which similar imagery is applied to groups of working class women associated with movements for universal male suffrage. So in August 1819, a cartoon of the Blackburn Female Reform Society, whose objective was "to assist the male population of this country to obtain their rights and liberties", shows the savage and grotesque character of male and female figures and, with a wealth of obscene detail, the sexual disorder associated with female reform (Cruikshank, George, 12 August 1819; Thomis, 1982: 92f.). At a much larger meeting a few days later, a meeting assembled in Manchester, on St. Peter's Fields, and was broken up by armed force, a meeting which became a day remembered and commemorated among reformers as Peterloo. We know that women did themselves play a ceremonial, even an allegorical role on this occasion—placed in white dresses, with flags, banners, caps of liberty, at the head of processions. The woman who was President of the Female Reform Society of Manchester, dressed in white, rode with the leader of the movement in his carriage (Rendall, 1985: 236).

The meaning of women's role in public action may have been changing. What might be a living allegorical role by some, might equally be interpreted as a learning process in the "public" space by others. What happened to that link, between allegory and female organization, a link still evident in the 1840s? In the public ceremonies of US cities studied by Ryan "the language of public ceremony became increasingly infused with gender terms", increasingly elaborated, and, she argues, infused with domestic values: though it would certainly also overlap with class and perhaps with ethnic values (Ryan, 1990: 56).

Similarly, a focus on the urban geography of nineteenth century cities, which follows Stansell's fine work on New York, might allow us to see how women occupied public space, and how that space was gendered (Stansell, 1986; Ryan, 1990: chapter 2; Hewitt, 1985). We might consider how women used such space: they would do so both in their domestic labour—fetching water, washing, hawking—in moving around the city to work and in their occasional leisure—chatting, public houses, dances, local parks. Their world was one of informal sociability, but also of mobility, in employment. There was nothing here of the female domestic sphere: women's lives were lived in the turbulent, crowded and intimate tenements and streets. But we may also see these streets as grounds for conflict between classes, in which the taming and domesticating of the women of the streets was the target of evangelical reformers, women and men. I would like to consider the boundaries of that public space for working class women in the new urban communities of industrial England. How far did conventions imposed by women themselves, in their neighbourhoods, regulate behaviour? What was the sexual geography, the map of danger and of pleasure—and who regulated it? Where were men likely to find the public spaces in which to construct their public presence—in public houses, workplaces, clubs, from which women were excluded? Our maps need to cover not simply a public/private distinction: but the intersecting contrasts of domesticity, of sociability, of paid and unpaid labour and of voluntary and organized association.

This would of course be a major contribution not merely to the history of nineteenth century feminism but to social history more broadly interpreted. It could mean the recovery not only of the changing common themes that governed the lives of working class women, but also those which bound them to resist alternatives, alternatives which might come from the alien experience of separate spheres, and which might pay little attention to cultural and social differences. Working class women might rather choose to ally themselves with men of the same class in their own understanding of their best interests, and community networks might form a barrier against the imposition of regulation by middle class women and men. That is not, however, to suggest that there were never circumstances in which cross-class alliances between women did not become possible: but those circumstances might well be exceptional.

Feminism: Identity, Difference and Dominance

Finally, in a look at the third possible direction which new work might take, I would suggest a focus on analyses of feminism which might point to questions of identity, of difference and of dominance. Feminist movements were not only about the possibilities of "sisterhood": they might mark out a territory of nationality, of class and of race. The history of the relationship between British feminist movements, and British nationalism, and imperialism, remains to be written. There are of course differences and dominance within the historiography of the United Kingdom itself: there is as yet no study of feminist movements in Scotland, Wales, or Northern Ireland though each presents complex and relevant questions (Owens, 1984; Murphy, 1988).

The wealth of published writing of the last twenty years has focused entirely on England. In a study of "Englishness" it has been pointed out how, though the qualities of the perfect Englishman might be clearly perceived, those of the Englishwoman are more elusive: her qualities were not perceived as being specifically English, rather those of domesticity, modesty, and civilizing potential inherent in womanhood, though she practised these virtues in a highly superior way (Mackay et al., 1986). They were, perhaps, identified less with nationhood, than with the race, the Anglo-Saxon race to which they belonged, their task to be its guardian and perpetuator. An historian of the emigration movement has written of the way in which "notions of imperial destiny and class and racial superiority were grafted on to the traditional views of refined English motherhood to produce a concept of the Englishwoman as an invincible global civilizing agent" by the turn of the century (Hammerton, 1979: 162-63).

What needs further examination is how nationalist, and imperialist discourses intersected those of feminism in different historical contexts. The kind of literature I have cited above could be directed precisely *against* feminism: which could be seen as a force undermining an imperial destiny. But aspects of it could well be reshaped, and turned: and there is indeed some evidence to suggest that a kind of feminist "orientalism" made of the "Eastern" or "Oriental" woman and the harem, a benchmark of subjection and difference, an index of the kind of decaying civilization, which Britain sought both to rule and to lead to progress. Harriet Taylor wrote of Asian women who "were and are the slaves of men for the purposes of sensuality", Millicent Fawcett that "in the semi-civilisations of the East we know that women are valued principally as inmates of the Seraglio" (Burton, 1990). We still have to examine and unpack such rhetoric, to distinguish its variants and its gendered nature.

A belated beginning has been made on such an analysis. So for instance, Clare Midgley has examined the part played by English women in anti-slavery agitation in the first half of the 19th century. Such women were drawn from the radical middle classes, and by the 1850s their networks "overlapped" that of feminist activists: their campaign was rooted in a discourse of evangelical mission, which constructed its own portrait of the suffering female slave as its object (Midgley, 1989; forthcoming). A survey of Josephine Butler's campaigns on behalf of Indian prostitutes suggested a feminist image of helpless Indian womanhood, a contrast against whom the greater progress and superior level of civilization of the women of the imperial country might be measured (Burton, 1990). Barbara Ramusack in an investigation of five British women activists in India has asked how far it was possible for women from one race or ethnic group, to promote effectively reforms or institutions designed to reform or modify the conditions of women from another group? Were women activists in India cultural missionaries, still in the early twentieth century imbued with an evangelical if secular zeal? Were they in Ramusack's phrase "maternal imperialists" who saw Indian colleagues rather as daughters? Or might they simply be good and useful allies, with helpful skills and contacts as some undoubtedly were? (Ramusack, 1990; Chaudhuri, 1990). These questions await answers: which are unlikely to be simple, or monolithic, or, we hope, even binary.

The History of Feminism

So there are diverse and exciting new possibilities for the history of feminism, and approaches no doubt to be transcended in their turn. Such a history cannot be divorced from contemporary debates and discussions, and indeed the approaches I have outlined have arisen out of that. New work will of course be grounded not entirely in these exciting new buzz-words, but also in the serious empirical and local studies, which alone can, I think, give substance to our concerns. It is only by giving such serious study to our predecessors that we can do them justice, in every way: and I have not intended, in what I have been saying of the need to understand the differences of the nineteenth century, altogether to lose our pleasure in the work and lives of those individual women. For they too could be self-reflexive, self-critical, understanding the contradictions and recognizing the patriarchal character of the societies in which they lived: they too could display those qualities for which we strive.

References

Sources

Anon. (28 February 1798), "The Hopes of the Party! Or the Darling Children of Democracy", listed as no. 9178 in Stephens and George (1798): VII, 425.

Barbauld, Anna (1826), *A Legacy for Young Ladies, Consisting of Miscellaneous Pieces in Prose and Verse*, London.

Cruikshank, George (12 August 1819), "The Belle-Alliance, or the Female Reformers of Black-bourn!!!", listed as no. 13257 in Stephens and George (1978): IX, 916-17.

Cruikshank, Isaac (10 February 1794), "A Peace Offering to the Genius of Liberty and Equality", listed as no. 8426 in Stephens and George (1978): VII, 75-76.

Stephens, F.G. and M.D. George (eds.) (1870-1954; British Museum Publications Ltd., 1978),

Catalogue of Prints and Drawings in the British Museum. Division I. Political and Personal Satires, 11 vols., London.

Wollstonecraft, Mary (1792: Harmondsworth Penguin 1975), *A Vindication of the Rights of Woman*, pp. 252-262.

Literature

Agulhon, Maurice (1981), *Marianne into Battle. Republican Imagery and Symbolism in France 1789-1800*, Cambridge: Cambridge University Press.

Bock, Gisela (forthcoming 1991), "Challenging Dichotomies: Perspectives on Women's History", Karen Offen, Ruth Roach Pierson and Jane Rendall (eds.), *Writing Women's History: International Perspectives*, London: Macmillan.

Burton, Antoinette M. (1990), "The White Woman's Burden. British Feminists and the Indian Woman, 1865-1915", *Women's Studies International Forum*, 13, no. 4, pp. 295-308.

Chaudhuri, Nupur and Margaret Strobel, "Introduction", *Women's Studies International Forum*, 13, no. 4.

Cott, Nancy (1977), *The Bonds of Womanhood. Woman's Sphere in New England. 1780-1835*, Yale: Yale University Press.

Cott, Nancy and Ellen DuBois (1989), "Comments on Karen Offen's article "Defining Feminism: A Comparative Historical Approach"", *Signs*, 15, no. 1, pp. 196-209.

Dauphin, Cécile et al. (1980), "Women's Culture and Women's Power: an Attempt at Historiography", *Journal of Women's History*, 1, no. 1, pp. 63-88.

Davidoff, Leonore and Catherine Hall (1987), *Family Fortunes: the Men and Women of the English Middle Classes 1780-1850*, London: Hutchinson.

Dodd, Kathryn (1990), "Cultural Politics and Women's Historical Writing. The Case of Ray Strachey's *"The Cause""*, *Women's Studies International Forum*, 13, nos 1 and 2, pp. 127-37.

Hammerton, A.J. (1979), *Emigrant Gentlewomen. Genteel Poverty and Emigration 1830-1914*, London: Croom Helm.

Hewitt, Nancy (1984), *Women's Activism and Social Change. Rochester, New York 1822-1872*, Ithaca and London: Cornell University Press.

Hewitt, Nancy (1985), "Beyond the Search for Sisterhood: American Women's History in the 1980s", *Social History*, 10, pp. 299-321.

Hewitt, Nancy (1988), "Sisterhood in International Perspective: Thoughts on Teaching Comparative Women's History", *Women's Studies Quarterly*, XVI, nos 1 and 2, pp. 22-32.

Hunt, Lynn (1984), *Politics, Culture and Class in the French Revolution*, Berkeley: University of California Press.

Jalland, Pat (1986), *Women, Marriage and Politics 1860-1914*, Oxford: Clarendon Press.

Kent, Susan Kingsley (1987), *Sex and Suffrage in Britain 1860-1914*, Princeton: Princeton University Press.

Kerber, Linda (1988), "Separate Spheres, Female Worlds, Woman's Place: The Rhetoric of Women's History", *Journal of American History*, 75, no. 1, pp. 9-39.

Kessler-Harris, Alice (1990), *A Woman's Wage. Historical Meanings and Social Consequences*, Lexington: University Press of Kentucky.

Landes, Joan (1988), *Women and the Public Sphere in the Age of the French Revolution*, Ithaca and London: Cornell University Press.

Levy, Darline Gay, Harriet Branson Applewhite and Mary Durham Johnson (1979), *Women in Revolutionary Paris, 1789-1795*, Urbana: University of Illinois Press.

Mackay, Jane and Pat Thane (1986), "The Englishwoman", Robert Colls and Philip Dodd (eds.), *Englishness, Politics and Culture 1880-1920*, London, Sydney and Dover: Croom Helm.

Maynard, Mary (1989), "Privilege and Patriarchy: Feminist Thought in the Nineteenth Century", Susan Mendus and Jane Rendall (eds.), *Sexuality and Subordination. Interdisciplinary Studies of Gender in the Nineteenth Century*, London: Routledge.

Midgley, Clare (1989), "Women Anti-Slavery Campaigners in Britain, 1787-1868", Ph.D. Thesis, University of Kent, Kent.

Midgley, Clare (forthcoming), "Race and Sisterhood: Women Anti-Slavery Campaigners in Britain, 1780-1870", Joan Grant (ed.), *Silent Voices: Historical Essays on Race and Gender in Britain*, London: Prism.

Mill, John Stuart (1970), *Principles of Political Economy with Some of Their Applications to Social Philosophy* (1848). Books IV and V, ed. D. Winch Harmondsworth: Penguin.

Murphy, Cliona (1988), *The Women's Suffrage Movement in Irish Society in the Early Twentieth Century*, Hemel Hempstead: Harvester/Wheatsheaf.

Offen, Karen (1988), "Defining Feminism: A Comparative Historical Approach", *Signs*, vol. 14, no. 1, pp. 119-57.

Owens, Rosemary Cullen (1984), *Smashing Times. A History of the Irish Women's Suffrage Movement 1889-1922*, Dublin: Attic Press.

Pateman, Carole (1988), *The Sexual Contract*, Oxford: Polity Press.

Pateman, Carole (1989), "Feminist Critiques of the Public/Private Dichotomy", *The Disorder of Women. Democracy, Feminism and Political Theory*, Oxford: Polity Press (first published 1983).

Poovey, Mary (1984), *The Proper Lady and the Woman Writer*, Chicago and London: University of Chicago Press.

Ramusack, Barbara (1990), "Cultural Missionaries, Maternal Imperialists, Feminist Allies: British Women Activists in India, 1865-1945", *Women's Studies International Forum*, 13, no. 4, pp. 309-321.

Rendall, Jane (1985), *The Origins of Modern Feminism. Women in Britain, France and the United States 1780-1850*, London: Macmillan.

Rendall, Jane (1987) (ed.), "Equal or Different? Women's Politics 1800-1914", Jane Rendall, *A Moral Engine? Feminism, Liberalism and the English Woman's Journal*, Oxford: Basil Blackwell, pp. 123-25.

Rendall, Jane (1989), "Friendship and Politics Barbara Leigh Smith Bodichon (1827-1891) and

Bessie Rayner Parkes (1829-1925)", Susan Mendus and Jane Rendall (eds.), *Sexuality and Subordination. Interdisciplinary Studies of Gender in the Nineteenth Century*, London: Routledge.

Riley, Denise (1988), *"Am I That Name?" Feminism and the Category of Women in History*, Basingstoke: Macmillan.

Rosaldo, Michelle Zimbalist (1974), "Woman, Culture and Society: A Theoretical Overview", Michelle Zimbalist Rosaldo and Louise Lamphere (eds.), *Woman, Culture and Society*, Stanford: Stanford University Press.

Rosaldo, Michelle Zimbalist (1980), "The Use and Abuse of Anthropology: Reflections on Feminism and Cross-Cultural Understanding", *Signs: Journal of Women in Culture and Society*, 5, no. 3, pp. 389-417.

Ryan, Mary (1990), *Women in Public. Between Banners and Ballots 1825-1880*, Baltimore and London: Johns Hopkins University Press.

Scott, Joan Wallach (1988), *Gender and the Politics of History*, New York: Columbia University Press.

Segalen, Martine (1983), *Love and Power in the French Peasant Family. Rural France in the Nineteenth Century*, Oxford: Basil Blackwell.

Sievers, Sharen (1989), "Six (or More) Feminists in Search of a Historian", *Journal of Women's History*, 1, no. 2, pp. 134-147.

Smith-Rosenberg, Carroll (1975), "The Female World of Love and Ritual: Relations between Women in Nineteenth-Century America", *Signs*, 1, pp. 1-29.

Stansell, Christine (1986), *City of Women. Sex and Class in New York, 1789-1860*, New York: Knopf.

Strachey, Ray (1928), *"The Cause". A Short History of the Women's Movement in Great Britain*, London: G. Bell & Sons.

Thomis, M. and Jennifer Grimmett (1982), *Women in Protest, 1800-1850*, London: Groom Helm.

Thompson, Dorothy (1976), "Women and Nineteenth Century Radical Politics: A Lost Dimension", Juliet Mitchell and Ann Oakley (eds.), *The Rights and Wrongs of Women*, Harmondsworth: Penguin.

Thompson, Dorothy (1986), *'The Chartists'. Popular Politics in the Industrial Revolution*, Aldershot: Wildwood House.

Turbin, Carole (1989), "Beyond Dichotomies: Interdependence in Mid-Nineteenth Century Working Class Families in the United States", *Gender and History*, 1, no. 2, pp. 293-308.

Patronesses, Gentlewomen, Feminists—and Common Wives.
Political Gender and Class Systems in Tampere during the Period of Industrialization

Aino Saarinen

What Is Political, What Is Politics

Helga Maria Hernes has pointed out that the entry of women into politics has often taken place via the kitchen (Hernes, 1987: 11). This argument relates directly to one of the most important methodological tenets of feminist and gender studies: that, as Linda Christiansen-Ruffman has stressed (1982), women's activity and actions must always be weighed against existing structures of opportunities, that the aim must be to identify both obstacles to and opportunities for women's politics. Obstacles and opportunities, in turn, point to the power strategies identified by Beverly Thiele (1986), to the exclusion and underestimation of women. The attention now shifts to the existence of a male gender and to the relationship of that gender to women's activity: to a search for persuasion and adaptation, for contradictions and tensions.

There is also another dual perspective on "kitchen politics"[1] which is sensitive to power systems and which also challenges established concepts. Anna Jonasdottir (1987) has two analytically distinct but nevertheless closely interwoven questions which constitute a very interesting approach: What is political? What is politics?

Jonasdottir describes the former as the "content aspect" of politics. Feminist critique of political research has challenged not only the answers that have been given to the questions on the political agenda, but indeed the whole agenda itself: In what ways does it reflect power strategies, what are the key problems, for whom are they problems? Which problems are given priority; which are neglected; which are completely omitted from the agenda? It is, of course, also important to look into the "form aspect" of politics, to explore the political arenas: In what kind of places, in what ways, and at what times has politics been possible for married and single women, for women of different social standing and in different social classes?

This article examines the structures which presented obstacles to and opened up opportunities for politics among upper-class women in Tampere during the latter half of the nineteenth century. It has been written as part of a major research project on the historical struggle for universal suffrage in the industrial city of Tampere.[2] In the words of Carole Pateman (1988a: 1-18), this period of modernization was not only one

Workers of the Finlayson Mills, 1896

of continuity but also represented a break, a tendency for paternal patriarchy to transform into a fraternal patriarchy. All in all, it should be clear from these concepts that the changes taking place in the gender systems were closely intertwined with the restructuration at the macro level of class systems; what we want to know is *how* they were related. How was women's political citizenship and political organization woven into the Tampere fabric, where not only class position but also various new ideas as well as linguistic, cultural, and national ties played an important role? And finally, how potent is the "local"[3] as an explanatory factor in a situation where the nation and modern state were still in the process of becoming?

The three case studies presented below span more than half a century, providing glimpses of the diversity and the local and historical characteristics of everyday life and politics in late nineteenth century Tampere. At the same time these studies cut across the development of women's organization. In the first case the focus is very much on one individual woman: the patroness of Finlayson, who was the dominant figure in the kitchen policy pursued at the Finlayson textile mills, commonly known as the "cotton heart" of the town. She symbolizes the first stage of industrialization in Finland, a process that was already well under way in continental Europe. The Association of Upper-Class Gentlewomen, the first registered women's organization in Tampere, is linked in important respects with the second stage of development, which was largely inspired by increasing trade in the 1860s and a movement towards national independence. With the growth and development of education and culture in the 1880s, the first pro-Finnish party was set up, bringing in its wake the first early feminists and finally, by the 1890s, the first feminist organization. In addition to the patroness, the gentlewomen, and the feminists, our case studies also feature "common wives", albeit in a silent role. Their turn will come later.

The Patroness's Domain: The Industrial Family Household

Prior to the 1906 reform when Finnish women gained universal suffrage and eligibility for office, they had very little, if any, real political influence; the power strategy was to exclude them as far as possible from the political sphere. This also applies to Constance von Nottbeck, the patroness of Finlayson, the biggest textile factory in the Nordic area, whose assets (excluding factory buildings) were estimated in the late nineteenth century at around six million Finnmarks (Hirsjärvi, 1950; Rasila, 1988).

The exclusion of women from political power was in many ways becoming increasingly obvious towards the end of the century. Legislative and constitutional reforms introduced in 1868 and 1877-78 abolished many class privileges, which meant that an increasing number of men representing the (urban) bourgeois classes gained state citizenship. In the nobility, the rules and regulations remained unchanged; therefore the Nottbecks were represented in the diet, as before, by the head of the family.

At the level of municipal government there were at least some disruptions in this fraternal development: in 1873 a decree was issued stating that while eligibility for office in municipal government was still to be restricted to men, women were now to be granted the vote—providing that they met all the relevant criteria with regard to citizenship, taxability, and self-determination. There were two different dimensions to self-determination, i.e. a class dimension and a gender dimension. The latter divided women by marital status: women who were legally incompetent under private law—married women—were excluded from political citizenship at the municipal level (Jutikkala, 1972; Saarinen, 1990). This provision unequivocally deprived the patroness of Finlayson of the vote.

Looking beyond these obstacles to political activity, the reverse side to this "private" and "natural" marital asymmetry also provided certain opportunities for exerting political influence. It is here that we find the channels and arenas in which the patroness of Finlayson exerted her powerful influence.

In the mid-nineteenth century Tampere was emerging as a modern industrial town. The whole process of industrialization was very much controlled from the outside: Finland remained under Russian rule (and economic policy), and most of the industry was in foreign ownership. At the cotton mills, the Scot James Finlayson was succeeded by the German Uhde and eventually by another German, Nottbeck, who came from St. Petersburg. In the 1840s, with the arrival of the young and glamorous lady Nottbeck,

The patroness of Finlayson:
Marie Elise Constance von Nottbeck, née *von*
Mengden

who descended from high Livonian-German nobility, social life in "Finland's Manchester" was surrounded by a new kind of charm and excitement. The patroness was
never involved in the organizations of upper-class women, although during the Crimean
War she did arrange sewing circles at her home for gentlewomen.[4] She did, however,
make a very strong impact on the lives of the factory workers. They made up a large
number of people: by the early 1870s one third of the town's population was working
for Finlayson, and by the time of the patroness's death two thousand out of the total
of five thousand industrial workers in Tampere were at Finlayson (Rasila, 1988;
Haapala, 1986: app. 1).

During these decades, a rather peculiar way of life emerged in Tampere, where
aspects of modern industry, on the one hand, and the paternalism of pre-modern class
society, on the other, were combined. The most obvious illustration of this intermediate
stage is represented by Finlayson's "industrial family household", where old bonds and
burgeoning freedoms were closely interlocked. It was also a domain specifically
designated by the existing structures of opportunity to the patroness of Finlayson. That
domain was further enlarged by the strong horizontal segregation of the labour markets:
textile and clothing industries preferred to have on their payroll single, unmarried
women. Towards the end of the century the vast majority of Finlayson staff—roughly
four-fifths of them—were women and children (Haapala, 1986: app. 5; Kanerva, 1946:
48).

Kitchen Politics and Control

In her agenda, the patroness followed the traditional obligations of paternalist society: it was considered the duty of the privileged and the wealthy to look after the under-privileged. During the morning the patroness—as she wanted people to call her—handed out food, clothes and money to needy people. There were also donations for general purposes, in connection with emergencies, and at Christmas.[5] On the other hand, in spite of the gradual modernization of class relations, the attention focused rather selectively on the factory's own workers.[6] In return, the patroness received good publicity and, from the workers, loyalty and gratitude, even affection.

To strengthen the sense of community among working-class families and to show her special love and appreciation for the children who worked at Finlayson, Mrs. von Nottbeck frequently arranged her own summer and Christmas parties. The factory brass band and choir, which were set up in the early 1870s, would in turn always arrange a concert on special occasions for the beloved patron Wilhelm von Nottbeck (Kanerva, 1972: 257-261; Haapala, 1986: 69-74). These parties and events were important occasions in that they formed an integral part of a continuing effort of ideological socialization from above,[7] the aim of which was to reproduce mental, emotional, and symbolic relationships of dependence. At the same time the patroness, in the same way as all women who were in a similar position, assumed partial responsibility for the social, cultural, and health-care services provided by the factory. Finlayson in particular was widely known as "a town within a town"; it was possible to live within its walls from the cradle to the grave. It had its own kindergarten, asylums for working girls and boys, a school, hospital, canteen, and old-people's home, a shop, bank, church, and a reading room—and of course residential quarters (Lindfors, 1938: 294-324; Haapala, 1986: 69-74).

These "welfare institutions" provided a more permanent platform for Constance von Nottbeck's charity and goodwill. In the local newspapers, for instance, she was praised for exempting some of her working boys from his asylum fees; she would personally pay for their upkeep. The latent agenda that went together with this and other similar feats of extraordinary charity was that it provided an opportunity for controlling ways of life and moral principles. The children at the kindergarten and in the asylums were punished in the name of the owners, even though the actual spanking came from hired caretakers (Kanerva, 1946: 152-162). The same pattern of paternal control extended to the older workers at the factory.

From the patroness, who had had an Hernnhutian upbringing, young couples received a Bible as a wedding present. The control was not restricted to the sphere of private life, but extended to activities within the burgeoning civil society. For example, as late as the 1870s the patroness still considered it inappropriate for her girls to sing in the Fennomanian choir—that conflicted with her understanding of sexual morality. Eventually the Finnish nationalist movement had to give in: the girls resigned and the whole choir sank into oblivion for several years. On the other hand, this was very much a two-way road: perhaps someone had complained to the patroness about the supervisor who had been harassing the girls and who was promptly dismissed. Among the older women at Finlayson, the patroness actively encouraged religious devotion, and gave direct financial support for missionary work among the workers. All in all the industrial family household at Finlayson wanted to see hard-working, loyal, morally righteous people who showed proper respect for both God and for the patron and patroness (Kanerva, 1972: 257-261; Aamulehti, 13.12.1884).

But where did Constance von Nottbeck not have a visible role? One such place was the Association of Cotton Mill Workers, which had been set up under the protection of the patron and which held its meetings on the factory premises. This socio-cultural association remained the responsibility of the patron, no doubt largely because it accepted male members only. It was not until 1872, after an anonymous letter-writing campaign in the local newspaper that Finlayson's women managed to change the rules. Women were now admitted as full members, but they were still excluded from its leadership (Kanerva, 1972: 143-150). This type of vertical segregation was to become a permanent structural characteristic of worker organizations in Tampere.

The First Independent Organization: the association of Gentlewomen

In a historical context Tampere is widely known in Finland as a "women's town", but as far as women's organization is concerned it was certainly not one of the pioneers. While women at one point accounted for as much as 60 per cent of the population in Tampere, the vast majority of those women were working-class girls from the Finlayson cotton mills (Rasila, 1984: 219-225), the proportion of upper-class gentlewomen remained relatively small, and it was they who in most cases started the process of organization among women. In the late 1880s there was only one official women's organization in Tampere, the Association of Tampere Gentlewomen, which had been established in 1866. In other Finnish towns the first associations dated back to the 1840s, and by the 1860s there were women's organizations in at least twenty other towns (Stenius, 1987: 165-167).

Why did it take so long for the women in Tampere to get organized? One reason, apart from the comparatively small number of gentlewomen, was no doubt the predominance of industrial family households. The underprivileged in Tampere remained under the patronizing care and control of a few major factories throughout the latter half of the nineteenth century, but this industrial-paternal way of life did not satisfy the future needs of the people. The Association of Gentlewomen in Tampere was far better placed to deal with the emerging new challenges, and it set out, in the same spirit as other similar organizations, to "resolve the problem of poverty and ignorance among the working people". The efforts of the Association no longer focussed on one factory but on the whole town and all its working people. Although this implied a detachment of charity from personal relations of dependence, it was still essentially a continuation of the patroness's policy in that it remained given from above. All attention now had to be directed to meeting the demands of the industrial capitalist community, which was expanding at an accelerating rate into the field of trade and small-scale industry. This required a continuous distinction between actors and the objects of action.[8]

The Association was very homogenous in terms of social composition; in practice the rules precluded membership from all except married women or widows of a high social standing. The single women who were admitted remained in assistant positions in the Association.

In the 1860s most of the gentlewomen in Tampere came from a Swedish-speaking background; the only notable exceptions a few foreigners who had moved into town. In quantitative terms, however, the Swedish-speaking population was very small indeed, as almost 95 per cent of the population in Tampere represented the Finnish-speaking majority. Therefore the membership consisted initially of only a handful of women; by 1880, a total of 56 women had joined up as members. Upon closer inspection it is clear that the Association attracted only a minor fragment of the upper classes in Tampere. The membership and particularly the Association's leadership consisted increasingly of the town's new Finnish-born crème de la crème: a special priority status was enjoyed by wives of merchants and of high officials in the administrative apparatus—the church, the army, the police and the judicial system.[9]

Private Spheres and Public Arenas

The Association's arenas of activity were characterized by a dual relationship to publicity: it remained at once in the background and made itself very visible.

The Association of Gentlewomen was preceded in the 1860s by a sewing society (Silmäys..., 1916), which operated within the private sphere and brought upper-class women together in an activity that was very popular and commonly accepted as a useful pastime. And since these meetings were held at private homes—instead of community halls, factory reading rooms, primary schools, or cafés, which later became popular meeting places for various mass movements and feminists—it was important that all members were more or less of the same social standing. This activity could be described as a form of intimate publicity: it was the response of women to men's clubs and in this sense reflected the structures of opportunity that were open to women.

Through the position of its members, the Association became part of the shifting borderline between the private and the public. The arenas of industrial family households were open only to a small number of people; the domestic world was becoming increasingly confined and increasingly a women's sphere. There remained only two main functions in that world, i.e. the management of the household and

Emma Hammaren, one of the Chairwomen of the Association of Tampere Gentlewomen who were married to local commercial councillors.

raising children; childhood was now being defined as a separate stage of life. Indeed, one might argue that the life of gentlewomen was becoming more and more domestic and more and more intimate, which of course was in stark contrast to the public life of working women and common wives in the factory tenements and in their collective kitchens (Saarinen, 1985; Rasila, 1984: 184-188).

The Association provided an important meeting place for these women who were becoming isolated in the private sphere. But as well as providing an intimate arena, the Association of Gentlewomen was in fact one of the most publicity-oriented organizations in civil society. The parties and lotteries and other events it arranged for charity put it at the centre of almost continuous public attention. Starting from the early 1880s, these women were appearing more and more often in the local newspapers, which ran extensive stories on these important events.[10]

While publicity obviously played an important role in mobilizing external support for the Association, it was perhaps even more important in translating charity into an organized political programme. At the same time, a separate politico-ideological sphere began emerging. For the community, the message was becoming very clear: the privileged elite of the town will continue to fulfil its obligations in the new society and to assume responsibility for the establishment as a whole (Stenius, 1987: 200ff.; Ramsay, 1989). And that responsibility, clearly, was recognized in Tampere and elsewhere as an important part of the future programme to build a new Finnish (albeit not necessarily a Finnish-speaking) nation.

"Male Activists"

The Association of Gentlewomen firmly established gender—femaleness—as a legitimate principle of organization. The strange thing about it all was that the most important driving force beind this organization were married women, who had been categorically excluded from official politics. And why did the Association attract male activists, even though the rules specifically defined it as a women-only organization?

It is necessary to consider the gentlewomen's agendas and arenas of activity against the whole gender system that prevailed in politics at that time. This draws our attention to the great enthusiasm of men. According to the Association itself, the initiative came originally from a priest, i.e. from the institution that was responsible for poor relief.

And that was not all. Up until 1899, the secretary of the Association, who was elected by outside the Board, was a man; the longest tenure was recorded for the town mayor who held the position for almost a quarter of a century. In the absence of minutes of meetings, we do not know exactly what kind of role the secretary played in the day-to-day work of the Association. At least he was responsible for issuing official announcements for the association's annual meetings, for writing its annual reports, and for liaising with the local press. The treasurer and auditors were also men, and they too were husbands of activist women and "professionals", i.e. distinguished businessmen.[11]

In search of an explanation, we must first turn to the obstacles that appear in the structures of opportunity. The 1734 Act that had been instituted during Swedish rule was still effective by prohibiting the public appearances of married women. In addition, marital legislation defined married women as financially incompetent.[12] So this, to a certain extent, explains the involvement of men in the first women's organizations; they were there to assume responsibility for public functions and for the management of finances. Perhaps this arrangement helped create an intermediate stage of change? The old and the new, the conventional and the radical were beginning to find each other; breaking the main rule—the privacy of married women—was fitted together with their entry into publicity with evident femininity.[13] A closer examination of the male activists points in other directions as well.

The male members of the gentlewomen's association were important political figures of the 1860s and 1870s in Tampere. In the 1880s, when the first political parties were being established, they were closely involved in building the Swedish-speaking front that consisted of a small economic and administrative elite, which maintained its class privileges well into the 1890s. Starting from the 1880s these same men also occupied top positions in a number of men-only organs, such as the merchants' association and the pro-Swedish party organ, the Swedish "conversation club"—and, needless to say, in the town council and the Diet (Rasila, 1984: 339-345, 421-447, 556-575).

Considering the existing structures of opportunity, it is clear that in this paternal

*Ida Yrjö-Koskinen, a teacher, a
founder member and a later Chairwoman of
the Tampere Women's Association and a
member of the Finnish Parliament*

world a leadership by married women was the only efficient way to run an organization. In short: married women, excluded from all official power organs and from the pro-Swedish civil society, were deprived of power, but they still had considerable political leverage. They had acquaintances and people in the family who were working in important positions and making decisions on their applications for financial support. To achieve the results they were looking for, these women did not have to resort to confrontation but could often use the subtler methods of persuasion.[14]

Did the drawing room arenas occasionally become bedrooms? There is no evidence of this in the historical documents that are available, for these were prepared for public use and prepared by men. There is also no indication of any conflicts. Nevertheless feminist critique suggests that a search for at least latent disagreements would be worthwhile.[15] It also encourages us to take a dual perspective on the channels of influence that were opened up to gentlewomen by the system of representation.

The Agenda: Reproduction of Class Relations

The agenda of the gentlewomen developed very much around the central functions that they had been assigned in their new family role. The first policy concerning children and education was actually formulated by the sewing society. The elementary school that was established in 1862 was originally open for girls only; it was closed down around the turn of the century because at that time there were a number of schools run by the municipal authorities. Four fifths of the children were from non-industrial working-class and artisan families for whom there had been no room in the factory's own schools. The school, according to the town mayor, was "of great value" to the town. This was followed by a Sunday school for girls and women. The major project of the 1880s was an orphanage; in 1885-1899 around 80 per cent of the running costs of this institution came out of the town budget. Both of these semi-public institutions depended on voluntary work by activists as well as on a small number of hired staff.[16]

There was one notable exception to the rule of organizational independence, and that was the children's workshop, which was set up in 1881. According to official history the idea for this project came from the women themselves, but it was organized by a separate association. The Board consisted for the main part of functionaries of the Gentlewomen's Association, but one third of the seats as well as top management were occupied by the magnates, with whom the women were already working in other fields.

The initial investment in the workshop came from the town authorities, which was quite exceptional. In fact, the town pledged to provide regular financial support for this project. This is hardly surprising in view of the fact that the purpose of the workshop was to help these children grow into self-respecting, hard-working citizens—which of course would also mean that they would no longer be a strain on the town's economy. The emphasis on moral work was clearly visible at the workshop's Christmas party, which always received good coverage in the local newspapers: on these occasions the gentlewomen—"these angels of charity"—would hand out gifts and clothes and religious literature to the children, all "basic necessities".[17]

The workshop's annual reports, the lists of gifts that were handed out and the speeches that were held on these occasions point to the reverse side of this philanthropy, its hidden agenda. What these lower social strata—or more precisely, these opposite social classes -were actually being given here was not only charity but also, and importantly, an interpretation of reality. Their sad plight was defined as a social and moral problem for which these people were themselves responsible; it was not an economic or a structural flaw in the system, which of course would have placed the blame on the upper classes.

A further example of cooperation between the male and the municipal authorities responsible for poor relief dates back to the early years. the association also revised its policy of charity by interventions in the private sphere, i.e. through visits to the homes of poor people. As in the case of the children's workshop, examples had already been set by other organizations at home and abroad.[18]

Apart from religious and moral advice, the visitor also had some money to hand out. This came mainly from donations and the proceeds of Christmas bazaars, and to some extent directly from the city council. A more systematic approach was soon developed to make the intervention more effective: the town was divided into 42 districts, each of which was covered by one or more gentlewomen. This arrangement remained effective until the early twentieth century, when the whole system of poor relief was completely reorganized. At this point the district gentlewomen became guardians who worked under the direct supervision of the authorities rather than the Association.

The functions of care and inspection were also in many ways linked together. The women in each district reported the need for work; in 1886-89 the Association arranged needle work for poor women. They informed the school, workshop, and orphanage about children who needed guidance or needed to be taken into custody. The Association's school often served as a meeting place for children from homes and from the gentlewomen's orphanage, workshop and even the city's poorhouse.[19]

Similar programmes were also developed by the sewing societies of the 1880s and 1890s, which had stronger religious undertones and which created the basis for the later development of the deaconness system. There was also cooperation in individual campaigns, or what may be described as sporadic mobilization (Christiansen-Ruffman, 1982). The gentlewomen of Tampere were constantly involved in such campaigns, whether these were for acquisition of a new concert grand or for raising money for starving people. They also did much work in support of men's organizations, even though they had been barred from those organizations either by direct exclusion or by means of vertical segregation. Would the new building for the volunteer fire-brigade ever had been possible without the lotteries arranged by the gentlewomen? (Järventie, 1959: 36-40; Sauramo, 1923: 59f.; Aamulehti e.g. 8.4.1882, 10.1.1892).

In spite of its continuing contributions the Association of Gentlewomen moved more or less out of the limelight in 1888 when the diet, referring to the great achievements of these associations, declared women—excluding married women—eligible for posts on municipal boards that were responsible for poor relief.[20]

Mobilization from Below—Incorporation from Above

The political issues that were tackled by gentlewomen were highly topical, and the politics they pursued was very creative and innovative; they were clearly willing and capable of "existing for others". They emerged as the epitomy of altruistic social and religious morality.[21]

The important thing, however, is that when the agenda of the Gentlewomen is seen in the more general context of their arenas and relations of activity and compared to the activity of men, then the harmony disappears and contradictions emerge. Would it be unfair towards these charitable ladies to talk about ideologized structures of opportunity? After all, this kind of agenda and these strategies of action were precisely what was generally expected of them, given their position and relationship to the economic and administrative elite of the town. Perhaps they were actually guided in this direction? There can be little doubt that the networks of personal contact which grew up within the Association and within its most important fora of cooperation created certain internal hierarchies. In Tampere the cultural mobilization of women from below came in contact with the incorporation from above by the male elite which held the economic, politico-administrative, and spiritual power; formally the autonomous Association became dominated by the external hierarchy.[22] The closeness of the relations is reflected in the fact that in revising their rules in 1889, the women decided to leave their funds, if the Association were to be disbanded, to the joint committee formed by the town minister, Chairman of the male representatives, and the town mayor.[23]

Within this vertical-horizontal divison of labour the setting of goals and the power remained in the hands of men, while the social and cultural work aiming at the realization of those goals was the responsibility of women. Indeed the overall picture was quite ambivalent. In terms of gender ideology the gentlewomen carried and pursued a strategy of assistance and complementation, a strategy resting on the notion that men and women are fundamentally different and that women are secondary, even incompetent.[24] On the other hand, although the gentlewomen were not making explicit calls for autonomy, their self-esteem, the appreciation bestowed on them by the people, and their own capacity for taking constructive action in society were all strengthened. Indeed it is legitimate to speak of the evolution from the 1860s onwards of a gender- and class-specific political citizenship. If we untie the links of the concept of citizen to the institutions open to men in the higher classes, it is directly comparable to the associations of men, whose work has naturally been recorded in the political history of Tampere.

Through their efforts the gentlewomen also ranked among the pioneers of the local welfare state—and on the other hand (and again in an ambivalent way) among the creators of the control state. All in all they are a good example of "Hegel's dilemma":[25] they were outside the state and the municipality and yet involved in creating these institutions through their own specific agendas and arenas.

This perhaps helps to explain why the Tampere Association of Gentlewomen was not defunct by the 1880s and 1890s. On the contrary, it showed signs of growth and development: membership figures peaked in 1895-96, when the Association had a total of 133 members, representing 0.4 per cent of the town's female population.[26]

According to the Association's "mayor-chair-secretary" these years saw the first germs of socialism in town. The city administrative court, under his supervision, was making national reputation for its interpretations of decrees, which effectively curbed the advancement of universal suffrage (Voionmaa, 1932: 352-393; Saarinen, 1990). The power positions of the economic and administrative elite and of the Swedish-speaking elite were falling apart; Tampere was in the grip of a fierce struggle for hegemony. The struggle was between a Fennomanian front which was built around a nucleus of intellectuals and the labour movement which was gradually dissociating itself from the powerful Swedes and, on the other hand, the "temperance people" who were, too, threatening the pro-Swedish "liquor and purse party". Women were also involved. They responded immediately to the call-up: the "angels of charity" showed an unwavering loyalty to their class and language bonds. Following the elections in 1893, learning about their defeat, the pro-Swedish gentlewomen urged all people who were starving after the cold winter to "go to the kitchens of the party that is now in power" (Sinisalo, 1932: 19-20).

A New Epoque Emerging: The Organization of Early Feminists

A new type of organization was born in 1890 with the establishment of Tampere Women's Association, which grew out of a national organization. After some hesitation (which was little more than a formality), the organization decided to ban male membership. This separatism was geared towards the aim of full autonomy; a central concern of early feminists was to maintain a non-hierarchical structure. A warning example was provided by the Tampere Pedagogic Society, where "the discussion is dominated by men".[27]

The reference that was made to the Pedagogic Society was important in another respect as well, in that the Association was committed to promote the interests of economically active and professional women. At the constitutive meeting, 12 of the 36 women present were teachers. Similarly, many of the married women had close connections with the intelligentsia. Only four founding members represented the town's economic elite. In other words there was only marginal overlap between the two associations in Tampere: only a few of the women who attended the meeting in November 1890 were also members of the Gentlewomen's Association. There was also very little cooperation between these two associations.[28]

The Women's Association was by no means a mass movement aiming to recruit a broad membership from all social strata. There were only three members who did not represent the upper classes. Language was no obstacle to participation, because of the availability of an interpreter so that either Finnish or Swedish could be used. The birth of the Association was indeed associated with the strengthening of the Finnish party. The struggle of the language parties in the 1880s mainly revolved around the school institution. It was also at this time that the first Finnish girls' school was opened. This was supported by the male leadership of the Fennomanian movement, which thus contributed to the development of local early feminism.[29]

In spite of the growth of the school the industrial town of Tampere was clearly an unfavourable environment for the recruitment efforts of the Women's Association; there was also no room for the Women's Union that later emerged as a serious competitior on a national level.[30] The average attendance at the regular meetings of the Women's Association was no more than fifteen women, while the figure for the annual meetings was between 14 and 35. In 1890-1902, the Gentlewomen's Association had membership figures that were twice as high as those recorded by the Women's Association. The latter's membership figure reached a peak in 1897, when its 68 members represented 0.2 per cent of the town's female population.[31]

The Women's Association also differed from the Gentlewomen's Association in terms of the marital status of its membership. This, too, represented a significant break with the past, in that two thirds of the founding members were unmarried. However, that this was still a transitional stage is clear from the fact that married women continued to occupy a central position at least in the formal hierarchy.[32]

The Agenda in the Public Sphere

The Association took an important first step in transcending kitchen politics by declaring itself a "women's right" movement. However, there remained a strong duality in the specific objectives that were written into its rules: on the one hand they called for autonomy, for full citizenship in the public sphere, and for competence in the face of law. On the other hand, this emerging feminism also wanted to carry on the tradition of the Gentlewomen's Association and through charity "improve the position of common wives" (Minutes of meeting in The Tampere Women's Association, 14.2.1894).

Why such an agenda—for what purpose was this organization needed? In the late nineteenth century the social position of women in the higher social strata was rather contradictory. Even working-class men were now getting somewhere, but women remained trapped in their given gendered position. At least for the Association's primary anchorage group (Siisiäinen, 1986: 142)—unmarried upper-class women who were seriously trying to earn their own living—this was a topical and very important point (Saarinen, 1985; Siisiäinen, 1986: 167-183).

In contrast to the Gentlewomen's Association, the Women's Association had the willingness and the power to defend its interests. The membership of the organization, as we already saw, consisted primarily of teachers, the biggest and most powerful professional group of women in the whole of Tampere. They had personal experiences of discriminatory gender structures in the public sphere; in institutions of higher educa-tion, for instance, only marginal positions were open to them. In elementary schools, they were faced with rigid vertical segregation in that all teaching positions to do with senior grades went to male teachers. Moreover, women were paid only two thirds of men's wages, even though the job was the same.[33] It is hardly surprising, then, that there were frequently discussions at their meetings of paid labour, of the relationship between men and women and of the family.

The Association failed to agree on a single unified position. This was not a matter of leadership disagreeing with other members or married women disagreeing with unmarried women. There was an ongoing debate among members. Some had adopted the position that women and men should continue to work separately in their respective spheres; some even felt that it was the duty of women to support and promote men in their pursuit of higher objectives. Nevertheless it was evidently the feeling of the majority that the Tampere Association should follow the example set by the parent organization and call for an opening of all occupations to both men and women. A particularly radical proposal (considering the historical context in which it was made) suggested that husband and wife should be made equally responsible for the family's livelihood and that they should receive equal pay for the same work. As in Helsinki, the Association gave its full support to co-education, so much so that its meeting "presided over the birth of the Finnish co-educational school" (Minutes of meeting in the Tampere Women's Association, e.g. 20.3.1893, 20.4.1893, 11.10.1894, 5.12.1895).

In its debates, the Association frequently attacked the traditional ideal that the role of breadwinner in the family belongs to men. The Workers' Association (established 1887) and the Association of Outdoor Workers (1893) both recruited a considerable number of women, but in both cases the leadership was in the hands of men. Workers were, for these organizations, men; women were workers' wives. This was also the bias on which political agendas were constructed, and accordingly the interests of men were given primary importance and those of women secondary (Saarinen, 1989; Siisiäinen, 1986: 185f.). So the task that remained for the Women's Association was to observe that there was "a special need in Tampere for a day nursery", after all around 6 per cent of the factory workers were women who were sole providers. However this idea, which was floated during the very first months of the Association, did not materialize until 1898 (Minutes of meetings in the Tampere Women's Association, 27.2.1891, 29.11.1895, 5.4.1897; Annual Report, 1898; Haapala, 1986: app. 5).

The Kitchen Agenda: From Private and Intimate to Political

The day nursery idea emerged from the reproductive day-to-day reality of working women, from female work (Halsaa, 1988), it was of importance to women, but absent from the male agenda. It represented at once continuity and change. The patroness and the gentlewomen continued their efforts to support poor children, but the feminists were the first to work for an organized system of daycare that would make it possible for women to take on full-time jobs. The day nursery idea is also an interesting example because it reminds us of the importance of the formal dimension of the agenda: what we have to ask is how the "time and place" of the problems prevent them from surfacing or how they facilitate this. The day nursery is also related to the private sphere. It is an example of a problem which is created by a distinction between the public and the private, to which men and women have a different relationship. Women did not have "househusbands" to look after their children while they were out working.

The successful jetty campaign serves as an example of a different type of time- and place-related problem. Writing under the pseudonym of "Someone" in the biggest daily of the Tampere area, the Chairperson of the Association said that "what the town really needs is not one huge washing jetty but several smaller ones". The male authorities responsible had not only failed to consider the long distances that women had to travel, but also the effects of the nearby sewage pipe (Minutes of meeting in the Tampere Women's Association meeting, 25.1.1897; Aamulehti, 24.1.1897).

The distinction between public and private was most deeply rooted in the issue of prostitution. The private home was facing a problem that was commonly described by the label of "public women". What is more, the whole issue was declared a taboo subject; in 1888, the nobility wanted the diet to deal with the subject in camera, whereas a bishop representing the clergy felt that decent and respectable women should not even know of its existence—let alone have young girls see a petition for its abolition, which was what the Finnish Women's Association was doing (Tuulasvirta-Kaleva, 1988: 28; Ohtonen, 1987: 30).

On the other hand, prostitution was very visible even in local terms. It was usually associated with unmarried and low-paid working-class women. In Tampere, the police records for the turn of the century include around 30 or 40 women. Newspapers frequently ran stories about the gaol sentences given to brothel operators and prostitutes who had been selling spirits; in the 1880s there was even pillorying and flogging. Nevertheless when the issue of universal suffrage was being discussed, prostitution was still considered a normal and acceptable source of income. In the 1896 municipal electoral register, six of the 323 women were listed as "general women" (Jaakkola, 1982: 235; Aamulehti, e.g. 6.8.1884, 18.1.1887, 3.2.1887, 7.7.1887, 10.1.1888, 24.4.1888, 3.5.1890, 13.11.1890; Electoral roll, 1896).

The Women's Association took the issue on its agenda from the very outset. At the initiative of the parent organization in Helsinki, the feminists in Tampere expressed their serious concern over the Medical Association's favourable statement in 1891 regarding the establishment an inspection centre. The feminist also rallied for a "chastity front" and in the mid-90s urged councilmen to take steps to prevent prostitution. In the early years of the twentieth century, the Association set up a special committee and wrote a letter directly to the Czar of Russia. There was not, however, complete unanimity on this issue. In fact the majority of activists were opposed to the proposal according to which women would no longer be allowed to work as bathing attendants for men, because that would have "excluded women from an occupation they have pursued from time immemorial" (Minutes of Tampere Women's Association meetings, 20.1.1891, 28.3.1892, 10.10.1892, 28.10.1892, 24.11.1892, 20.4.1903, 19.1.1904; Annual Report, 1895).

The Women's Association was no doubt primarily motivated in its effort by an honest concern for the family, its calls for increased public control and education were no doubt motivated by the serious aim of establishing a more settled and peaceful social order. However, it is quite obvious that the upper-class feminists also wanted to pull down the double standards of morality that were built into the inspection legislation, because the Association insisted that the inspection should be extended to male customers. This proposal caused a reversal in the interests of medical experts and men in general. They were primarily concerned with the health of women, of future

children and of the prostitutes, not only the health of men. At the same time the proposal made morally visible those whom the gentlewomen perhaps did not want to see:
the men in their own social strata. In the end, although it referred to "fallen women",
the Women's Association did not accuse the profession but highlighted the difficult
economic and social conditions under which prostitutes had to live.

Women's moral policy has often been interpreted within the context of the "from
victimization to guilt" pattern proposed in "malestream" critique (Siltanen and
Stanworth, 1984: Introduction). Most writers have concluded that it boils down to
moralism, an inauthentic policy. And if it has been acknowledged as a policy, then it
has been labelled as a conservative one. One important thing that is bypassed in these
interpretations is the double standards of sexual morality that prevailed among the
upper classes of the nineteenth century. The image of women's maternal or almost
childlike innocence and passivity complemented those of full-grown, experienced men;
the sexuality of men was always potentially active and was not to be reduced to
fatherhood. In addition, the sexuality of respectable women was restricted to the
intimate sphere of matrimony, whereas men had the freedom to satisfy their needs
whereever and whenever they pleased.[34]

The Double Strategy of Emancipation

The requirement of an absolute sexual morality that is equally applicable to women
and men is a far-reaching and profound demand. It is part of the entire gendered
power system and integrated into the critique of bipolar female and male images. It
is not an apolitical programme, nor is it marginal or conventional; it is a radical idea
that goes straight to the crux of the issue. It is also a radical idea when we consider
the formal dimension of the agenda. Anti-prostitution politics implied a direct
confrontation with traditional notions of conventionality, which said that the public
treatment of sexuality was strictly a male affair.[35]

But how were the other interests of common wives filtered down into the politics
of the feminists? This question has long remained without serious attention in research
on early feminism in Finland.[36] Yet particularly in the case of Tampere it is a very
important question. The agenda of the Women's Association was in practice a philan-
trophic one. There is no simple and straightforward answer. That there was at least
some sisterly sensitivity is demonstrated by the requirement that inspections be carried
out by female doctors, so as to make it "at least less intolerable for the prostitutes".
The Association supported the proposal of granting illegitimate children the same legal
status as legitimate children. It set up a summer camp for working-class girls, because
the teachers knew full well that at home they had less time for themselves than boys;
they, too, had the right to a childhood. The next step was to arrange a summer camp
for factory women, who deserved a break and recreation: the modern concept of wage
labour was gradually breaking through. Gymnastics courses were arranged as a

counterbalance to the physical monotony of industrial work. The general programme for women's education included courses in arithmetic and reading. The tradition of giving advice in household management was also carried on, but using a new method: lecturing (Tampere Women's Association Annual Reports, 1890-1902).

So the philantrophy of the "teacher association" that worked "in-between" classes was, in contrast to the more maternalistic patronizing of the patroness and the gentlewomen, of a more modern nature, and it provided the necessary ingredients for a change that was based on knowledge and education. However, the social homogeneity of the activists eventually led to the emergence of a latent agenda—a policy that may be described as a double strategy of emancipation. As in the case of Helsinki, these trends are most clearly visible in the issue of the housemaids.[37]

The Association held that the mistress must assume responsibility not only for the moral education of her maids, she must also "make sure they do not go on strike". The Association took a negative stand on the requirement for shorter working hours: "at least in families with small children" this was impossible. These problems, that concerned domestic work and mutual power relations between women, were not insignificant, because in Tampere housemaids represented the second biggest occupational group. In the early 1880s there were 400 of them, while 20 years later the figure had soared to 1,700. Something of this relationship is also revealed by the fact that when at the turn of the century as many as a couple of hundred working-class women came into contact with the Association, they were directed to a separate reading and sewing circle (Minutes of Tampere women's association meetings, 4.2.1891, 2.12.1893, 23.3.1900, 25.1.1901, 20.2.1901, 18.3.1901, 22.4.1901, 13.5.1901; Haapala, 1986: 83).

At last we have an explanation for the discrepancy between the name and the rules of the Association: The "women" were the upper-class feminists themselves, while the "common wives" were excluded, although this was done with some discretion: they represented a special group of women whose position would be gradually improved under the close supervision of feminists. The strong merger of the feminist cause and philantrophy was indeed a rather contradictory phenomenon. On the one hand it reflected women's orientation to "being for others" as well as sisterliness. On the other hand it also contained ideologized structures of opportunity: perhaps it helped make up for the exclusion of women from other struggles?[38] At the same time the interest that was shown in the agenda of the Women's Association towards sisters representing lower social strata was no doubt also in part due to the specific ideological basis of early Finnish feminism: the common good—building a unified nation—was set over and above individual rights in the Hegelian Fennomanian movement which was also joined by local feminists through its mother organization. The factor of "locality" must also be taken into account in the explanation. During the 1880s the Finnish front needed an organization to match the Gentlewomen's Association, which was taking care of the working class; and at the turn of the century it was necessary to take the working class into consideration, because the potential recruitment basis in Tampere was very broad indeed.[39]

Confrontation and Sisterhood

We still need to explore the arenas, means and working methods of early feminists in Tampere; this will help to complete the picture.

From the historical material that is available on the Gentlewomen's Association, it is impossible to say how the public activity of women affected their activity as mothers and housewives. The situation is different in the case of the Women's Association. We learn from the minutes of their meetings that they also discussed the strategy—as applied by the temperance movement—of "home missions"; they did not, however, go as far as working-class women and consider a "love strike". It was generally believed that the desired results could be achieved by talking things over. The common wives' strategy of public punishments against drunken husbands were completely out of the question; that would have been a disgrace (Minutes of The Tampere Women's Association meetings, 17.4.1891, 25.1.1897; Saarinen, 1989; Aamulehti, 1.6.1866).

The policy pursued by the Women's Association was not, however, concerned only with public structures or directed at other people, it was also directed at themselves. This is yet another point where the Association differed radically from the gentlewo-men: what they were seeking was not only development but a break in development, an inner change in oneself. This requirement transformed all loci of activity into potential arenas of politics, and introduced an element of temporal continuity. Politics was not a separate sphere but an aspect of life. In its discussions on wage labour and the family, the Women's Association was outlining a new individualistic woman. The aim was a process of cultural socialization regulated from below. There was a strong determination to hold on to "femaleness" and to revise the definition it had been given by "men or women who are not interested in the cause of feminism" (Minutes of Tampere Women's Association meeting, 28.3.1895).

In the early years of the Association, disputes over meanings produced perhaps the most visible confrontation in the local civil society and in the Finnish nationalist movement. The initial impetus came from a lecture that had been given at the folk high school on marriage and the family. It has always been difficult for women to make public appearances and speeches, especially in front of mixed audiences and in subjects on which there remains disagreement. In the 1880s common women had al-ready taken this step and spoken at temperance associations and in the street; now, it was the turn of upper-class women. The Women's Association arranged a counter-lecture "for the same audience, in the same place" (Minutes of Tampere Women's Association meeting, 8.3.1897; Aamulehti, 23.3.1897; Saarinen, 1989).

One of the most important things that the upper-class women of Tampere learned from the Women's Association—and that they had not been taught by the Gentle-women's Association—was how to say "no". The relationship of the Association to community-level publicity thus acquired features of a dual strategy. On the one hand it was working to undermine vertical socialization (W.F. Haug, 1979), the position of women in a mixed audience. The Association taught its members the kind of skills they would be needing in modern civil society, which was based on active participation and argumentation. On the other hand, it was creating an exclusive publicity for women. Early feminists served as a link for a process of horizontal socialization, which was tying activists in Tampere to global networks of ideologies, mobilization and organizations.

Again there is a clear difference in comparison with gentlewomen. Although the Gentlewomen's Associations relied largely on contacts extending from one region to another, and perhaps even on international contacts, they never had any national organization, not to speak of a programme. Feminist organizations, by contrast, were from the very outset oriented to setting up an organization that would cover the entire country (Stenius, 1987: 294-318). With their central associations and regional subdivisions, they represented a rather fixed and hierarchic type of organization.

Women activists in Tampere invited speakers and lecturers both from Finland and from abroad although this, admittedly, was still rather rare. Having a good command of many foreign languages, they were also able to arrange meetings where lectures originally delivered in Kuopio, Helsinki, Stockholm, and even Chicago were read and discussed. In addition, the Association distributed Finnish as well as foreign magazines and books. Unlike the mass organizations then operative in Tampere, it did not publish a journal of its own, nor dit it have its own speaker society (Minutes of Tampere Women's Association meetings, 7.3.1893, 25.10.1893, 1.11.1894, 1.11.1897, 3.2.1899, 27.3.1899, 1.4.1901, 18.11.1901; Aamulehti, 8.4.1890, 15.4.1890, 26.9.1890; Saarinen, 1989).

Perhaps these were not considered necessary? That is, the organization had all the necessary resources to make their case well beyond their own ranks. A future novelist reported on the Association's meetings in the local newspapers. Lectures were also readily available from the ranks of the Association's many teachers, although on the subject of health care and menstruation it was necessary to find an outside expert. The choice was a female doctor. Was this an attempt to concretize the demand for opening all professions to women? Or was it the Association's objective to create an ideal speech situation, a new type of women's publicity on intimate subjects, which allowed for a confidential treatment of subjects that still remained rather delicate and perhaps even shameful?[40]

Towards Public Power

Many women activists still remained interested in exploiting every opportunity to exchange views in more private settings as well. Thus the proposal to discontinue morning visits met with fierce resistance on the part of a number of members. Their argument certainly made sense: these were excellent opportunities to talk about topical issues of the day (Minutes of Tampere Women's Association meeting, 5.12.1894). There are of course no written documents on these visits or on the conversations that went on among working-class women in their collective kitchens. Nonetheless they serve as one example of the kind of arenas that started to emerge in the everyday life of common wives; arenas that do not always correspond to the male fora that were largely moulded by their work and its strictly scheduled rhytm.[41]

Following the example of its parent organization, the Women's Association in Tampere was nevertheless determined to break into the arena of public power, the state apparatus. In the short run women encouraged each other to use the rights they had. Throughout the 1890s the Tampere activists continued to make appeals, both through personal contacts and through adverts placed in newspapers, for women to turn up at electoral campaigns. These were necessary appeals in that, although the women leadership of the Association had no vote, teachers represented the biggest individual group of women in Tampere who qualified as full citizens in municipal elections: in 1896 they numbered 64, which was one fifth of the electoral roll (Minutes of Tampere Women's Association meetings, 7.12.1891, 23.1.1893; Electoral Register, 1896; Saarinen, 1990).

Universal suffrage did not rank among the women's priority issues until 1903-04. The Women's Association remained extremely quiet if one considers the progress of the reform at the state and municipal level in the male civil society. The struggle culminated in the mass petitions filed by the Worker's Association and the Finnish Club, which had been established in 1891. Both petitions called for universal suffrage for men; universal included men only (Sinisalo, 1932: 26-27).

This was hardly surprising in view of the fact that there was a strict gender division in the top strata of the pro-Finnish civil society. Since the 1880s there had been a silent acceptance of feminism, and in many ways it was even supported. In return for this favour, civil society wanted to have women lend their contribution to the nationality and language struggles through workers' associations and temperance movements. Indeed women who were close to the Women's Association played a visible role in sporadic mobilization. However, by adopting a strategy of exclusion the Finnish Club, which was the central organ of the Finnish Party, was helping to reinforce a brotherly tendency. Working-class men were admitted as members from the very beginning, but women had to wait until a rewriting of the rules after the general strike in 1905 (Sinisalo, 1932: 149).

Nevertheless the early feminists did have certain privileges of their own: at least

eight of the 12 chairpersons, deputy chairpersons, secretaries and treasures in 1890-
1902 were married to a founding member and top-ranking figure in the Finnish Club.
It was hardly surprising, then, that Tammerfors Aftonbladet, the leading organ for the
Swedish party, accused the Women's Association of campaigning for the Finnish
Party—an allegation that was firmly rejected by the Association, although there had
been talk about concentrating votes for the "nationally-minded".[42]

Obviously these connections were not completely meaningless. The Club's agenda
was largely characterized by the exclusion and marginalization of women's interests.
It did briefly discuss the issues of prostitution and women's suffrage, which were
probably introduced on the agenda via these marital connections. As the Finnish Party
gained an increasingly strong power position, these connections were no doubt very
useful when applications for grants were submitted to the municipal authorities
(Sinisalo, 1932: 22-23, 113; Rasila, 1984: 578-582).

Working-class women in Tampere did not have such unofficial and indirect
channels at its disposal, let alone any formal and direct means of influence; on the
1896 electoral roll, there were only three women with a working-class occupation. And
as far as the diet was concerned they had even less political leverage, while the
Women's Association had informal channels of influence through husbands. By the
1890s the bourgeois classes of Tampere were already represented by the pro-Finnish
intelligentsia. Many of them were husbands of early feminists, and they sponsored
various bills concerning women's eligibility for office in municipal elections and
private and economic liberties (Ääniokeus... [Elecoral Register], 1896; Saarinen, 1990;
Voionmaa, 1932: 362-368).

The Women's Association wanted to avoid the growth of an internal hierarchy. It
did not remain completely immune to external relations of domination, although this
of course was a two-way road. Feminists were at least to some extent aware of the
risk of corporatism. In spite of the financial support they had received, they declined
the invitation of city councillors to work as inspectors of poor relief. It was also clear
that everyone was behind the call for universal suffrage—even those who had strong
doubts about the ability of women to do serious scientific work.[43]

In summary: in terms of the ideology of gender the Women's Association was to
a certain extent ambivalent. It involved a strategy of equal value that aimed at
maintaining separate spheres but at the same time at eradicating their internal
hierarchies, and it even showed traces of the strategy of assistance and complementation. At the same time the Association was very much a "women's rights" organization. It was the first association to deny the dependence of women on men, both in
the family and in the state: that is what early feminists wanted to build themselves,
without male representatives. Indeed they set up strategies to counteract women's
exclusion and underestimation in a way, which resulted in strategy of emancipation that
adopted a critical stance on the world of men. Thus it challenged the strong liberalist-
patriarchal (fraternal) double rationality (Pateman, 1988b) of the time as well as the

underlying bipolar images of gender. The Association formulated its aim of universal suffrage in terms of a double strategy until the general strike, for the call was for suffrage on equal conditions for men and women.

Epilogue

The dialectics of control, and—viewed from Tampere, a mere coincidence—the Russo-Japanese war interfered in the course of events. When the development that was controlled from above got out of hand and was transformed into a revolution coming from below, a group emerged on the state arenas, which was different both in terms of its gender and in terms of its class position: the common wives. Their political citizenship had evolved elsewhere and in more revolutionary forms, in the workers' and temperance movements; only part of this had been visible through the patroness, the gentlewomen and early feminists.

The 1905 general strike, a great feat of strength both for the nationalist front and for the labour movement, was all-encompassing: everyone joined in. The strike even united the women of Tampere for a moment. The Association of Gentlewomen, in which the younger patroness of Finlayson had been involved, was not directly taking part in the struggle for freedom, but it undertook to look after the children who would need care and attention during the strike. Upper-class feminists found their way into the radicalized women's section of the Tampere Workers' Association. Now even the Women's Association, going against the "step-by-step policy" favoured by the parent organization and the Old Finnish party, was working for universal suffrage, even eligibility for office (Tampere Women's Association membership list, 1897; An-teckningar, 1866-1898; Annual Report, 1905).

On Thursday, November 2nd, the strike committee—which included working-class women—spoke to an audience that had gathered at the Central Square in Tampere using this prophetic opening line: "Finns! Citizens! Brothers! Sisters!" Women were only a few days away from the *Promised Land*.[44]

References

Sources

A. Archives:

Äänestysluettelo kunnallisvaaleissa Tampereella 1896. (Voionmaan kokoelma).

Tampereen kaupunginarkisto:
Tampereen Työväenyhdistys (TTY). *Johtokunnan ja kuukausikokousten pöytäkirjat 1886-1896.*
Tampereen Ulkotyöväenyhdistys (TUTY). *Johtokunnan ja yleiskokousten pöytäkirjat 1893-1896.*

Tampereen kaupungin veroluettelo 1895.
Tampereen köyhäinhoitohallituksen pöytäkirjat 1882-1902.
Tampereen seurakuntien arkisto.
Tampereen seurakuntien rippikirjat 1890-1902.
Naisten Tampere—sateenvarjoprojektin arkisto. Historiatieteen laitos, Tampereen yliopisto.

Tampereen Rouvasväenyhdistys:
Anteckningar rörande Fruntimmersföreningen Tammerfors, 1866-1898.
Årsberättelser 1876-1900.
Silmäys Tampereen Rouvasväenyhdistyksen toimintaan v:na 1866-1914. A.B. Tammerfors Nyheterin kirjapaino, Tampere 1916.

Tampereen Naisyhdistys:
Kokouspöytäkirjat 1890-1905.

B. Newspapers:
Aamulehti, 1882-1902.

Literature

Alfthan, Märtha von (1966), *Seitsemän vuosikymmentä Naisasialiito Unionin historiaa.* Unioni Naisasialiitto Suomessa ry.

Bagguley, Paul, Jane Mark-Lawson, Dan Shapiro, John Urry, Sylvia Walby and Alan Warde (1990), *Restructuring: Place, Class and Gender*, London: Sage.

Christiansen-Ruffman, Linda (1982), "Women's Political Culture and Feminist Political Culture", paper presented in research committee 32, 10th World Congress of Sociology, Mexico City.

Haapala, Pertti (1986), *Tehtaan valossa. Historiallisia tutkimuksia 133, Suomen historiallinen seura*, Tampere: Vastapaino.

Haapamäki, Hilkka (1986), *Tampereen Suomalaisen klubin jäsenten sosiaalinen tausta vuosina 1891-1905.* Suomen historian pro gradu -tutkielma. Tampereen yliopisto.

Halsaa, Beatrice (1987), "Har kvinnorna gemensamma intressen?", *Kvinnovetenskaplig tidskrift*, 4.

Hernes, Helga Maria (1987), *Welfare State and Woman Power*, Oslo: Norwegian University Press.

Haug, W.F. (1979), "Umrisse zu einer Theorie des Ideologischen", Manfred Behrens et al. (eds.), *Über Ideologie*, Arguments-Sonderband, 40. Argument Verlag, Berlin.

Hirdman, Yvonne (1988), "Genussystemet—reflexioner kring kvinnors sociala underordning", *Kvinnovetenskaplig tidskrift*, 3.

Hirsjärvi, Kyllikki (1950), *Ylhäistä elämää Tampereella.* Tampere. Tutkimuksia ja kuvauksia IV. Tampereen historiallisen seuran julkaisuja VIII. Hämeen kirjapaino, Tampere.

Hollis, Patricia (1987), *Ladies Elect. Women in English Local Government 1865-1914*, Oxford: Clarendon Press.

Jaakkola, Jouko (1982), *Työväestö ja sosiaalinen poikkeavuus*. Suomen historian lisensiaatti-tutkimus, Tamperen yliopisto, Tampere.

Jallinoja, Riitta (1983), *Suomalaisen naisasialiikkeen taistelukaudet*, Werner Söderström, Osakeyhtiö, Helsinki-Juva.

Jonasdottir, Anna (1987), "I kvinnors intresse: Förtrycksfri form och öppet innehåll", Aino Saarinen, Eva Hänninen-Salmelin and Marja Keränen (eds.), *Kvinnor och makt. Kvin-noperspektiv på välfärdsstaten*, Samhällsvetenskapliga forskningsinstitutionen, Tammerfors Universitet, serie B 48, Tampere.

Jutikkala, Eino (1972), *Säätyvaltiopäivien valitsijakunta, vaalit ja koostumus*. Suomen kansanedustuslaitoksen historia IV. Eduskunnan historiakomitea. Valtion painatuskeskus, Helsinki.

Järventie, Martti (1959), *Uskon ja rakkauden työtä. Tampereen kaupunkilähetyksen 75-vuotishistoria*. Tampereen kaupunkilähetys, Tampere.

Kanerva, Unto (1946), *Pumpulilaisia ja pruukilaisia*, Helsinki: Tammi.

Kanerva, Unto (1972), *Liinatehtaalaisia ja "tehtaanmaistereita"*. Tampere-Seura. Tampereen Keskuspaino, Tampere.

Lerner, Gerda (1979), "The Political Activities of Antislavery Women", *The Majority Finds Its Past*, Oxford: Oxford University Press.

Levas, Naemi (1957), *Augusta Lundahl-Wallenius*. Tampere. Tutkimuksia ja kuvauksia V. Tampereen historiallisen seuran julkaisuja IX. Hämeen kirjapaino, Tampere.

Lindfors, Gustav V. (1938), *Finlayson-fabrikerna i Tammerfors. I. 1820-1907*, F. Tilgman.

Manninen, Juha (1987), "Rakkaus sivistystapahtumana", *Dialektiikan ydin*, Pohjoinen, Oulu.

Ohtonen, Virva (1987), *Elisabeth Stenius-Aarneenkallio, kuopiolainen naisasianainen*. Snellman-instituutin B-sarja, Kuopio.

Pateman, Carole (1988a), *The Sexual Contract*, Oxford: Polity Press.

Pateman, Carole (1988b), "The Patriarchal Welfare State", Anne Philips (ed.), *Democracy and the Welfare State*, Princeton: Princeton University Press.

Puoli vuosisataa naisasiatyötä. (1934) Suomen Naisyhdistyksen 50-vuotisjuhlajulkaisu 1884-1934. Otava, Helsinki.

Ramsay, Aleksandra (1989), "Huvudstadens hjärta" Licenciatavhandling i Finlands och Skandinaviens historia, Helsingfors Universitet.

Rasila, Viljo (1984), *Tampereen historia II. 1840-luvulta vuoteen 1905*. Tampereen kaupunki, Tampere.

Rasila, Viljo (1988), *Finlaysonin tehtaan vanha "palatsi"*. Tampere. Tutkimuksia ja kuvauksia IX. Tampereen historiallisen seuran julkaisuja XIV, Tampere.

Rendall, Jane (1987) (ed.), *Equal or Different*, Oxford: Basil Blackwell.

Saarinen, Aino (1985), "Naisliikehdinnän ensi askeleet Suomessa—naiset "hyvinvointivaltion" pioneereina, Aino Saarinen, *Vapautta naisille!*, Tutkijaliitto, Helsinki.

Saarinen, Aino (1986), "Naistutkimus—frakkiin vai hameeseen?", *Politiikka*, 4.

Saarinen, Aino (1989), *Morgonrodnad och rösträtt. Arbetarkvinnorörelsens framväxt i Tammerfors*, Arbetarhistoria, 3.

Saarinen, Aino (1990), "Veljeystendenssi ja kamppailut äänioikeudesta Tampereella vuoteen 1902. Brotherly Tendency and Struggles for Universal Suffrage in Tampere Up Until 1902" (manuscript).

Sauramo, A.V. (1923), *Tampereen vapaaehtoinen palokunta 1873-1923*. Tampereen kirjapaino-osakeyhtiö, Tampere.

Scott, Joan W. (1988), "Deconstructing Equality-versus-Difference—Or, the Uses of Poststructuralist Theory for Feminism", *Feminist Studies*, 1.

Siisiäinen, Martti (1986), *Intressit, yhdistyslaitos ja poliittisen järjestelmän vakaisuus*. Jyväskylä Studies in Education. Psychology and Social Research 57. Jyväskylän yliopisto, Jyväskylä.

Siltanen, Janet and Janet Stanworth (1984) (eds.), *Women and the Public Sphere*, London: Hutchinson.

Sinisalo, Uuno (1932), *Tampereen Suomalainen klubi 1891-1931*. Tampereen Kirjapaino-osakeyhtiö, Tampere.

Stenius, Henrik (1987), *Frivilligt, jämlikt, samfällt*, Skriften utgivna av svenska litteratursällskapet i Finland, nr. 545, Helsinki.

Sulkunen, Irma (1987), "Naisten järjestäytyminen ja kaksijakoinen kansalaisuus", Risto Alapuro et al. (eds.), *Kansa liikkeessä*, Kirjayhtymä, Helsinki.

Thiele, Beverly (1986), "Vanishing Acts in Social and Political Thought: Tricks of the Trade", Carole Pateman and Elisabeth Gross (eds.), *Feminist Challenges*, Boston: Northeastern University Press.

Tuulasvirta-Kaleva, Tiina (1988), *Prostituoitujen valvonta- ja rankaisusäännökset 1875-1909*. Suomen historian pro gradu—tutkielma, Tampereen yliopisto, Tampere.

Walkowitz, Judith (1980), *Prostitution and Victorian Society*, Cambridge: Cambridge University Press.

Voionmaa, Väinö (1932), *Tampereen historia itämaisesta sodasta suurlakon aikoihin*. Tampereen työväen kirjapaino, Tampere.

Notes

1. The term is here employed as a loose metaphor for women's politics which is bound up with the agendas and arenas of the private sphere.

2. Within this project I have already published an article describing working-class women and the labour and temperance movements of 1882-1902 [*Morgonrodnad och rösträtt*, Saarinen 1989; in Swedish]. Currently I am finishing a manuscript which is concerned with male organizations [*Brotherly tendency and struggles for universal suffrage in Tampere up until 1902*, Saarinen 1990; in Finnish]. The study is part of two different umbrella projects: *Women's Tampere* and *The Gender System of the Welfare State*.

3. For a discussion on the "local", see Bagguley et al. 1990. I am indebted to *Tiina Tuominen* who drew my attention to British locality resarch.

4. Hirsjärvi (1950) says that formally the patroness was a member of the Gentlewomen's Association, although she is not mentioned in the Association's membership list, see

Tampereen Rouvasväenyhdistys [The Association of Tampere Gentlewomen] (TRY), Anteckningar [Notes] 1866-1898.

5. Hirsjärvi, 1950. For more on charity, see Ramsay, 1989: 77-90. Local newspapers provide an abundance of information on charity in Tampere.

6. As late as the 1850s Finlayson's workers were hired on an annual basis, see Kanerva, 1946: 38-44.

7. On ideological and cultural socialization, see W.F. Haug, 1979.

8. For the rules, see Anteckningar... [Notes], 1866-1898; on the associations, Stenius, 1987: 168-169.

9. Membership list, Anteckningar ... [Notes], 1866-1898; on marital relations, see Silmäys... [An Overview], 1916. According to Ramsay (1989: 91-99) the Association in Helsinki also had pro-Finnish women members representing the intelligentsia. There were certain exceptions in Tampere as well. For instance, there was one Chairwoman who had connections with the Fennomanian movement through her mother and her family. This clearly points to the importance of women's networks, see Levas, 1957.

10. The data here have been collected from Aamulehti issues from 1882-1902.

11. Silmäys... [An Overview], 1916; see also Kanerva, 1972: 257-261; Aamulehti, 13.12.1884; Anteckningar... [notes], 1866-1898; Aamulehti, 1882-1899, especially 23.5.1885. By the 1890s the women seemed to have taken control of their own bookkeeping.

12. Stenius, 1987: 78. In Germany, for instance, women were still barred from membership of political organizations and parties as late as the nineteenth century; see Greven-Anschoff (1981: 27).

13. For the categories of "Privatheit" and "Öffentlichkeit" as part of gender domination, see Greven-Anschoff, 1981: 22-27.

14. For a description of methods of persuasion and influence, see Lerner, 1979. Another telling point about structures of opportunity is the fact that the Association's Christmas collection box was placed in a chemist's shop owned by one of the activist's husbands.

15. The same point is raised by Ramsay, 1989: 121, who has studied the work of the Association in Helsinki.

16. Silmäys... [An Overview], 1916; TRY Annual Reports, 1876-1899, especially 1882.

17. Workshop Annual Reports, see Aamulehti e.g. 8.3.1882, 14.4.1883, 22.4.1884, 16.4.1885; Silmäys [An Overview], 1916; on the Christmas parties, Aamulehti e.g. 4.1.1882.

18. Silmäys... [An Overview], 1916; on Helsinki, see Ramsay, 1989: 109-116; more generally, Saarinen, 1985; on England, Hollis, 1987: 1-28.

19. Silmäys... [An Overview], 1916; TRY Annual Reports 1876-1899, especially 1884.

20. Aamulehti, 31.3.1888. The first woman to be elected to this board in 1894 was a merchant who was active in both the major women's organizations in Tampere and who had recently been widowed. These women had previously been represented on the Board of Directors of some of the private girls' schools. Minutes of the Board of Poor Relief, 1889-1894; Aamulehti, e.g. 18.4.1885.

21. This is stressed by Ramsay, 1989: 7-10; see also Saarinen, 1985.

22. On internal and external hierarchies, see Siisiäinen, 1986: 41-54; on incorporation, see Hernes, 1987: 51-52. For comparison reference can be made to the study on Helsinki by Ramsay (1989).

23. Proposals to revise TRY rules, Aamulehti, 31.10.1889.

24. This line of argumentation is analysed in Manninen (1987). It creates a basis for the distinction between strategies of equal value on the one hand and strategies of assistance and complementation on the other.

25. This is from Pateman, 1988b. The concept of dual citizenship proposed by Irma Sulkunen (1987) would be appropriate here, although it is not unproblematic. Although the concept has been developed in the context of gender studies, it has approached the empirical sphere on basis of concepts of politics and the political that are not considered theoretically. This clearly affects Sulkunen's interpretations particularly of moral and kitchen politics.

26. Tampere Association of Gentlewomen (TRY) membership list, Anteckningar [Notes], 1866-1898; Silmäys... [An Overview], 1916; Annual Reports, 1880-1898. For these years there are no annual demographic statistics on women and men; the figures here are estimated based on Rasila (1984: 223), which gives figures at five-year intervals. The same applies to the statistics presented later.

27. Finnish Women's Association, 1884-1894: 2. There remain some historical minutes of the meetings of Tampere Women's Association, see 2.5.1892, 2.12.1893.

28. Data are available on only 24 women; minutes of the founding meeting of Tampere Women's Association, 20.11.1890; TRY membership list, see Anteckningar [Notes], 1866-1898; confirmation certificates of Tampere congregations 1890. On the National Women's Association, see Jallinoja, 1983: 72, 82, 85.

29. See articles in the Finnish party's Aamulehti, e.g. 28.1.1882, 10.4.1884, 20.10.1887, 1.6.1889.

30. Another relevant factor was no doubt that the Union's party-political reference group was represented by the Young Finns, who never won a very strong footing in Tampere. See Jallinoja, 1983: 46-50 and Rasila, 1984: 580-581.

31. There are no membership lists available. New members were occasionally entered in the minutes of the Association's meetings, but not always. Membership statistics are given in the 1890-1902 Annual Reports of the Tampere Women's Association. The number of female members in mass organizations was of course several times greater in the 1890s, see Saarinen, 1990, more generally Sulkunen, 1987.

32. This is stressed by Ramsay, 1989: 7-10; see also Saarinen, 1985. Tampere Women's Association Annual Reports, 1890-1902; Jallinoja, 1983: 71.

33. Tampere tax register, 1895; on the teachers of primary schools, see e.g. Aamulehti, 4.11.1891; more generally Saarinen, 1985.

34. For a more detailed discussion, see Walkowitz, 1980.

35. Walkowitz (1980: 179) also describes how difficult it was for women to talk about prostitution especially to mixed audiences. On bipolarity, see Scott, 1988.

36. As an example, see Jallinoja, 1983, for a critique, Saarinen, 1987.

37. With the concept of double strategy I want to stress the latent agenda, the protection of one's own interests as part of the struggle against discrimination and "being used". On the issue of the housemaids, see von Alfthan, 1966: 153-158.

38. Another important reason why the Women's Association failed to develop into a major organization lies in the general rule formulated by Helga Maria Hernes (1987: 57) that there are always more women in organizations which have supportive roles than in those that are opposed to other organizations or that are in direct competition with other organizations.

39. See minutes of the Tampere Women's Association meeting, 22.4.1901. Generaly speaking: this specific contradiction between liberalist individualism and the Fennomanian movement which displayed a Hegelian orientation has so far remained unstudied in the history of early feminism. In addition, the feminist movement has been reduced to a "Helsinki-national" phenomenon, see Jallinoja, 1983.

40. Minutes of Tampere Women's Association meetings, 28.9.1893, 20.2.1895, 24.1.1902. The concept of ideal speech situation is from Habermas, see Siisiäinen, 1986: 183-184.

41. This has been stressed e.g. by Rendall, 1987.

42. Minutes of Tampere Women's Association meeting, 23.1.1893; Annual Reports, 1892-1902. On marital relations, see confirmation certificates of Tampere segregations, 1890-1902; Haapamäki, 1986: Appendices 1 and 2.

43. Minutes of Tampere Women's Association meetings, 5.12.1894, 18.5.1900. There remain no data on The Association's accounts, and therefore no similar estimate can be made as in the case of The Gentlewomen's Association.

44. The religious-utopian expression was used by the Chair of the Finnish Women's Association, Aleksandra Gripenberg, 1.10.1906, the same day as the new Parliament Act was enforced (Puoli vuosisataa..., 1934: 29-30).

Women's Culture and the Continuity of the Women's Movement

Leila J. Rupp and Verta Taylor

Scholars have traditionally depicted the history of the women's movement in the United States and other Western industrialized nations as discontinuous (Flexner, 1959; Evans, 1977; Chafetz et al., 1986). According to this scenario, the movement emerged in the nineteenth century, died out in the 1920s with the attainment or blockage of suffrage, and reemerged along with the other sixties movements—or what have been dubbed the "new social movements"—in a kind of "immaculate conception" (Klandermans, 1986). Supposedly, a forty-year lull in feminist activity separated the two waves of mobilization. Recent empirical work on the US civil rights movement (McAdam, 1988), the US left (Isserman, 1987), the US and international peace movement (Foster, 1989; DeBenedetti, 1990), and the women's movement (Spender, 1983; Cott, 1987; Rupp et al., 1987; Black, 1989; Rupp, unpublished) challenges the view that the new sixties movements emerged out of nowhere, suggesting that the break between the new social movements and earlier waves of political activism is not as sharp as previously assumed. Increasingly we have evidence to support a view of the women's movement, in particular, as continuous from the mid-nineteenth century to the present, despite fluctuation between stages of mobilization and what we term "abeyance" (Taylor, 1989).

We propose that a central factor for the continuity of the women's movement is the persistence of women's culture. We focus on two abeyance cycles of the American women's movement—women's rights activism in the 1940s and 1950s and contemporary lesbian feminism—and on the international women's movement from its late nineteenth century origins to its reestablishment after the Second World War in order to explore the role that women's culture played in sustaining the women's movement in unfavorable environments. We suggest, further, that women's culture, because it is essentially an expression of collective identity, creates an atmosphere during abeyance phases that is particularly prone to conflict over identity. Thus women's culture has a complex impact on the history of the women's movement.

Data

Our discussion focuses on three cases on which we have done or are currently doing research. The data on the US women's rights movement from 1945 to the mid-1960s come from archival collections of organizational and personal papers and from interviews. Archival data consist of personal letters, organizational correspondence, minutes, reports, and publications relating to women's rights activity. Our 57 interviews with leaders and core members of the most central groups working for women's rights include 45 open-ended, semi-structured, tape-recorded interviews conducted between 1979 and 1983 and 12 transcribed interviews conducted by other researchers and available in archival collections. Complete documentation can be found in Rupp and Taylor (1987).

The data on the contemporary US lesbian feminist movement come from published primary materials and interviews with participants. The written sources include books, periodicals, and narratives by community members; and newsletters, position papers, and other documents from lesbian feminist organizations. Twenty-one in-depth, open-ended interviews were conducted with informants from Boston, Provincetown, and the rural Berkshire region of western Massachusetts; Portland, Maine; Washington, D.C.; New York City; St. Petersburg, Florida; Columbus, Yellow Springs, Cleveland, and Cincinnati, Ohio; Minneapolis; Chicago; Denver; Atlanta; and Charlotte, North Carolina. Fuller discussion is available in Taylor and Whittier (forthcoming).

The data on the international women's movement from 1888 to 1950 come from archival collections in the US and England. The research focuses on international women's organizations working in concert on a variety of issues, including suffrage, equality, peace, labor, and morality, is still in progress (Rupp, unpublished). Our discussion here is based on the records of 10 international organizations (the International Council of Women, the International Alliance of Women, the Women's International League for Peace and Freedom, the International Federation of Working Women, Equal Rights International, the Open Door International, the World Woman's Party, the Peace and Disarmament Committee of the International Women's Organisations, the Pan American International Women's Committee, and the International Assembly of Women) as well as the personal papers of 21 women involved in these and other organizations. Although all of the papers are located in US or British archives, they do include the correspondence of a number of European (and to a lesser extent Latin American and other) women.

Theoretical Considerations

An overemphasis on origins has blinded social movement scholars to the "carry-overs and carry-ons" (Gusfield, 1981: 324) between stages of social movement activism. Although a few analyses of movement maintenance and transformation look to external factors, notably the changing structure of political opportunities and shifting economic and demographic conditions (Garner, 1977; McAdam, 1982; Barkan, 1985; Jenkins et al., 1986), most consider primarily internal organizational dynamics (Zald et al., 1966; Gerlach et al., 1970; Kanter, 1972; Gamson, 1975; Staggenborg, 1988). At the micro-

The Women's International League for Peace and Freedom, depicted with their banners during a mass meeting in Madison Square, January 20th, 1932. The meeting was held prior to the sailing for Europe of two of the US delegates to the disarmament conference at Geneva.

level, pre-existing links and organizational ties among individuals have emerged as the most significant determinant of persistent activism (Morris, 1984; Rosenthal et al., 1985; McAdam, 1986; McAdam et al., 1988). What is still missing, however, is attention to the way in which the production and maintenance of meaning within groups affects continued participation. This leads us to consider what historians have called the "women's culture" of the women's movement.

Disagreement among US women's historians about the role of women's culture in movement formation calls attention to lack of clarity in use of the term. DuBois (1980), who defines women's culture as "the broad-based commonality of values, institutions, relationships, and methods of communication, focused on domesticity and morality and particular to late eighteenth- and nineteenth-century women", warns against the tendency to romanticize a culture that accepted the dominant values of the larger male-dominated society. For her, women's culture and feminism stand in a dialectical relationship.

In contrast, Carroll Smith-Rosenberg (1980) insists that a culture must have "its own autonomous values, identities, symbolic systems, and modes of communication". Setting aside the term "women's culture" and the question of its relationship to feminism, Smith-Rosenberg suggests that feminism cannot develop outside a "female world" in which women create rituals and networks, form primary ties with other women, and develop their own world view. In a similar vein, Freedman (1979) argues that the strength of the American women's movement in the late nineteenth and early twentieth centuries depended on the construction of a public female sphere of separatist institutions based on the private middle-class women's culture. The decline of the women's movement in the 1920s, she suggests, can be partly attributed to the de-valuation of women's culture and the decline of separate female institutions.

To muddy the waters still further, in the contemporary American women's movement "women's culture" has come to mean a specifically feminist culture, that is, the culture of the movement itself. We leave aside here the question of the relationship of women's culture outside the movement—which historians assume disappeared by the early twentieth century—and focus on women's culture within the women's move-ment. We define women's culture as the values, rituals, relationships, and alternative institutions of the women's movement that express the solidarity of women and women's equality with (or superiority to) men. This women's culture, we argue, plays an important role in sustaining the women's movement through periods of less overt activity.

Continuity of the Women's Movement: The American Case

The women's movement in the US, we argue, has a continuous history from the mid-nineteenth century to the present. In describing the history of the women's movement, it is useful to distinguish two types of stages: mobilization and abeyance. As Lofland (1985) points out, mobilization is best viewed on a continuum from "warm" to "white-hot". This formulation corrects the popular misconception that movements by definition are numerically large and mass-based and calls attention to variations in patterns of movement growth. Movements also, however, undergo the process of demobilization, which we have elsewhere analyzed as abeyance (Taylor, 1989). The term "abeyance" depicts a holding process by which movements sustain themselves in non-receptive political environments and provide continuity from one stage of mobilization to another. A movement in abeyance is made up of a cadre of activists, mainly recruited in an earlier round of mobilization, engaged in activism around the same challenge. Abeyance structures are important because they link one upsurge of activism with another. Through promoting the survival of activist networks, sustaining a repertoire of goals and tactics, and promoting a collective identity that offers participants a sense of mission and moral purpose, an abeyance phase of a social movement contributes to continuity.

The continuity of the American women's movement has been obscured until recently because most scholars have focused on cycles of mobilization. Historians have traced the emergence of the women's movement in the mid-nineteenth century out of abolitionism and other reform efforts (Flexner, 1959; Berg, 1978; DuBois, 1978). The annual women's rights conventions of the pre-Civil War era, held in different locations throughout the northern states, substituted for social movement organizations until the emergence of what DuBois (1978) refers to as an "independent women's movement" in the years immediately following the Civil War (Phillips, unpublished). At this point, women in the emerging movement formed two opposing organizations out of conflict over the relationship to their abolitionist and labor movement allies. In the succeeding years, the movement slowly gained adherents and respectability as its goals came to seem less radical and its activities less out of synch with mainstream culture (Kraditor, 1965).

By the turn of the century, the movement was moving into a phase of peak mobilization as the two original groups merged into an increasingly mass mainstream organization; at the same time, smaller militant groups, influenced by the British suffragettes, began to flourish (Buechler, 1986; Lunardini, 1986). The attainment of suffrage in 1920, however, helped to fragment the mass movement of the 1910s. The militant branch of the national movement, the National Woman's Party, launched a relentless campaign to pass an Equal Rights Amendment (ERA) to the constitution. Never a mass organization, the Woman's Party increasingly defined itself as a feminist vanguard or elite and alienated both its socialist allies and moderate feminists by its implacable opposition to protective labor legislation for women. The mainstream branch of the movement formed the non-partisan League of Women Voters and, while advocating a broad range of reforms, spearheaded the opposition to the ERA. Other activists in the suffrage campaign channeled their efforts into new or growing organizations that did not have an explicitly feminist agenda but promoted a vast range of specific causes that, in part, grew out of expanded role options available to women (Cott, 1987). Although a variety of organizations continued to work on behalf of women, the Woman's Party captured the feminist agenda by alone continuing to claim the title "feminist".

As the American movement splintered in the years after the First World War, the international women's movement seemed to flourish. The International Council of Women, founded in 1888 at the instigation of US suffragists, had brought women together from a number of countries to work on a variety of issues on which they could agree. In 1904, suffragists within the organization, impatient with the conservatism of some Council branches and leaders, formed the International Woman Suffrage Alliance to work specifically for suffrage. During the First World War, pacifist members of the Woman Suffrage Alliance called a meeting that ultimately led to the formation of the Women's International League for Peace and Freedom. The war seemed to spur international organizing among women: the 1920s and 1930s saw a proliferation of international women's organizations concerned with peace, equal rights, and labor, giving rise to coalitions of international organizations designed to coordinate women's efforts in lobbying the League of Nations in Geneva. The outbreak of war in 1939 seriously disrupted international organizing among women, although existing groups reestablished international contacts after the cessation of hostilities in 1945.

To a certain extent, international activity among women can be seen as a response to dwindling national efforts. Stymied or discouraged at home, national leaders sometimes turned their attention to the international arena. Thus, the 1920s and 1930s, a period of abeyance for most national women's movements in the industrialized world, saw increased organizing on the international level. But mass mobilization of women was never an object of the international movement; participation necessitated international travel to attend meetings or conferences, and this constraint shaped both the numbers and the social composition of the membership. From 1888 to the end of the Second World War, US and northern European (especially British, Dutch, and German) women with the resources to travel internationally and/or the status to serve as representatives of their groups dominated the international organizations, although the leadership sought representation from women throughout the world. Thus, the international women's movement, even in periods of increased activity, shares basic characteristics with abeyance phases of national movements.

From the end of the Second World War to the resurgence of the American women's movement in the 1960s, the women's rights movement in the US consisted of a number of organizations and networks of women, most of them old, white, middle or upper class, well-educated professionals who had developed a commitment to feminism in the early years of the twentieth century. Centered around the National Woman's Party, a small number of women with the time, financial means, and other kinds of resources to commit themselves to the feminist cause kept the movement alive. Lacking an active membership, feminists attempted to give the appearance of a mass base and used strategies such as lobbying and letter-writing that could be carried out by the leadership and core membership without support from a large membership. The movement, which had ties to the suffrage struggle through both its personnel and its organizational history, focused its efforts primarily on passage of the Equal Rights Amendment (ERA), advocacy of women in policy-making positions, and proselytizing on behalf of women's history. It facilitated continuity between two cycles of mass activism, most visibly by keeping alive the ERA, which women's rights activists brought to the attention of emergent organizations in the 1960s.

The resurgent American movement grew from two separate sources (Freeman, 1975). What came to be known as the liberal branch, which coalesced around President Kennedy's Commission on the Status of Women (1961-1963) and the new National Organization for Women (founded 1966), had ties to the existing women's rights

From the International Women's Suffrage Alliance Congress in Copenhagen, 1939. At the first table from the left facing the photographer, Sigrid Amnitzbøl (Denmark), K. Bompas (UK, Secretary), Malaterre Sellier (France), the author Karen Blixen (Denmark), M. Corbett Ashby (President) and Edel Saunte (Denmark, Chairwoman of the Danish Women's Society). Across the table Rosa Manus (Holland), wearing glasses and a hat, and Frantiska Planinkova (Czechoslovakia).

movement (Rupp et al., 1987; Harrison, 1988). The radical branch had roots in the civil rights and New Left movements (Evans, 1979). The liberal branch consisted primarily of national-level, hierarchically-structured, formal organizations; the radical branch was an amorphous, decentralised network of primarily local, autonomous groups characterized by lack of formal organization and hierarchy. The former took a reformist stance and, early on, focused on legal change. The latter advocated the transformation of the major structures of society through consciousness-raising and militant actions.

Throughout the 1970s, the American women's movement grew and expanded its focus. Despite the continued differences in the structure of national mass-membership organizations and small local groups, the goals and strategies of what began as two quite distinct branches began to converge as the liberal branch embraced such issues as reproductive freedom, the fight against violence directed at women, and lesbian rights, and the ERA came to serve as a rallying point for the entire movement (Ferree et al., 1985; Taylor, 1988). But the movement also increasingly confronted challenges from within over issues of race, class, and sexuality as women of color, poor and working-class women, and lesbians criticized the traditional biases of the movement.

Recent scholarship argues that such conflict ultimately led to the demise of radical feminism and its replacement by what its critics have dubbed "cultural feminism" (Echols, 1989; Ryan, 1989). In contrast, we envisage what has been proclaimed the death of feminism as another abeyance phase of the movement, in this case one in which lesbian feminist communities sustain a commitment to feminist activism (Taylor et al., forthcoming).

As lesbians in both the liberal and radical branches of the women's movement encountered hostility from and engaged in conflict with heterosexual feminists, they formed separate lesbian groups. The Furies, founded in Washington, D.C. in 1971, marks the beginning of lesbian feminism (Echols, 1989). Other groups sprang up shortly after in New York, Boston, Chicago, San Francisco, and other urban localities around the country. Throughout the 1980s, lesbian feminist groups proliferated even in smaller communities, especially those with major colleges and universities.

National publications, events, organizations, and celebrities tie together local lesbian feminist communities, which engage in a range of actions—from protest to more institutionalized tactics in the political arena—to achieve social change. As the mass women's movement receded in the 1980s, an elaborate network of feminist counter-institutions, including rape crisis centers, battered women's shelters, bookstores, newspapers, publishing and recording companies, and recovery groups, remained, increasingly driven by the commitment of lesbian feminists. These groups and others, established in the 1980s, form the institutional base of a community that channels women into a variety of actions geared toward personal, social, and political change.

Such a brief overview can do no more than sketch the cycles of mobilization and abeyance that characterize the history of the American women's movement. What is important for our purposes is the role that women's culture played in both sustaining activism and provoking conflict throughout this history.

Women's Culture in Abeyance Cycles

The women's culture of the international women's movement, the American women's rights movement of the 1940s and 1950s, and lesbian feminist communities in the US since the 1970s shared four basic features: an affirmation of "female" values, the use of ritual, an emphasis on women's relationships, and the creation of separatist organizations and institutions.

Female Values

Women involved in the international women's movement paid homage to the idea that women across national boundaries shared basic female values. Most often they linked those values to motherhood, which they believed made women natural advocates of peace. As the bearers of life, they asserted, women longed to save lives by eliminating war. Because women lacked political power throughout the world, the evils of war could only be laid at the doorsteps of men.

Although motherhood emerged most often as the basis of women's solidarity, some women active in the international movement linked women's values to a universal sense of injustice. Whatever the bond, women throughout the movement resorted to the language of sisterhood to describe women's common interests. "Sisterhood" across the boundaries of race, class, ethnicity, nationality, and culture implied that women as a group, in contrast to men, shared something fundamental. Whether this was "mother-consciousness" or a shared commitment to "culture, justice, civilization, and beauty", whether it was a biological or cultural tie, it served as the basis for women's organizing on the international level.[1]

American women's rights activists in the post-1945 period also asserted the importance of female values. Although the (ERA), the major goal of the movement, provided for identical treatment for women and men under the law, there was a strong current of belief among women's rights activists that women and men are fundamentally different. Such a view, which had been prominent in the American women's movement in the nineteenth century, had eroded by the mid-twentieth century and thus distinguished those who held it in this period from those who accepted the dominant conviction that women are human first and female second. A core of women in the National Woman's Party put women's gender identity first because they believed that women are in fact superior to men. In a way reminiscent of international activists, some pointed to the Second World War as an inevitable consequence of women's exclusion from policy-making, arguing that the entrance of women into positions of power would transform society in basic and desirable ways. Although they spent little time dwelling on the origins of gender-based discrimination or on the responsibility of men as a group for the social system, they did on occasion express anti-male sentiments, complaining, as one woman did, of masculinity, "man-mindedness", "masculine egotism", and "sex bigotry".[2] As in the international movement, women expressed their relationships to one another in terms of sisterhood.

Far more explicitly than women in the international women's movement or the American women's rights movement, contemporary American lesbian feminists affirm female values by proclaiming their superiority over those of men. A large body of scholarly and popular writings valorizes egalitarianism, collectivism, an ethic of care, respect for knowledge derived from experience, pacifism, and cooperation as essentially female traits. In contrast, an emphasis on hierarchy, oppressive individualism, an ethic of individual rights, abstraction, violence, and competition are denounced as fundamental male values. The belief in these essential differences between women and men is expressed, as in the other cases, as the basis of sisterhood. Community members refer to one another as "sisters" and assert, in the words of a movement slogan, that "sisterhood is powerful". Thus, from quite different perspectives, the women's culture of these three phases shared a basic belief in female values and the sisterhood of women.

Ritual

A second component of women's culture is ritual. Rituals are symbolic expressive events that communicate something about social relations in a relatively dramatic way. By reinforcing collective values, they reaffirm the moral order (Wuthnow, 1987).

Rituals played an important role in the international women's movement as an expression of international ties. The movement functioned primarily through meetings of organizational officers and periodic congresses that brought women together from throughout the world. At such congresses, rituals such as banquets, teas, receptions, and entertainment sought to meld women into a cohesive group. But, ironically, expressions of nationalism could not be eliminated. The display of national flags held a central place at such congresses, and local arrangement committees provided characteristic national entertainment (Bosch, 1990).

Other rituals also attempted to express international connections. International organizations devised ceremonies for their constituent national members to perform at the same time throughout the world. The headquarters of international organizations in Geneva between the wars sponsored teas and receptions for the international community. Individual organizations sponsored contests for the best design of a membership pin that would be produced, sold, and worn as a symbol of internationalism. In addition, international leaders periodically set off on world tours in an attempt to arouse interest in their organizations. In all of these ways, the leadership and membership sought to create and cement ties among women of diverse backgrounds.

Relatively homogeneous national movements did not confront the same obstacles to the creation of a common culture, but they also used ritual to express solidarity. The National Woman's Party, the core of the American women's rights movement, developed an elaborate series of rituals enacted at the Alva Belmont House, national headquarters in Washington, D.C. Public rituals—teas, receptions, and parties—celebrated feminist heroines and achievements of the past, honored women politicians or sponsors of the ERA, or marked victories in the on-going struggle to pass the ERA. Celebrations of feminist foremother Susan B. Anthony's birthday or of the ratification of the suffrage amendment served to link current activity to the legacy of the women's movement. How important the rituals at Belmont House remained even after the resurgence of the women's movement in the 1960s is suggested by the fact that women's groups continued to hold functions there throughout the 1970s.

Ritual, both public and private, also plays an important role in the contemporary American lesbian feminist community. At the local and national levels, public rituals consist of cultural events such as concerts, films, poetry readings, exhibitions, plays, and conferences. Most prominent at the national level is the annual Michigan Woman's Music Festival, a five-day all-female celebration that attracts up to 10,000 women for musical performances, workshops, support groups, political strategy sessions, healing circles, and the sale of feminist paraphenalia. The National Women's Studies Association Conference is another annual cultural event that goes far beyond an academic conference by not only providing a forum for feminist performances but also by featuring open debate over central movement issues that periodically gives way to virulent conflict. Other rituals, such as Take Back the Night Marches, occur in local areas but tie communities together through the use of the same strategy.

In addition, lesbian feminists construct what might be viewed as private rituals in response to the central tenet that "the personal is political". The politicization of everyday life is, in many respects, the hallmark of lesbian feminism. Every aspect of life—where one lives, what one eats, how one dresses—can become an expression of politics. Activists engage in symbolic displays that challenge conventional standards of gender behavior that subordinate women. Dress and mode of self-representation, in particular, are used to strike a blow against reigning standards of beauty. Such private rituals, like the public rituals of the other cases, represent an important element of women's culture.

Relationships

Women's culture in all of these cases also involves the formation and validation of relationships among women. Such relationships might range from the comradeship of common participation to the creation of "mother-daughter" ties to lesbian or other marriage-like relationships.

Friendships that grew out of common work in the international women's movement were important in creating solidarity among relatively diverse women. Women came to know one another from repeated meetings at international congresses, visits to each others' homes when travelling abroad, serving on committees together, or travelling together on organizational business. When an international congress took place, the organizing committee provided hospitality for foreign visitors in individuals' homes whenever possible. Thus international work necessitated periodic but intense contact among women. Women throughout the movement commented on the importance to them of the friendships they made through international participation.

Some women formed more intense ties. Leaders especially seemed to call forth great devotion from women involved in the movement. When a younger woman attached herself to an older one, they might conceptualize their relationship in terms of a mother-daughter bond. Dutch activist Rosa Manus, for example, formed such a relationship with American leader Carrie Chapman Catt.[3] Other women came to the movement in existing relationships with women. The German activists Anita Augspurg and Lida Gustava Heymann, for example, were known throughout the movement as a couple and, at least to European women, as a lesbian couple.[4] Other prominent couples included Americans Anna Howard Shaw and Lucy Anthony and Englishwomen Margaret Rhondda and Helen Archdale. What is significant about such relationships is that they were accepted within and validated by the movement.

Women's relationships were quite similar within the American women's rights movement of the 1940s and 1950s. Women formed friendships as they attended meetings, lobbied together, or visited each others' homes to work on particular projects. Women who lived and worked at the National Woman's Party headquarters, the Belmont House, became, for some, the "Woman's Party family". They developed ties that they described as mother-daughter or sororal relationships. In fulfilling their functions as family members, women provided financial and emotional support, celebrated holidays with one another, and vacationed together. Many who did not live at the house on a regular basis came to do organizational work or lobbying, thus participating on a temporary basis in the "family".

Just as in the international movement, women coupled with other women played an important part in women's rights activity. Women who lived together in marriage-like relationships and worked together in the movement found their relationships treated as any heterosexual partnership might be. Some seemed to form communities with other similar couples, visiting each other on a regular basis. Former Vassar College roommates and National Woman's Party members Alma Lutz and Marguerite Smith shared a Boston apartment and summer home, "Highmeadow", in the Berkshires from 1918 to Smith's death in 1959. Mabel Vernon, a militant suffragist and worker for peace, and her "devoted companion" Consuelo Reyes, who had met through the Inter-American Commission on Women, spent every summer at Highmeadow with them. Woman's Party members and animal rights activists Alice Morgan Wright and Edith Goode, described as "always together", visited on occassion.[5] Such relationships could facilitate work for women's rights, while participation in the movement provided acceptance for women whose relationships might be declared deviant by the larger society, despite the fact that these women did not, as far as we know, identify as lesbians (Rupp, 1980).

By definition, women's relationships are central to the contemporary American lesbian feminist community. But these relationships are conceptualized not only as personal but also as political, as captured in the classic slogan, "feminism is the theory and lesbianism is the practice". For some lesbian feminists, this means that lesbianism is defined by woman-identification and resistance to patriarchy rather than by sexual attraction to or involvement with women. Not all members of the lesbian feminist community are sexually involved with women, and not all women who have sex with women are part of the community. Lesbian feminist community members tend to form intimate relationships with other politically-committed women. They also construct family-like ties with one another, celebrating holidays, birthdays, commitment ceremonies, and anniversaries with other members of the community.

Women's relationships in these three cases suggest not only the centrality of ties among women to women's culture, but also the significant role that woman-identified women have played in the women's movement throughout its history. Only since the emergence of lesbian feminism have lesbians made their presence known in the women's movement, but the participation of women who have primary bonds with other women is not new. This helps to explain the contemporary charge in the US that one "has to be a lesbian to be a feminist". Even to hostile outsiders, the strength of women's relationships within the women's movement is evident.

Organizational Separatism

A final component of women's culture is organizational separatism. Although women may work within gender-mixed organizations for a variety of women's issues, the all-female nature of women's movement organizations is important.

In the international women's movement, women organized in separate organizations as a consequence of their belief in female values and as an outgrowth of separatist organizing on the national level (Darrow, unpublished). Perhaps more significant, the international women's organizations banded together in the 1920s and 1930s, forming coalitions to coordinate their effort. By such actions, they expressed the conviction that a women's peace organization, for example, had as much or more in common with a women's equal rights group than with male or mixed-gender peace organizations. Despite increasing pressure in the twentieth century for women's organizations to merge with men's groups or accept male members, the international women's organizations retained their separatist structures (Boynton, unpublished).

Likewise, organizations in the American women's rights movement confronted the question of admitting men but remained committed to working with women for women. The National Woman's Party came under particular attack because its wealthy benefactor, Alva Belmont, had included a clause in her bequest revoking her legacy if men ever joined or participated in the organization. This periodically raised hackles in the 1950s, when domesticity, motherhood, and suburban togetherness figured so prominently in American women's social scripts. The leadership of the Woman's Party persistently rejected proposals to admit men, dismissing the notion as "an injury" or simply "fantastic".[6]

Lesbian feminism takes separatism a step farther. Not only are lesbian feminist organizations for women only, but a central goal of the community is the creation of separate institutions to serve as islands of resistance to the dominant society. Often men, and even male children over a very young age, are explicitly excluded. Lesbian feminist separatists attempt to withdraw from men and male society in every way as a means of building personal strength and creating institutional alternatives that might serve as the basis of a truly feminist society.

Although the extent of separatism is much greater in the lesbian feminist community, organizational separatism plays a role in the women's culture of all three cases. Even if women's organizations cooperate with mixed-gender groups, the identity as a women's organization remains important.

We find, then, that the assertion of female values, the use of ritual, an emphasis on women's relationships, and organizational separatism characterize the women's culture that was created in all three quite different phases of the women's movement. What all these stages have in common is the absence of mass mobilization. Although we do not mean to suggest that women's culture is only important when the external climate is inhospitable, we do think that in abeyance phases, or in contexts such as the international arena, the importance of women's culture expands. Without a great deal of activity by large numbers of participants, the shared culture of those trying to sustain the movement becomes central.

Conflict in Abeyance Phases

Women's culture as we have analyzed it is a manifestation of collective identity: the shared definition of a group that derives from members' common interests, experiences, and solidarity (Taylor et al., forthcoming). Collective identity defines the boundaries of a group, provides a structural explanation for its position, and suggests means to renegotiate or alter the disadvantaged position. The elements of women's culture that we have identified express in various ways the solidarity of the "group called women" (Cassell, 1977). Collective identity not only helps the movement to survive, but it can also heighten conflict within the movement. Since who one *is* eclipses what one *does*, conflicts over identity become crucial.

In all of the cases that we have considered, conflicts erupted to threaten the solidarity of women. In the international women's movement, the most serious conflicts concerned the relationship of national (or ethnic) identity to the collective identity of the women's movement. Although participants asserted the solidarity of women across national and ethnic boundaries, when world war broke out or struggles for national liberation heated up, women in the international movement did not always see their interests lying with other women. During the First World War, some German and French women refused to participate in the International Congress of Women called in The Hague; the head of the major national women's organization in Germany explained that during a struggle for national existence, "we women belong to our people and *only* to them".[7] A Belgian woman who attended but refrained from voting echoed this sentiment, proclaiming, "I am Belgian above all".[8] In the aftermath of the war, women in the international organizations sought to bring about a reconciliation, and there were symbolic displays of unity, but continuing expressions of nationalism led American Carrie Chapman Catt to conclude in 1922 that "there was no longer any internationalism left in the [International Woman Suffrage] Alliance".[9]

Questions of national or ethnic identity were equally problematic in the colonial and dependent countries, where growing nationalism challenged imperialist control. A Syrian woman and a French woman clashed over the consequences of French rule in Syria at the International Congress of Women held in Chicago in 1933.[10] At a board meeting of the International Woman Suffrage Alliance in 1939, Dutch Jew Rosa Manus faced off with Egyptian feminist leader Huda Shaarawi over the question of continued Jewish emigration to Palestine.[11] Whether in the colonies, in politically independent but economically dependent countries, or in the leading industrial nations, women's national or ethnic identities led to clashes with their "sisters".

In response to such threats to international women's solidarity, international organizations attempted to suppress or avoid conflict by forbidding discussion of questions considered "purely national".[12] This did not, of course, solve anything. Thus, creating a group identity depended on ignoring national or ethnic identities, something that was particularly unlikely in time of war or a national struggle for independence.

In contrast to the broad program and relative diversity of the international women's movement, the American women's rights movement was positively homogeneous and focused. Yet the most serious crisis in the history of the National Woman's Party erupted in 1946, just as the post-war reaction was shutting down options for women. A rebellious group within the organization challenged the established leadership, eventually forming an opposition faction and attempting to wrest control of the organization's resources through the legal system. The focus of attack was Alice Paul, the founder and leading light of the Woman's Party. But what was at stake was the nature of the organization. Would it be run democratically or autocratically? Would it be large or a small vanguard group? Would it adopt modern techniques or continue to use traditional methods? The opposition identified itself as democratic, interested in mass membership, and modern, denouncing Alice Paul and her supporters as the "Conservative Group".

The opposition group lost its case in court in 1947 and the Woman's Party continued on, although work on the ERA had ground to a halt and the membership had declined. But the issues had not been settled, and they reemerged in the early 1950s. This time the new chairman of the organization took up the banner of democracy, recruitment, and modern methods, unsuccessfully challenging Alice Paul's covert control. Flinging charges that Woman's Party members held "archaic" notions of "exaggerated feminism" and were "harried or misfit women" unable to get along with men, the defeated chairman attacked the very basis of the Woman's Party culture.[13] Thus this conflict, like conflicts within the international women's movement, focused on questions of group identity.

Identity politics—and conflicts—are even more central to contemporary American lesbian feminism. The questions of identity that plagued the international women's movement apply here: race, class, and ethnic loyalties create dilemmas for women of color, working-class and poor women, and Jewish women who are community members and find themselves fighting racism, élitism, and anti-Semitism in the women's movement.

In addition, the lesbian feminist community is beset by a conflict over sexuality. What originated as a struggle over pornography is now referred to as the "sex wars". Not only do lesbian feminists disagree about the appropriate balance between "sex as danger" (an emphasis on rape, incest, battering, and pornography) and "sex as pleasure" (including a validation of pornography, prostitution, sadomasochism, and role-playing), but these disagreements carry over into the expression of lesbian feminist identity. The dominant sex-as-danger position is associated with "political correctness" in dress and behavior: comfortable, practical, non-feminine styles, and relationships in which politics take precedence over sexuality. In contrast, the "pro-sex" advocates or "sex radicals" advocate sexual expressiveness and sometimes adopt fashions traditionally associated with the sex trade or prostitution. Some working-class women, like African-American, Asian-American, and Latina women, criticize the hegemonic cultural style of the "politically correct" faction as an imperialist imposition of white, middle-class standards. Conflict over these questions can be bitter and has, in the past, disrupted conferences and cultural events. Like the conflicts over race, class, and ethnicity, the conflict over sexuality focuses on how one defines oneself in relationship to the women's movement.

What is central to conflict in these three cases, then, is the question of identity. Because identity is so crucial to women's culture in abeyance phases of the women's movement, the struggle to define that identity can be fierce. In the international women's movement, the difficulty of elevating gender identity on the international level above national or ethnic identity created conflict and limited potential recruitment. In the American women's rights movement, conflict over the nature of the organization and its membership almost destroyed the National Woman's Party. And disputes about race, class, ethnicity, and sexuality threaten to tear US lesbian feminist communities apart.

Conclusion

The threat of conflict within the women's movement brings us full circle, back to the question of continuity. We have argued, based on the American case, that the persistent social cleavage of gender in industrialized Western nations has given rise, at least since the mid-nineteenth century, to a continuing, if variant, organized collective effort to bring about social change. The women's movement, we suggest, can best be seen as fluctuating between stages of mobilization and abeyance as hostile political and social climates replace more receptive ones.

In abeyance phases, or in the international context, where mass mobilization was by definition impossible, women's culture has played an important role in sustaining movement organizations through inhospitable times. Although we have focused on abeyance cycles, we do not mean to suggest that women's culture is only important when the women's movement is in the doldrums. Further research might fruitfully examine the role of women's culture in mobilization cycles and the relationship between abeyance and mobilization cultures.

In the cases we have examined, we find the culture of the movements sharing similar characteristics, despite great differences between the international women's movement, the American women's rights movement of the 1940s and 1950s, and contemporary American lesbian feminism. All three cultures asserted the existence of female values, used ritual to express solidarity among women, validated women's relationships, and emphasized organizational separatism. These aspects of women's culture point to the centrality of collective identity in abeyance phases.

New social movement theorists posit that attention to cultural concerns and expressive elements—sometimes referred to as "identity politics"—is unique to recent European and American movements (Cohen, 1985; Touraine, 1985; Melucci, 1989; Epstein, 1990; Kauffman, 1990). Earlier movements, in contrast, are depicted as directed primarily toward changes in the political arena. We believe that the distinction between politics and culture or between "doing" and "being" has been reified in existing conceptualizations, causing scholars of social movements to overlook the importance of "identity politics" in earlier movements. The creation of a shared culture that undermines conventional understandings of a dominated group is essential for maintaining activists' involvement in sustained social protest (Mueller, 1987). Women's culture plays this role in abeyance phases of the women's movement.

Although both "doing" and "being" can be conceptualized as a part of activism, one may take precedence in a particular stage of movement development. In an abeyance phase, "doing" declines in importance, and the questions of who one is and how one defines oneself in relation to other women rise to the surface. This, in turn, creates a situation in which conflict is likely to emerge. We find that conflict over issues of identity erupts during abeyance phases, since identity is what holds the movement together. In the international women's movement, tension between national or ethnic identity and gender identity is inherent, but global war and the rise of national liberation movements heightened the conflict. The American National Woman's Party, faced with rapidly-declining opportunities for the achievement of feminist goals in the aftermath of the Second World War, erupted into conflict over the conception of the organization. And contemporary American lesbian feminism is beset by conflict over race, class, ethnic, and sexual identity.

Thus, to return to the question of the role of women's culture in the women's movement, we find that women's culture plays a complex role, both holding the movement together and provoking conflict among the keepers of the faith. At least in the cases we have explored, the movement survived such conflict, although it exacted a toll in terms of numbers and diversity of adherents. That survival might have both positive and negative consequences for later rounds of mobilization: positive because abeyance phases keep alive important aspects of earlier mobilization phases, negative because they carry legacies of exclusion and conflict. But in any case, the significance of women's culture and conflict for movement continuity suggests how foolhardy we are to think about the future without knowing about the past.

References

Barkan, Steven E. (1985), *Protesters on Trial: Criminal Justice in the Southern Civil Rights and Vietnam Antiwar Movements*, New Brunswick, N.J.: Rutgers University Press.

Berg, Barbara J. (1978), *The Remembered Gate: Origins of American Feminism*, New York: Oxford University Press.

Black, Naomi (1989), *Social Feminism*, Ithaca: Cornell University Press.

Bosch, Mineke (1990), "Comment: All Over the Map: Development and Conflict in International Women's Networks", Berkshire Conference on Women's History, New Brunswick, N.J., June 10, 1990.

Bosch, Mineke and Annemarie Kloosterman (1990), *Politics and Friendship: Letters from the International Woman Suffrage Alliance, 1902-1942*, Columbus: Ohio State University Press.

Boynton, Virginia R. (unpublished), "Surviving Adversity: The US Section of the Women's International League for Peace and Freedom during World War II", M.A. thesis, Ohio State University, 1990.

Buechler, Steven M. (1986), *The Transformation of the Woman Suffrage Movement: The Case of Illinois, 1850-1920*, New Brunswick, N.J.: Rutgers University Press.

Cassell, Joan (1977), *A Group Called Women: Sisterhood and Symbolism in the Feminist Movement*, New York: David McKay.

Chafetz, Janet Saltzman and Anthony Gary Dworken (1986), *Female Revolt: Women's Movements in World and Historical Perspective*, Totowa, N.J.: Rowan and Allanheld.

Cohen, Jean L. (1985), "Strategy or Identity: New Theoretical Paradigms and Contemporary Social Movements", *Social Research*, 52, pp. 663-716.

Cott, Nancy F. (1987), *The Grounding of Modern Feminism*, New Haven: Yale University Press.

Darrow, Sheila (unpublished), "It Takes More Than Ideology to Make a Movement: The Women's International League for Peace and Freedom, 1915-1922", M.A. Thesis, Antioch College, 1990.

DeBenedetti, Charles (1990), *An American Ordeal: The Antiwar Movement of the Vietnam Era*, Syracuse, N.Y.: Syracuse University Press.

DuBois, Ellen (1978), *Feminism and Suffrage: The Emergence of an Independent Women's Movement in America, 1848-1860*, Ithaca, N.Y.: Cornell University Press.

DuBois, Ellen (1980), "Politics and Culture in Women's History", *Feminist Studies*, 6, pp. 28-36.

Echols, Alice (1989), *Daring to Be Bad: Radical Feminism in America, 1967-1975*, Minneapolis: University of Minnesota Press.

Epstein, Barbara (1990), "Rethinking Social Movement Theory", *Socialist Review*, 20, pp. 35-66.

Evans, Richard J. (1977), *The Feminists*, London: Croom Helm.

Evans, Sara (1979), *Personal Politics: The Roots of Women's Liberation in the Civil Rights Movement and the New Left*, New York: Knopf.

Ferree, Myra Marx and Berth B. Hess (1985), *Controversies and Coalition: The New Feminist Movement*, Boston: Twayne Press.

Flexner, Eleanor (1959), *Century of Struggle*, Cambridge: Harvard University Press.

Foster, Catherine (1989), *Women for All Seasons: The Story of the Women's International League for Peace and Freedom*, Athens: University of Georgia Press.

Freedman, Estelle (1979), "Separatism as Strategy: Female Institution Building and American Feminism, 1870-1930", *Feminist Studies*, 5, pp. 512-529.

Freeman, Jo (1975), *The Politics of Women's Liberation*, New York: David McKay.

Gamson, William A. (1975), *The Strategy of Social Protest*, Homewood, Il.: Dorsey.

Garner, Roberta Ash (1977), *Social Movements in America*, Chicago: Rand-McNally.

Gerlach, Luther P. and Virginia H. Hine (1970), *People, Power, and Change: Movements of Transformation*, Indianapolis: Bobbs-Merrill.

Gerson, Judith M. and Kathy Peiss (1985), "Boundaries, Negotiation, Consciousness: Reconceptualizing Gender Relations", *Social Problems*, 32, pp. 317-331.

Gusfield, Joseph R. (1981), "Social Movements and Social Change: Perspectives of Linearity and Fluidity", Louis Kriesberg (ed.), *Research in Social Movements, Conflict and Change*, vol. 4, Greenwich, Conn.: JAI Press, pp. 317-339.

Harrison, Cynthia (1988), *On Account of Sex: The Politics of Women's Issues 1945-1968*, Berkeley: University of California Press.

Isserman, Maurice (1987), *If I Had a Hammer: The Death of the Old Left and the Birth of the New Left*, New York: Basic.

Jenkins, J. Craig and Craig M. Eckert (1986), "Channelling Black Insurgency: Elite Patronage and Professional Social Movement Organizations in the Development of the Black Movement", *American Sociological Review*, 51, pp. 812-829.

Kanter, Rosabeth Moss (1972), *Commitment and Community*, Cambridge: Harvard University Press.

Kauffman, L.A. (1990), "The Anti-Politics of Identity", *Socialist Review*, 20, pp. 67-80.

Klandermans, Bert (1986), "New Social Movements and Resource Mobilization: The European and the American Approach", *Mass Emergencies and Disasters*, 4, pp. 13-38.

Kraditor, Aileen (1965), *The Ideas of the Woman Suffrage Movement, 1890-1920*, New York: Columbia University Press.

Lofland, John (1985), "Social Movement Culture", John Lofland (ed.), *Protest: Studies of Collective Behavior and Social Movements*, New Brunswick, N.J.: Transactions, pp. 219-239.

Lunardini, Christine A. (1986), *From Equal Suffrage to Equal Rights*, New York: New York University Press.

McAdam, Douglas (1982), *Political Process and the Development of Black Insurgency*,

1930-1970, Chicago: University of Chicago Press.

McAdam, Douglas (1986), "Recruitment to High-Risk Activism: The Case of Freedom Summer", *American Journal of Sociology*, 92, pp. 64-90.

McAdam, Douglas (1988), *Freedom Summer*, New York: Oxford University Press.

McAdam, Douglas, John D. McCarthy and Mayer N. Zald (1988), "Social Movements", Neil Smelser (ed.), *Handbook of Sociology*, Newbury Park, C.A.: Sage, pp. 695-737.

Melucci, Alberto (1989), *Nomads of the Present: Social Movements and Individual Needs in Contemporary Society*, Philadelphia: Temple University Press.

Morris, Aldon (1984), *The Origins of the Civil Rights Movement: Black Communities Organizing for Change*, New York: The Free Press.

Mueller, Carol McClurg (1987), "Collective Consciousness, Identity Transformation, and the Rise of Women in Public Office in the United States", M.F. Katzenstein and C.M. Mueller (eds.), *The Women's Movements of the United States and Western Europe*, Philadelphia: Temple University Press, pp. 89-108.

Phillips, Brenda D. (unpublished), "The Decade of Origin: Resource Mobilization and Women's Rights in the 1850s", Ph.D. Dissertation, Ohio State University, 1985.

Rosenthal, Naomi, M. Fingrutd, M. Ethier, R. Karant and D. McDonald (1985), "Social Movements and Network Analysis: A Case of Nineteenth Century Women's Reform in New York State", *American Journal of Sociology*, 90, pp. 1022-1054.

Rupp, Leila J. (1980), "Imagine My Surprise: Women's Relationships in Historical Perspective", *Frontiers: A Journal of Women Studies*, 5, pp. 61-70.

Rupp, Leila J. and Verta Taylor (1987), *Survival in the Doldrums: The American Women's Rights Movement, 1945 to the 1960s*, New York: Oxford University Press.

Rupp, Leila J. (unpublished), "Conflict in the International Women's Movement, 1888-1950", paper presented at the Berkshire Conference on Women's History, New Brunswick, N.J., June 10, 1990.

Ryan, Barbara (1989), "Ideological Purity and Feminism: The US Women's Movement from 1966 to 1975", *Gender and Society*, 3, pp. 239-257.

Smith-Rosenberg, Carroll (1980), "Politics and Culture in Women's History", *Feminist Studies*, 6, pp. 55-64.

Spender, Dale (1983), *There's Always Been a Women's Movement This Century*, London: Pandora Press.

Staggenborg, Suzanne (1988), "Consequences of Professionalization and Formalization in the Pro-Choice Movement", *American Sociological Review*, 53, pp. 585-606.

Taylor, Verta (1988), "The Future of Feminism: A Social Movement Analysis", Laurel Richardson and Verta Taylor (eds.), *Feminist Frontiers II*, New York: Random House, pp. 473-490.

Taylor, Verta (1989), "Social Movement Continuity: The Women's Movement in Abeyance", *American Sociological Review*, 54, pp. 761-775.

Taylor, Verta and Nancy E. Whittier (forthcoming), "Collective Identity in Social Movement Communities: Lesbian Feminist Mobilization", Aldon Morris and Carol Mueller (eds.),

Frontiers of Social Movement Theory, New Haven: Yale University Press.

Touraine, Alain (1985), "An Introduction to the Study of Social Movements", *Social Research*, 52, pp. 749-787.

Wuthnow, Robert (1987), *Meaning and Moral Order: Explorations in Cultural Analysis*, Berkeley: University of California Press.

Zald, Mayer and Roberta Ash (1966), "Social Movement Organizations: Growth, Decay, and Change", *Social Forces*, 44, pp. 327-341.

Notes

1. Mrs. Ambrose N. Diehl, "Welcome Address", International Council of Women, *Report of First Post-War Council Meeting*, Philadelphia, 1947; L.G. Heymann and Anita Augspurg, "Antwort des Deutschen Komitees auf einem Schreiben des Französischen Komitees", No. I, Aug. 20, 1915, Fannie Fern Andrews papers, Schlesinger Library, Radcliffe College, box 30, folder 365.

2. Rose Arnold Powell, Diary entry, November 2, 1960, box 1, v. 8; Rose Arnold Powell to Mary Beard, June 23, 1948, box 2 (27); Rose Arnold Powell to Anita Pollitzer, January 13, 1949, box 3 (50); Rose Arnold Powell, diary entry, April 15, 1947, box 1, v. 5; all in Rose Arnold Powell papers, Schlesinger Library; Fannie Ackley to Mildred Palmer, September 19, 1950, National Woman's Party papers, reel 97.

3. See, for example, Rosa Manus to Catharine McCulloch, June 2, 1910, Dillon Collection, Schlesinger Library; Rosa Manus to Clara Hyde, April 28, 1923; Carrie Chapman Catt to Rosa Manus, September 18, 1931; Rosa Manus to Carrie Chapman Catt, October 5, 1932; all in Carrie Chapman Catt collection, reel 4, Library of Congress; Rosa Manus to Josephine Schain, April 19, 1932, box 6, Josephine Schain papers, Sophia Smith Collection, Smith College.

4. See, for example, Emily Balch to Alice Paul, September 17, 1943, National Woman's Party papers, reel 174; Rosika Schwimmer to Alice Park, January 7, 1944 (?), Alice Park papers, box 1, Hoover Institution, Stanford University; Mineke Bosch, with Annemarie Kloosterman, *Politics and Friendship: Letters from the International Woman Suffrage Alliance, 1902-1942*, Columbus: Ohio State University Press, 1990.

5. Alma Lutz to Florence Kitchelt, July 29, 1959, Florence Kitchelt papers, box 7 (178), SL; Press release from Mabel Vernon Memorial Committee, and obituary in Wilmington *Morning News*, September 3, 1975, in Mabel Vernon, "Speaker for Suffrage and Petitioner for Peace", conducted in 1972 and 1973 by Amelia R. Fry, Suffragists Oral History Project, Regional Oral History Office, University of California, 1976; Nora Stanton Barney to Alice Paul, n.d. (May 1945), National Woman's Party papers, reel 86.

6. Marion May to Alice Paul, May 19, 1949, National Woman's Party papers, reel 95; Marion Sayward to Alice Paul, September 22, 1959, National Woman's Party papers, reel 105.

7. Letter from Gertrud Bäumer, "Some Letters from those not adhering to the Congress", International Women's Committee for Permanent Peace, *International Congress of Women, The Hague - April 28th to May 1st 1915, Report*, pp. 306-310.

8. Speech by Eugenie Hamer, "Report of Business Sessions", April 30, 1915, International Women's Committee for Permanent Peace, *International Congress of Women*, 1915.

9. Carrie Chapman Catt, "Diary of Tour of Europe, October to November 1922", Carrie Chapman Catt papers, Library of Congress, reel 2.

10. *Our Common Cause - Civilization: Report of the International Congress of Women including the series of round tables, July 16-22, 1933, Chicago, Illinois* (New York: National Council of Women of the US, 1933), pp. 148-154, 161, 168-169.

11. Rosa Manus to Carrie Chapman Catt, July 31, 1939, Catt papers, Library of Congress, reel 4.

12. See the Constitution of the International Council of Women, the by-laws of the International Woman Suffrage Alliance, and the rules for debate of the International Congress of Women in 1915.

13. Ethel Ernest Murrell, Biennial Report, n.d. [June 12, 1953], National Woman's Party papers, reel 99.

Christian and Competent Schoolmistresses: Women's Culture at the Aarhus Training College for Women Teachers 1909-1950

Hanne Rimmen Nielsen

> Our backs are straight and light our stride,
> and thankful are our minds.
> With morning prayer and evensong
> our days are framed.
> We bend down and pray,
> we prepare ourselves
> prepare for service on this Earth
> (The third stanza of the "Training College Song",
> written by Astrid Astrup in 1923).

It is the aim of this article to apply a perspective of cultural totality to a section of the women's movement, viz. the Aarhus Training College for Women Teachers, which was founded as an evangelical[1] training college in 1909. In a broader sense I shall focus on the women teachers in Aarhus, a large provincial town in Denmark. The training college for women teachers as well as the women teachers in Aarhus are both viewed as parts of the work-based women's culture, which was characteristic of women teachers and other groups of educated an independent women in the period from the end of the nineteenth century to the middle of this century.

The women's culture represented space as well as experience. The women worked primarily in female dominated spheres of work, such as girls' schools. Many of them lived together, and many were active in various women's organizations, e.g. organizations for women teachers, the Danish Women's Society (Dansk Kvindesamfund), and the YWCA (KFUK). The training colleges for women teachers were seen by the young women as a possibility to enter into a work and living arrangement for the duration of their education before embarking on the life of a teacher.

The women's culture and the training colleges for women teachers were based on specific ideas about woman's nature and mission in life. These ideas emphasized traditional feminine characteristics and virtues together with a new focus on intellectual training and on activity and extroversion in the young women.

How does this reconstruction of women's culture in a historically well-defined period relate to the study of the history of the women's movement? If by the women's movement we understand the organized activities of women aimed at changing and improving their conditions, then the work and struggle of the women teachers at the Aarhus Training College for Women Teachers and in the wider context of municipal life can definitely be seen as a part of the efforts of the women's movement. Whether this struggle can be defined as feminist is another and more awkward matter. This depends on whether one wishes to define feminism as an encompassing or a narrow concept. I, myself, prefer the encompassing definition proposed by Olive Banks, who understands the feminist movement as "any groups that have tried to change the position of women, or the ideas about women" (Banks, 1981: 3). Instead she aims at exploring the several variations or "Faces of Feminism". Banks distinguishes between three major traditions: 1. The evangelical, Christian feminism. 2. The feminism of the Enlightenment or the feminism of equal rights. 3. Socialist feminism. In Scandinavia the terms difference and equality have been widely used, and they can reasonably be identified with the first and second traditions distinguished by Banks (Hirdman, 1986; Melby, 1984 and 1990). At the Aarhus Training College for Women Teachers the emphasis was on difference, but this did not mean that ideas of or demands for equality did not exist. If we consider all the women teachers in Aarhus, both ways of thinking existed in a variety of combinations. Equal rights thinking was powerful among many women teachers.

However, if one should apply the more narrow definition of feminism of, say, Nancy Cott, there is serious doubt whether the evangelical teachers at the Aarhus Training College for Women Teachers can be characterized as feminists (Cott, 1987: 4f.). They probably could not be said to constitute a conscious opposition to the hierarchy of gender, although at some occasions they certainly did form an opposition to the male leadership. Likewise, they probably did not conceive of women's situation as a social construction but rather as a God given plight. There is no doubt, however, that they identified as women, that they felt part of a women's community, and that they wished to change the conditions of women. You might conclude then that there were at least some feminist aspects in the thinking and behaviour of these women. Such feminist aspects could later develop into a genuine feminist identity, and in fact, many women teachers employed at the schools in Aarhus did grow into staunch feminists fighting for their rights in the 1920s and 1930s.

The Concept of Women's Culture

A cultural historical perspective on the women's movement puts women's communities in different historical periods and contexts into focus. Thus it becomes possible to look at the history of the women's movement from a broad perspective. The women's movement is not only made up of the large national women's organizations. It also consists of women's networks with a basis in everyday life.

Women's history shares the broad anthropologically inspired definition of culture with a large section of general historical research. In recent Scandinavian historical research the discussions have been concerned with a paradigm of cultural history that is supposed to have taken over from the paradigm of historical materialism of the 1970s (Jensen, 1990). The new research in cultural history defines culture primarily as a phenomenon of consciousness, as "collective consciousness", as "a system of significations and symbols" and as "the experience, knowledge and values shared by human beings that they re-create and change in their social behaviour" (Frykman et al., 1984: 15; Ehn et al., 1986: 13). Taking this general cultural perspective as my point of departure I shall focus on the analysis and understanding of women's lives in a perspective of cultural totality and on identifying the subjective dimension of the thoughts, feelings and psychical conflicts of women.

The connection between anthropology and women's history is also obvious in French research on women's history. The interest here has focused mainly on the analysis of women's culture in the traditional peasant communities (Verdier, 1981; Dauphin et al., 1986; Corbin et al., 1989).

The concept of women's culture as a specific terminology in women's history has primarily been developed in an American context. The identification of a specific women's culture originally emerged from the research done on the history of American middle-class women in the nineteenth century. Historians such as Carroll Smith-Rosenberg and Nancy Cott have pointed to the existence of a specific women's world and women's culture based on the social division of men and women in separate spheres (Smith-Rosenberg, 1975; Cott, 1977). Later on the term "women's culture" was applied to a larger variety of situations. For instance the perspective was shifted from the family based women's culture of the nineteenth century to the shared activities of younger women in the labor force. This was the case in Martha Vicinus' book *Independent Women* (1985). This book analyzes the communal working and living arrangements of single women in England from 1850 to 1920, and it is in this context that it considers, e.g., orders of nuns, nurses, teachers and women working together on policies concerning women.

Martha Vicinus' book signalled a new look at women's culture, which was now considered in the context of the public sphere as well as the private sphere. She claimed that women carried their specific culture with them as they moved into the public sphere to work there. Other historians have studied the women's culture, which came into existence alongside with specific women's institutions and organizations. The new "public women's sphere", which was created, enabled the women to strengthen their positions of power in the face of the male dominated political institutions (Freedman, 1979). But the communities of women gave strength and life to the internal structure of the feminist movement, too (Rupp et al., 1987).

Thus the history of the concept of women's culture has been characterized by an increasingly broad application, both in terms of chronology and in the understanding of the phenomenon of women's culture itself. Simultaneously, the 1980s have seen critical considerations of the term. Among these several American historians have recently pointed to the fact that it is a characteristic aspect of the use of the concept from the mid-eighties and onwards that we focus far more on the social relations between the sexes, than we used to. At the same time, there is a tendency to tie women's culture to a spatial or local context in a new way (Hewitt, 1985; Kerber, 1988). I have developed my own concept of women's culture in the dialectics of the theoretical discussions and my empirical work on a specific women's culture. The concept covers four dimensions that I consider necessary in the reconstruction of empirical women's cultures (Nielsen, 1990a and 1990b):

1. The physical and symbolic space of the women's culture.
2. The ideas of the women's culture, e.g. the ideas of equality and difference.
3. The relationship between the women's culture and the general culture. Conflicts, and alliances with men.
4. The dynamics of women's culture. Generations and generational conflicts.

The following has been structured according to the four dimensions of women's culture. I have applied this model to a historically and geographically well-defined women's culture, viz. that of the Aarhus Training College for Women Teachers and the women teachers in Aarhus during the years from 1909 to 1950.

The Women's Space

The Aarhus Training College for Women Teachers was founded as an evangelical college in 1909. Aarhus is the second largest city in Denmark. At the time of World War I it counted 65,000 inhabitants.

Since the Danish women had been admitted to the teaching profession in 1859, a series of private training colleges for women teachers had been founded. In 1909 there were two such training colleges in Copenhagen, viz. N. Zahle's and Femmer's colleges, and two in Jutland, the Horsens Training College for Women Teachers and Th. Lang's Teacher Training College. In addition, women were admitted to certain, co-educational colleges, whereas the four male teacher training colleges that were subsidized by the state and several private male colleges did not admit women. Only in 1918 did women get their own state subsidized teacher training college, the Ribe State Teacher Training College for Women. This college was the result of many years of struggle in the women's movement to get the government to fund a college for women. The demand for a government subsidized teacher training college for women was raised for economic reasons—it was cheaper to receive the education at a state college than at a private college—and it had an important symbolic function—it expressed women's demands to be recognized as important contributors to the general school system.

The women's answer to their exclusion from the government subsidized teacher training colleges was to establish their own colleges. The oldest and most important of these was Natalie Zahle's Teacher Training College of 1860.[2] The college was a kind of "mother" college to the others, and Theodora Lang, for instance, who founded a college in the town of Silkeborg in 1896, was a student of and had close relations to Natalie Zahle.[3] This was also the case with Astrid Blume who became the principal of the college in Aarhus. Before she came to Aarhus, she was employed at Th. Lang's Teacher Training College in Silkeborg.

Most of the women teachers educated before 1930 received their education at colleges for women only. The total number of women teachers grew in the period from 1870 to 1930 from 20 to 40 new teachers per year to approximately 250 per year. At the beginning of the century three quarters of these were educated at colleges for women only. Around 1930 two women out of three still chose to attend training colleges for women teachers. A growing number, however, chose the private co-educational colleges, and from 1930 the women's colleges started to decline. Several colleges (Th. Lang's, the Aarhus College, and the one in Ribe) went co-educational in the 1930s and 1940s, and two women's colleges, Horsens and Femmer, were closed down.

In 1934 at least 83 of a total of 141 women teachers employed at the elementary schools in Aarhus were educated at the five training colleges for women teachers.[4] 38 had attended the Aarhus Training College for Women Teachers. Note that the male and female teachers in Aarhus had been almost totally segregated in their education. Most of the men had attended teacher training colleges for men only.

In Denmark there was a strong tradition for single sex education until World War II. Both the educational system of the larger cities and, as we have seen, the education of female and male teachers were by and large set up as a single-sex education. However, there were important exceptions to this tradition: the village schools and certain types of further education, e.g. the universities, had a tradition for co-education.

The Origin and the Founding of the Training College for Women Teachers

The Aarhus Training College for Women Teachers is typical of the private training colleges for women in Denmark. Several of the teachers at the college undoubtedly considered themselves involved in the girl's school tradition epitomized by Natalie Zahle and Theodora Lang. The essence of this tradition was to reform the education of girls within a single-sex educational system. And the women involved went along with the tradition of sex segregation in schools. But the Aarhus Training College for Women Teachers had other roots as well. These were to be found in the evangelical movement and in the tradition of religious revival, which the evangelical movement was part of. This meant that the Aarhus Training College was not originally founded by women, who aimed at improving women's educational opportunities. The initiative came from a circle of evangelical men in Aarhus, and for many years the college was governed by a Board of men only. What, then, moved these men to found a teacher training college for women?

The Aarhus Training College for Women Teachers around 1910. Above the entrance, the inscription "Kvindeseminarium" (Training College for Women Teachers) is clearly visible.

The main objective for these men was to help provide the Danish elementary school with devoted Christian teachers. They thought they could do this by educating women teachers, because they realized that the young women represented a body of unexploited resources in this respect. Besides, the evangelical movement supported sex segregated training colleges, for in this movement the ideology of gender was based on the concept of difference. They believed that God had created women and men differently and with different tasks in life. They had already founded two evangelical colleges for men, and now they found that it was time for a college for women. In this way the evangelical movement, which held a rather conservative view on the position of women, paradoxically contributed to the creation of new educational possibilities for women and thereby, in a certain sense, to the agenda for women's emancipation.

The case was slightly different for the evangelical women. They, too, wished to contribute Christian teachers to the elementary schools. But in addition to this, they were much more concerned with women's own interests: to create an attractive opportunity for the education of young women. And the emphasis was on "justice", or in other words they wished that the college should contribute to the creation of equal rights between women and men in schools, church and society. As time passed it was the women, who most consistently worked to develop and maintain the college. I shall return to the conflicts that were sparked by the different interests of men and women in keeping the college female.

The objective of the evangelical movement to educate young women to the teaching profession resulted in the founding of a teacher training college for women only. A large sum of money was collected among the friends of the evangelical movement, and a building was erected and inaugurated in 1910. The principle of the building was that it should provide the principal, the teachers and the students with facilities for working and living together. A female principal was employed. Her name was Astrid Blume. And it was agreed that the teaching staff should preferably be female. This was considered the best basis for educating devoted and competent schoolmistresses. At a teacher training college for women the young women would be influenced by mature, Christian women. It was believed that it would be particularly important for the principal to have a nurturing and friendly relationship with the young women. Such an experience would develop their personalities to the improvement of their work as teachers. So far men and women agreed in favoring a teacher training college for women only.[5]

This women's space, which was created by an official evangelical ideology, was soon filled up with the women themselves and their ideas. I shall concentrate on the spatial dimension of the women's culture and return to its ideas later.

The Physical and Symbolical Women's Space

The spatial or physical dimension—the college as a place of work, a home and an opportunity for women to be together—can give us important information about life and community at the college. The building itself established the basic conditions for the behaviour of students and teachers, and it provided them with the opportunities to enter into an intimate community with women, a women's culture. The women's culture was a response to the demands of the official ideology. The college was at one and the same time public and private space, and it can because of its specific circumstances have eased the breaking away of the young women from a traditional women's space and helped them get used to a public sphere of work.

There are photos, drawings and descriptions of the building itself. From this material one can sense the integration and intimacy of the institution—which is quite contrary to the large and impersonal educational institutions of today. The principal lived there together with approximately 25 students. A number of students lived in town but often participated in the meals and in meetings besides classes. Altogether the college counted between 75 and 100 students around 1920.

The building was organized in the following way: The dining hall, kitchen and accomodation for the maids were situated in the basement. On the ground floor and the first floor there were classrooms, a library, an office and the faculty lounge. On the first floor there was also a common room, i.e. the community lounge. The second floor accomodated the students in double and single rooms, and here was Miss Blume's private apartment, where she lived with her foster-children. There was no sharp division between public and private space. Only the bedrooms provided the students with the probably much needed privacy.

Every room has a story to tell. But the material only to a certain extent makes it possible to reveal the arrangement of the rooms. The arrangement of the classrooms is particularly interesting. A few photos and oral reports testify to a very traditional arrangement with a blackboard, a highly elevated lecturer's desk, and rows of students' desks. The traditional arrangement coincided with a very traditional and authoritarian pedagogy, which did not distinguish itself in any important sense from that of the elementary schools. The same authoritarian teaching, the same swotting, the same control over the students.

The dining hall, the library and the lounge provided the framework for certain types of social activities: the meals, the communal preparation for classes, meetings and general socializing. The meals and certain meetings were regular. For instance there were regular meetings in the lounge on Saturday nights, often these featured women missionaries. But, of course, there must have been more informal ways for the teachers and the students, or the students themselves, to be together. The college garden also provided opportunities for social gatherings.

To some extent it was possible to live a life outside the control of the teachers in the student accomodation. It was usual to gather in the rooms at night, and it was also possible to withdraw to solitude there, particularly if one was lucky enough to have a room of one's own. But the main impression, according to contemporary and later accounts, is of a close-knit community, which is usually described in positive terms.

The close-knit community of the training college was emphasized by a relative distance to the surrounding community. As an institution the training college had to maintain contact with the local community and with the schools and churches in Aarhus. Most of the teachers and a number of students lived in town. The temporarily engaged teachers were normally employed at the municipal schools as well, and in connection with their teaching practice all students had to cross the street to Finsensgade's School close by and become acquainted with teachers and pupils there. The training college had close contact with Skt. Johannes Church nearby, and many students attended the YWCA in the northern part of town. But nevertheless, the main impression was that the college functioned as a somewhat closed world. Many students did not get into town very often but lived their lives at the college during the three to four years of their education.

The women's space was not just a physical reality. The division into a male and a female space symbolized the polarization of masculinity and femininity. The training college was organized around a series of female values, symbols and rituals. The Training College Song, for instance, expressed some of the values connected with life as a student and as a teacher: the bright, happy, active femininity that rests on a

The graduates and teachers of 1917. The Principal Astrid Blume is standing in the second row, second from the right, wearing glasses. Hulda Pedersen, the biology teacher, is standing behind her, in a white dress with a black belt. Olga Paulsen, the influential teacher of Danish language, is sitting in the front row, second from the right in a white dress. Notice the dresses of the graduates: Most are wearing long, white dresses in a sort of romantic style. Their long hair is brushed back in a knot. Their dresses express the culture, femininity and seriousness that were part of the ideal of the woman teacher.

foundation of religious devotion, seriousness and diligence. The celebrations and the shared recreational activities were used to emphasize the community of the women. There are extraordinarily many references to Miss Blume's efforts to create traditions and rituals to bring the students and teachers closer to each other. It was as if the women's space was to be given its own history that possibly functioned as an invocation against future co-educational ideas. Daily life was scheduled around regular routines that emphasized the ideal of hard work and frugality. For example, food was nourishing and plentiful, but in no way exciting. The dresses expressed culture and femininity, but also signalled moderation and seriousness. These outer rituals and symbols blended into a larger totality and a world of ideas that were to transmit certain norms and values to the students in the course of the years they attended the training college. I shall return to this later.

The women's space of the training college continued to hold importance for many of these students, even after they had left it. They returned on speech days and anniversaries, they communicated with each other via a shared diary in which they wrote about themselves, they kept up their friendships, and they reunited with their classmates for 25th, 40th and 50th anniversaries. Two retired teachers from the class of 1926 with whom I am in contact were gathered with their former classmates in 1986 for a 60th anniversary.

I shall end by a quotation, in which Kristine Nordby, a former student from the class of 1923, explains what the college meant for her and many others:

For us it is the building itself, the beautiful, white boarding school high on the hill, even though additions to the building have changed its appearance, and even though we no longer can detect the inscription above the entrance.[6] Don't we all have the experience of being suffused with an inexplicable warmth when we, upon reaching the foot of the hill, detect the building up there—especially if we have not been there for a while? And the Training College to us means the light and airy classrooms that for four years witnessed our victories and failures, it means the wide stairways with the double banisters that often would speed up our ways to the main entrance, and the large common room.

Still more the Training College to us is the institution filled with traditions, which we feel a part of and therefore share a responsibility for.

But most of all it is the place where we gather. It was so then, and it should continue to be so—for the sake of the college, but most of all for our sake ...

But strongest are the memories when we meet where they were created. And every time we do, we feel rich in memories and grateful towards the place that gave them to us, and we experience the feeling of community and mutual connection to the institution that can and ought to be the place where we get together.[7]

The Ideas of the Women's Culture. The Ideal of the Woman Teacher

The physical reality of the women's space was basically connected to a series of ideas about women's nature and tasks in life. I shall argue that the women at the training college participated in the creating of a new role model for their generation of women, the first generation of educated and independent women. This role model relied on the ideas of difference as well as equality. The notion of difference was deep and ingrained and was nourished by traditional conceptions of femininity and by religion. But this did not did mean that the women renounced equal rights. They demanded to be heard in the schools and in society, but this was to happen through their own institutions and organizations and on their own conditions. In the new role model they combined the heritage from their fore-mothers and from religion with new aspects that made place for an active and extrovert femininity and for individual development. I shall exemplify this by looking first at the struggle for the Training College for Women Teachers, then at the ideal of the woman teacher and at some of the teachers who tried to give the ideal existence.

The Struggle for the Training College for Women Teachers

The Aarhus Training College for Women Teachers had been founded as a college for women only in full agreement with the men and women behind it. Later it appeared that there were certain conflicting interests behind the agreement. Several times the women had to defend their training college and the existence of the boarding section. The course of the events shows that the evangelical women were ready to fight for their rights and for equality, and that they did so from the point of view of difference. Soon after the founding of the college the College Board began to consider co-education. Behind these considerations were economic rather than idealistic reasons. The college needed to attract more students, and it appeared that the easiest way to do this was to admit male students. The reason was that the period around World War I was a critical time for the teacher training colleges. Less students enrolled, because an overproduction of teachers made it very difficult for the newly graduated to find teaching positions.

As early as 1917 Astrid Blume, the principal, had to defend the idea of a training college for women. In a letter to the Board she rejected the idea of co-education, and she even went as far as to stake her job to prevent it. Her letter was a significant plea for the necessity of a training college for women, where the young women could be under a "female influence" while studying. Astrid Blume wrote:

I am convinced that young women need to be under the influence of women teachers while they study ... They need to be taught, I dare say brought up, by cultivated, competent women, who can give them values they would never get from men, because of their way of tackling the classroom subjects, because of their understanding of the needs of the young women ... Add to this the fact that the treatment of many of the most valuable subjects taught must suffer from being taught to mixed groups. How differently one can enter into questions when young men and women are separated. This goes for pedagogy, the study of literature, hygiene, many aspects of religion, etc., etc. ...[8]

The change to co-education was avoided this time, but surfaced again in connection with the death of Astrid Blume and the appointment of a new principal in 1924. The Board probably had the ulterior motive of going co-educational when in 1924 it decided to appoint a male principal, Jacob Høyer. The opposition to this appointment was evident inside as well as outside the college. 45 students signed a petition stating that they wanted a woman principal, more specifically they wanted Olga Paulsen, a teacher at the college whom they thought would be the right person to continue the work of Astrid Blume. The female and male teachers at the college were of the same opinion. They wrote to the Board that they wished to continue the traditions of the college and its good atmosphere and keep the college as a training college for women teachers under the leadership of a woman.

Outside the college the situation gave rise to an intensive debate in the letters to the editor of the daily newspaper "The Christian Daily" (Kristeligt Dagblad). In several of the contributions by women there was clear evidence of women's rights thinking. The plans to alter the college were seen as an attack on women. At the same time, most of the contributors preferred a women's college for educational reasons. Several of the male contributors supported this point of view.

For Jacob Høyer, the new principal, the widespread opposition to a male principal meant a difficult start at the college. Evidence points to the fact that several of the students regarded him with antipathy and open animosity.

The college went co-educational in 1932, but this time it did not give rise to any significant debate. The new generation of women students at the college was not very interested in this issue. These were different times, and the ideal was more and more for women and men to work together on an equal footing. The idea of difference faded into the background in favor of ideas of equality, or perhaps in favor of ideas that a person's sex is of minor importance in education.

The Ideal of the Woman Teacher

The ideal of the woman teacher reflected both the demands that the official ideology of the training college put to the new teachers and the women's own thoughts about this. For the young women, the ideal of the woman teacher grew into a professional identity, which was shared by a whole generation of women teachers. In the following I shall discuss the elements of the ideal woman teacher.

I shall take as my starting point the case of an appointment of a female teacher at the college in 1924. This case involves the most important elements of the official ideal. In a series of letters the members of the Board discussed the various candidates for the vacancy as a physical education teacher. For instance, Mr. Lambertsen, who was a teacher at Haslev Teacher Training College, one of the other evangelical colleges, recommended a young teacher Ebba Munk-Sørensen on the basis of the following considerations:

In my deliberations whether I could recommend a woman teacher for the college in Aarhus, I have stopped at one of our students, who is now graduating. She is an unusually cultivated and mature human being, 25 years old. She graduated in languages from Haslev High School, passed a philosophy examination cum laude and spent some years in Copenhagen, before she entered this college. She is the daughter of a merchant in this town, her father ... died suddenly last winter. She is not from a home of believers, but she herself is definitely a believer (she is best friends with Karin Bang—the daughter of the reverend Bang. Karin Bang also attends this college) but besides she is a person with a great understanding of the difficulties of young people in religious issues, and she will always be a woman with a strong personality, who will impress people whereever she goes (she is hardworking, but not pushful) and culturally ...

She is an intelligent person—makes an impression of competence—and has an unusual energy, so that she will always get a lot out of what she undertakes.—She is a good student in physical education and in particular she is good at teaching P.E. ...

And though I hesitate to predict a woman's future in relation to a man, I tend to think that she will bypass men—not because she hates men, but because all her burning energy is directed at work as a calling, which she will engage in and sacrifice herself to.[9]

According to the opinions of Lambertsen and others of suitable women teachers for the vacancy, a clear image of the ideal woman teacher emerges: First of all she must be a believer and capable of influencing others. Secondly she must be bright, energetic, and see work as a calling. Thirdly she must have a pleasant personality, be cultivated and capable of mixing with people. Preferably she is of a cultured family and has made valuable friendships. Such a teacher would be a suitable person to promote the evangelical movement, because she "would influence others with her strong personality", and because she would put all her energy and power into her work. In other words, she would be ready to "sacrifice" herself for the cause, and would be able to do so, because she would usually be unmarried.

Miss Munk-Sørensen did not get the job. She later went to Ribe School, worked as the leader of the YWCA, and was still unmarried in 1934 (*Dansk Skolestat*, 1934, vol. 3: 770). Another applicant with qualifications much like Miss Munk-Sørensen's was also rejected. A third applicant decided to accept a better paid position at the municipal school system in Aarhus. Finally the Board chose an applicant, Miss Karen Brøns, who distinguished herself by having very fine qualifications as a P.E. teacher. It is characteristic of the decision of the Board that technical and economic considerations counted the most. The ideal of the devoted and competent schoolmistress had to yield to the regard for the reputation and economy of the college.

The ideal of the woman teacher was significant in other ways. There is no doubt that the ideal was effective in relation to the future teachers. One may wonder what was so attractive about an ideal, which meant that one sacrificed oneself. But it is important to stress that the ideal also contained opportunities for the more active and powerful aspects of the female role. This became obvious when the young women looked to the teachers in front of them at the college. In the following I shall relate the histories of three teachers, who we know functioned as important role models for the students. All three of them were singled out as very competent teachers, and at the same time each of them represented a specific aspect of the ideal woman teacher.

Astrid Blume (1872-1924)

Many people pointed to Astrid Blume as the ideal Christian teacher. And as principal of the training college she received a lot of respect. She was a very extrovert person with many interests. At a time when few women had the courage to speak up in

Astrid Blume with her foster-children.

public, Astrid Blume was a very popular public speaker in many different contexts. Her example must have proved to other women that it was possible to expand the range of activities for Christian women teachers.

Astrid Blume was out of a well-known evangelical family, and her father was the reverend P.E. Blume. She graduated as a teacher from N. Zahle's Training College for Women Teachers in Copenhagen and went to Th. Lang's Teacher Training College in Silkeborg where she grew close to the principal, Theodora Lang, and her friend, Anna Hølzermann. In 1909 she was asked to take on the job of directing the Aarhus Training College for Women Teachers, and after painful deliberations she accepted, apparently more out of a sense of duty than because she felt like it. It turned out to be a difficult task she had taken upon herself, not least because of the many conflicts with the Board about the status and the bad financial state of the college. She wore herself down doing this work, but she also had success and carried her ideas into action in a continuous struggle with the patriarchs in the evangelical movement.

As principal, Astrid Blume went along with the ideas of difference in the women's movement. She played the role of a *mother*, in spite of the fact that there were some aspects of her management that indicated a more impersonal style. There are many statements to the fact that she united the nurturing and the authoritarian in a way that instilled *respect as well as love*. She inspired others to imitate her: "... How wonderful she was in her personal way of talking about the duties of a teacher. Our hearts glowed and you promised yourself to always try to become as whole and honest—as conscientious and dutiful as Miss Blume herself appeared to be". (Olga Jørgensen, the Anniversary Publication, 1934: 41).

Outside the college Astrid Blume's deepest engagement was in the work of the YWCA and in the Santal Mission (i.e. the India Mission). But she was also active in the women's movement. She supported the work of the Danish Women's Society and was active in the suffrage struggle.[10] Apparently there was no contradiction for Astrid Blume in working for the dissemination of the Gospel and working for women's rights.

It was the duty of the devoted and competent woman teacher to work on all these fronts, both inside school and church and outside in relation to the solving of important social problems.

Hulda Pedersen (1875-1961)

Hulda Pedersen is an important name in the history of the women's movement in Aarhus. For many years she was a prominent member of the Aarhus section of the Danish Women's Society, of which she was the chairman from 1917 to 1931. During this period the Danish Women's Society was the largest and most important women's rights organization in Denmark. The Society was founded in 1871, the Aarhus section in 1886. But Hulda Pedersen was active in many different organizations, e.g. in the Aarhus Women's Suffrage Association (1907-1915), and the Social-Liberal Party, which organized many of the middle-class, progressive women of the women's movement. One of her great interests was Home Economics, and the goal was to establish an academic program for Home Economics for women. This goal was reached in 1945 when a special education was organized at the University of Aarhus. However, she worked in many other areas too. She was a formidable organizer and fund-raiser and organized among other things the establishment of the Danish Women's Society's House in Aarhus. She was interested in sex education, in the youth work in the Danish Women's Society, in women's participation in politics and much more.

Besides this great involvement with women's politics, Hulda Pedersen was—first and foremost—a teacher. For many years (1908-1942) she was employed at Christians-gades Girls' School, which was the municipal secondary school for girls. When the Aarhus Training College for Women Teachers was founded in 1909, Hulda Pedersen was employed as a temporary teacher of natural history, and until 1932 she was one of the staunch supporters of the college.

Hulda Pedersen was the teacher at the college, who most unambiguously repre-sented the woman question. On several occasions she lectured the students about the goals of the women's movement. She did not have the obvious religious motivation, which characterized most of the teachers, but she still wanted the woman question to respect and integrate traditional Christian and family values. Her background as a minister's daughter may explain why she continued to see the family and religion as

Left, Olga Paulsen; right, Hulda Pedersen.

fixed points in her life. Hulda was strong in her conviction of equal rights, but behind this was the still more basic idea of difference.

Hulda Pedersen was an ambitious and inspiring teacher, and she was very much liked. Many teachers still alive remember her and mention her as one of their most important role models.

Olga Paulsen (1878-1947)

In many ways Olga Paulsen was poles apart from Hulda Pedersen, both as a person and in her understanding of the woman question. One of the colleagues of the two teachers described the difference between them like this: "... I learnt to respect the indefatigable energy and care that she (Olga Paulsen, HRN) put into her work, as the woman of duty and orderliness that she was ... While Miss Paulsen personified the old-fashioned, meticulous femininity, her colleague, who was the same age as her (Hulda Pedersen, HRN), epitomized a grand and stormy weather. She was quick in movement, speech and thought". (Svend Mogensen, *Aarhus Seminarium 1909-59*: 23).

For Olga Paulsen the woman question first of all meant working for women in the context of church (even though she was also a member of the Danish Women's

Society). She put most of her efforts into the Women Teachers' Missionary League (LMF—Lærerindernes Missionsforbund), in which she was the chairman of the national organization from 1918 to 1947. The members of the Aarhus section met for prayer and religious communion, and the organization worked to send out and support women teachers, who travelled as missionaries. Several young teachers from the Aarhus Training College for Women Teachers went out as missionaries to China and India during this period.

Olga Paulsen belonged to a group of teachers for whom the personal relation to God and the community of the devout was the most important part of their lives. They practiced a Christianity that combined devoted withdrawal and outward activity. For the believers, who could get strength in prayer and community, the aim was to subsequently go out and change the world.[11] In this endeavor towards high aims, towards "perfection", there was no room for women's feeling of inferiority. The implication of Olga Paulsen's attitude was that women had the same spiritual potentials as men and the same possibilities to work for practical results in their field. The women's organizations should safeguard the position of women in Christian work.

Olga Paulsen preferred to live in a woman's world, but she was not afraid of competing with men. She had professional ambitions, but in 1924 she was disregarded for the position as principal at the Aarhus Training College for Women Teachers. In 1928 she was the second woman elected member of the Board of the Danish Missionary Society. It was during her period in office that the female missionary work flourished, and the work was suffused with a genuine enthusiasm.

The First Generation and the Ideal of the Woman Teacher

The majority of the women teachers who were educated at the Aarhus Training College for Women Teachers in the 1910s and 1920s did their work without drawing attention to themselves, and they have not left any material or assessments to do with how they practiced or perhaps rejected the ideals of the college. Some, however, have assessed the significance of their time at the college, and in some cases we can judge the impact of the ideal of the woman teacher on the basis of their practice as teachers. Tentatively, we may conclude that there is a group of teachers who upheld the ideals of the college many years after leaving it. I shall give some examples of the fates of women teachers, to illustrate how they lived out the ideal.

Two teachers whom I have interviewed, Anna Mousten and Jensine Thomsen (born in 1905 and 1904) realized the ideal of the devoted and competent schoolmistress in their practice. And still both represent the ideals, which they encountered at the Aarhus Training College for Women Teachers in their youth. Today they still live within the women's culture of their own generation. This shows the non-synchronous[12] development in the conditions of women, who live in the same historical period and in the context of the same general culture.

Anna Mousten and Jensine Thomsen came from evangelical homes, and both have spent their lives in the spirit of Christianity. They have been devoted to their religion and competent as teachers. Anna Mousten was employed at the municipal schools of Aarhus, Jensine Thomsen at various village schools in western Jutland. Both teachers identified with work and let it fill up their lives. The interest in and love for the children always came first. They are both still in contact with old pupils and the schools they were employed at. Both were active within the two organizations the YWCA and LMF (the Women Teachers' Missionary League), and Jensine Thomsen is still active within LMF. Their recollections give a strong impression of active and enthusiastic lives in the service of the schools and of culturally active participants in social life at large.

The stories of the two old classmates about the class of 1926 give us reason to assume that they are not unique in this way of living. Even though the class was not completely homogenous, the communal spirit and the identification with the ideal of the woman teacher were strong. Anna Mousten and Jensine Thomsen are still in contact with some of their classmates.

Anna Mousten and Jensine Thomsen were among those struggling to retain a female principal in 1924. Their ideal teacher was Hulda Pedersen.

There is another type of material, which can give an impression of how a large number of teachers personified the ideal woman teacher. I have been through a large number of applications from women teachers in the archives of the municipal school system in Aarhus (the applications from the teachers, recommendations and the reports of the authorities), and on the basis of this I shall conclude that the ideals of the training college and the school authorities in Aarhus were very similar. The ideal teacher as understood by the school authorities was a kind of secularized version of that of the college. The Christian teachers were highly motivated, hard-working and cultivated, and the municipal school authorities were interested in employing them. But it worked the other way round, too. For in the long run, the college was probably influenced by the emphasis on professional expertise and the lack of interest in the religious element of the school authorities.[13]

The ideal woman teacher was secularized, but in the inter-war period it still makes sense to talk about an ideal female teacher as distinct from the ideal male teacher. The material basis of the ideal woman teacher was the sex segregated school and the existence of a particular culture among the women teachers in Aarhus.

The Women's Culture and the General Culture

It is possible to distinguish analytically between women's culture, men's culture and a general culture. By general culture I understand the totality of relations of gender, class and more, which the individual human being participates in.

Gerda Lerner, the American women's historian, puts it thus that women always live within a women's culture as well as a general culture (Lerner, 1979). Women live within the general culture and contribute to the shaping of history, just like men. But at the same time it is possible to say that women live within a women's culture based on the evidence that women have different experiences and therefore another consciousness than men. This means that the task of women's history becomes twofold: to study women's culture in its specificity, and to study the ways in which the women's culture interacts with the general culture.

The Training College for Women Teachers and the General Culture

All is not said and done by characterizing the Aarhus Training College for Women Teachers as a women's culture. We have to take into consideration the relationship of the college to wider cultural contexts such as the evangelical culture and local culture. These cultural contexts were represented in different ways in the everyday life of the college. First of all in the shape of the College Board, which consisted of evangelical men only. Secondly in the presence of male teachers at the college. In time these teachers acquired more influence than they had had at the start, and from 1924 the college had a male principal. Thirdly the college was part of a local community and a set of local schools. Finally the college was part of a larger, national system of schools and teacher training colleges.

Woven into the relations of the women's culture with the evangelical men, the male teachers and local groups were gender, class and religious dimensions. If we take as an example the relation to the evangelical men on the College Board, it becomes clear that there were identical and contradictory interests. The religious interests were identical. The evangelical men and devoted teachers and students at the college had as their goal to further the Kingdom of God on earth and the work of the evangelical movement in society. The class interests were the same, too, since both men and women can be regarded as members of the same upwardly mobile middle class. On the women's part it was particularly obvious that the teacher training was a means—one of the best—to become upwardly mobile. The contradictory interests were to be found in the different interests of the sexes. For the women the teacher training college and the community of women represented some clearly emancipatory potentials. But this was unsettling to the men, especially when it became clear that the women went their own ways and valued their own community. The result was a conflict about the future of the female college. In several turns—i.e. when the male principal was chosen in 1924, and when the college went co-educational in 1932—the men were successful in putting an end to the status of the college as a college for women only. The solution to the conflict was a defeat for the women, and in the long run the result was the gradual disappearance of the women's culture.

Women Teachers' Culture in Aarhus

After graduation, the young teachers had to say goodbye to the women's space of the college. But for those who got employment in larger towns there was an opportunity to enter into new spaces for women, into a larger women's culture.[14] In the following I shall describe the larger women teachers' culture in Aarhus that the teacher training college was a part of.

The first and most basic female space that the young women teachers who were employed at the municipal school system in Aarhus were to function in was the *sex segregated school*. In connection with practical training at the college they had already become acquainted with Finsensgades School, which was a so-called co-educational school for girls and boys, but in practice sharply divided into a girls' section and a boys' section with their own entrances and with their own school yards. As a rule the women teachers taught the girls and the male teachers the boys. The female teachers had their own common room, as did the male teachers.

The municipal school system in Aarhus was sex segregated until the 1950s. There were three girls' schools, three boys' schools and four co-educational schools of the same type as Finsensgades School, described above. As mentioned above the female teachers mostly taught the girls and the male teachers the boys. In 1920 there were 129 female teachers and 158 male teachers at the municipal schools in Aarhus.

The women teachers supported the system of sex segregated schooling. Most of them thought that the women teachers had special tasks to take care of in the socialization of the girls. They were to transmit an ideal femininity to the girls. The teachers had, however, another motive for supporting the sex segregated schools. Sex segregation was their best argument in favor of employing more women teachers. If girls were to be taught primarily by female teachers, boys by male teachers, then it would be reasonable to employ an equal number of each. Besides, the girls' schools in particular gave the women teachers opportunities to reach positions of real power in school matters. There was even a possibility that the women teachers could become senior mistresses/principals at these schools. The first senior mistress in Aarhus was appointed in 1916. She was Theodora Müller of Christiansgades School.

With the transition to co-education in the period from 1946 to approximately 1960, part of the basis for power for the women teachers disappeared.

The Aarhus Association for Women Teachers was another female space that got the women teachers of Aarhus together. The association was started in 1920, after the male teachers had left the general association in a protest against the passage of the bill for equal wages.[15] The new Association for Women Teachers soon proved to be a bastion for women's increased power and influence in school, and at the same time it became the frame around a flourishing organizational life. During the interwar period there was strong opposition between female and male teachers. The women teachers fought for their rights in three main areas: 1. In defence of equal wages. 2. In the effort to have

The common room at the girls' school, Paradisgades School, 1910.

as many female as male teachers appointed and to ensure the right to work for married women teachers. 3. In the struggle for women teachers' right to promotion.

Up through the 1940s and 1950s the women teachers repeatedly rejected the suggestion of the male teachers to merge the male and the female teachers' associations. Not until 1965 was the merger a reality, even though many older women teachers kept up their warnings against letting go of the independence of the women. Very soon after the merger women teachers had difficulties in manifesting themselves in the general Aarhus Teachers' Association.

The women teachers had other shared organizational contexts as well. The first generation of women teachers must be characterized as a very active group, and the individual teacher was often active in various organizations besides the daily work at school. Many were members of the *Danish Women's Society* (established in 1886 in Aarhus), and the teachers made up an important and dominating group in this organization. In 1917 there were at least 83 teachers in the membership of the Aarhus section of the Danish Women's Society. The total membership of the section was 395.

The Danish Women's Society had been the most important Danish organization for women's rights since it was founded, and the organization worked in many areas to enforce equal opportunities for men and women. At the same time it is important to emphasize that the organization was also influenced by the ideology of difference, e.g. in its work for Home Economics and for improving the conditions for mothers and housewives. The society organized independent women as well as housewives. In all of this, the teachers put in a great deal of important work. It is also important to emphasize that the Society was an important social context for many of its members.

Many teachers were active in the religious women's organizations, first of all the *YWCA and LMF—The Women Teachers' Missionary League* (the Aarhus sections were established in 1891 and 1909, respectively). In these organizations the women could be helped in the strengthening of their own religious beliefs, and they could perform useful work for others. In the YWCA many teachers worked as section leaders in youth work, and work was here a kind of continuation of their socializing efforts at school. The activities of LMF were directed at missionary work among heathen women, and the teachers could participate in these efforts either by travelling as missionaries or by supporting the work in other ways. I wish to repeat my emphasis on these organizations as very significant social and religious communities.

As women's communities the various organizations took care of related needs and functions. There are many examples of overlapping membership of e.g. the Danish Women's Society and LMF, even though most of the members put their main efforts into one organization according to background and temperament. There were different women's cultures among the teachers, but they overlapped. The Aarhus Training College for Women Teachers clearly belonged to the "religious" women's culture. Among the teachers in Aarhus, however, the mobilization on the issue of "the woman question" created the largest community for women.

Beside their work life and organizational life, the teachers had their *private lives and private communities*. There is not a lot of material to throw light on this area, but certain things are clear. Most of the women teachers were unmarried, though the number of married teachers grew in time. In 1920 the membership of the Aarhus Association for Women Teachers counted 105 unmarried and 24 married teachers. In 1950 the number of women teachers had reached 247, including 90 married teachers, but still the unmarried outnumbered those in matrimony.

The membership lists of the Association for Women Teachers and the Danish Women's Society reveal that many teachers lived with either another woman teacher or a sister. There are several examples of teachers living in life-long relationships. Neither was it unusual that a teacher adopted a foster-child. As a young woman, Hulda Pedersen lived with different colleagues. Later she bought a house and lived with her two sisters and her father. Olga Paulsen lived with a sister. Anna Mousten lived with her mother. Many women teachers met privately, went on vacations together and travelled together.

The women's culture that I have tried to describe flourished in the interwar years. The sex segregated schools and the conflicts with the male teachers formed the material basis for the women teachers' culture. But the women themselves were responsible for the specific construction of the women's space and the ideas of the women's culture. This women's culture dissolved after 1950. With the transition to co-education and the folding of the Aarhus Association for Women Teachers, part of the foundation for a specific women's culture disappeared. The women, too, had changed. They had grown more individualized and no longer felt that they needed the community of other women in the same way.

The Relationship between the Culture of the Women Teachers and the Local Culture

The individual teacher in Aarhus was not just part of a women's culture but also of a more general local culture. Here different class interests could mingle with gender. The relationship between male and female teachers was, as mentioned, full of conflict in the interwar period, and the two groups marked their disagreements by organizing themselves in two professional associations. Nevertheless the women teachers chose to remain within the national association, The Danish Teachers' Union, and thereby they signalled that they shared professional and class-related interests with the male teachers. For instance shared interests in the professionalizing of the teaching profession and in their social status.

If the women teachers married—and approximately one in five did, especially with male teachers—their interests were in this way related to various family oriented and social goals.

In the school, too, gender and class interacted. In Aarhus, e.g., there were two girls' schools predominantly for the girls of the working class and a posh municipal secondary school for the girls of the middle class. At Paradisgades School and Frederiks Allé's School, which were dominated by working-class girls, it was the idea of a housewifely femininity, which was taught to the girls. The girls' best hope would be—so they were told by the woman teacher—to enter domestic service after the seventh grade and later marry and become housewives. At Christiansgades School, which taught its pupils to the 10th grade, the ideal was another. Here the teachers sought to imprint in the girls the ideal of the educated and independent woman. It was an ideal that the teachers themselves personified to the girls, and that reflected the experience of the teachers in terms of gender as well as class. The ideal of the educated and independent woman promised both upward social mobility and sexual equality. The girls were told that this goal was to be reached only by diligence, hard work, and sexual abstinence.

The Dynamics of the Women's Culture. Generational Conflicts

In the course of the 1930s it became clear that the college students and the women's culture were changing. It is possible to reconstruct two specific generational patterns of reaction in the female student during the period from approximately 1909-1950. In this context I use the word generation about a group defined by a shared formative experience. In order to delimit a generation, it is necessary to look at year of birth, family background, experiences in education, work, marriage and relations with girlfriends, religious and political attitudes, attitudes in women's politics and activities, etc., etc. (Lagemann, 1979; Ware, 1981; Banks, 1986).

The two generations must be seen as ideal types not to be found in their pure forms in the empirical material. But it is possible in the material from the Aarhus Training College for Women Teachers to identify both generations and get an impression of the conflicts that followed in the wake of the entry of the second generation of students on the stage in the 1920s and 1930s.

The first generation were those who had participated in the making of the college and of the women's culture.[16] Anna Mousten and her friends had felt at harmony with their teachers. The ideal of the "devoted and competent schoolmistress" became a guiding principle for this generation.

The second generation did not in the same way form a community with their teachers. The position of the female teachers was weakened, and the new male management was in opposition to the students on several issues. For many the ideal of the devoted and competent schoolmistress had lost its appeal and its power to impart behavioural patterns. When the college went co-educational in 1932, it meant that the young women now had to settle into a mixed context. The second generation can be characterized as more individualized, they were more secularized and had a freer sexual morality. Contrary to the first generation, they did not feel that they needed a specific women's culture.

Just as the experiences of Anna Mousten and Jensine Thomsen could illustrate the experiences of the first generation, Ellen Pind Olesen can illustrate the ideals and experiences of the second generation. Of course, it is necessary to see these different life stories as mere illustrations of broader tendencies.

Ellen Pind Olesen (born 1905) graduated from teacher training college in 1927. She was out of a family of teachers in Aarhus, and she describes her family as interested in music, with a social awareness and no particularly religious interests. Ellen Pind Olesen had graduated from high school, before she entered teacher training, and this was probably the reason why she experienced the teaching there as boring, teacher dominated and characterized by swotting. She describes herself as lazy, in contrast to most of her classmates, who studied real hard. She did not like the evangelical "spirit" of the college and loathed the "obligatory" mission meetings every Saturday evening. There was a feeling of solidarity in her class, and she made several good friends. But she also felt a distance between herself and many of the devoted and hard-working classmates.

In my interview with Ellen Pind Olesen she describes herself as a "loner", an individualist, who often followed her own nose, both at college and later. For instance she had never been interested in the work of the women's organizations. As a teacher it was first of all the teaching and the children that had her interest. At Christiansgades School in the 1930s she had experienced a generational difference among the women teachers, in which she and two other young teachers were in opposition to an older generation of women teachers very much engaged in the woman question (Hulda Pedersen and others). The young teachers wanted—among other things—to modernize the teaching. They were less prudish in their attitude to the dress of the pupils and to sexual matters, and finally, they were not very interested in the woman question.

Ellen Pind Olesen can be seen as an early representative of the modern, individualistic type of woman who became more common at the training college in the course of the 1930s and 1940s. Her family and educational background provides some of the explanation why she experienced the college differently than the majority of her classmates. Her great interest in literature and art might provide another part of the explanation. But as all transitional figures, Ellen Pind Olesen also had her feet planted in the old ways. Her opposition to the training college did not include the fact that it was for women only, and today she still favors sex segregated schooling.[17] Both as a teacher at a girls' school and as a single woman she stayed a part of the old women's world.

Conflicts at the Teacher Training College in the 1930s and 1940s

In the archives of the Aarhus Teacher Training College there is a strange and interesting material written by principal Høyer. In three grey notebooks, the principal has written down his thoughts about a number of students and situations of conflict from 1926 to 1945. In the following I shall refer to examples from this material in order to illustrate the differences of norms among the principal and the students and among groups of students.

The material can give us a sense of the shadowy sides of the college. There were students, who for different reasons did badly at the college. It was not unusual for a student to do badly and leave the college without a certificate. Illnesses and nervous conditions were apparently quite common. Several became ill with tuberculosis, and mere fear of this disease could lead to nervous conditions. Over-exertion could also lead to nervousness or hysteria. In turn, nervous conditions could give rise to conflicts with the principal or the other students. Spiritual tenseness and religious crises were common, but were always seen as positive. In the understanding of the college a religious crisis was one of the ways in which one could reach the faith.

The most interesting part of the material, however, is that which deals with various types of conflict between the principal and the students. The material reveals principal Høyer to have been an engaged and temperamental person, but also an authoritarian, and somewhat touchy and rigid person. In some of the situations of conflict between the students and the principal, there arose a kind of intensity, in which the outburst was followed by the weeping of the student, her regrets and explanations and the forgiveness of the principal, which resulted in a kind of mutual understanding and closeness. That was that, according to Høyer. The real danger was in relation to the young women, who were rebellious and did not regret their behaviour.[18]

February 1927. Without warning Edith Petersen broke down in a geography class and wept and wept. In a later conversation she declared that she was afraid of me. I was very unsettled by this, and in the time to come I avoided her, until I felt forced to talk to her again. This was good and evened out the problem. During this conversation she told me that a large number of students in her class had sat down in a circle and prayed for me. This gave me great joy.

February 1938. Towards Lise Lotte Schou I wish that she does not use lipstick any more; that is not the type of young woman that we want here. In the middle of my talking about this, she interrupts with the words: I have a paper to hand in!—very huffed. I ask her to just listen to what I have to say. She answers that I am not on to everyone who uses it (= lipstick, HRN). I ask her to stay away from me with her insults. "I think it is me who has a reason to be offended", she answers. "Your insults are of no concern to me", I answer, and give her an indirect warning with a reference to the recommendation, she needs to get later.

The case of Eva Møller concerned more than the relationship between an individual student and the principal. It involved a struggle about the boarding section and showed that among the college students there were now at least two groups with different attitudes to the religious foundations of the college.

In the spring of 1932, Eva Møller entered the boarding school and the class of students preparing for admission to the training college. After the summer vacation she lived with Ingrid Bech, and there were disturbances in the hall after 10 p.m. and always in her room so that in the end I had to threaten with expulsion if this was to continue ...

Eva Møller and her friends wished to be mistresses over their own domains—the boarding rooms and the common room—and they were not interested in entering into a close relationship with the principal and his family. "Eva Møller explained that young people nowadays are different". However, it soon turned out that there was also another group there, a group more rooted in the old ways, which was on a good footing with the principal. Eva Møller accused this group of currying favour with the principal, and the situation in the boarding section was soon described as "intolerable". The provisional solution to the matter was that Eva Møller was given notice and had to leave. But this did not return the boarding section to the old times, for the disagreements between the two groups remained active and pointed to the fact that the college was heading for new times.

In the material there are descriptions of several conflicts that involved a whole class. These conflicts from the time around 1940 first and foremost concerned the authoritarian leadership of the principal in the face of the demand of the class for respect and participation in decision-making. The fact that there was now a number of male students at the college appears to have contributed to making the conflicts less personal and more about principles. The conflicts also showed that the students could now gain a certain influence by sticking together.

After the admittance of male students to the college a new "danger" appeared, viz. the danger of infatuations and perhaps even sexual relations between the students. In 1944 and 1945 the first two cases appear in the material. The first and most serious case concerned a female student, who had become pregnant. The father was another student. The case ended as both were told to leave the college. In evangelical circles such cases were regarded as a male as well as a female offence.

The other case was of a less serious character and must have concerned a quite common problem. It was about a date at the college. Høyer caught two students in the act in one of the classrooms on a late evening. The worst part about it was not the crime itself, but the fact that the two involved thought that they were within their rights to be dating in class at that late hour! In this, as in other areas, the norms were changing. The changes came to the college from outside, and they came with the students.

At the Co-educational College

After 1930, co-educational teacher training colleges gradually became the most common. In the course of time most female and male colleges went co-educational. The assessment of the parliament in 1948, when the conversion of the Ribe State Teacher Training College for Women to a co-educational college was discussed, was that it was a "development which is connected to the fact that female students increasingly prefer co-educational training colleges".[19] In 1948 the idea of specific training colleges for women was considered hopelessly old-fashioned among most of the young women, and it was seen as a remnant of the early days of the women's movement. It was now natural for modern young women to mix with young men in daily life.

It is much more difficult to learn something about the conditions of the female college students at the Aarhus Teacher Training College after 1932 than before. The women teachers now occupied less prominent positions than before, and the female students, too, appear less visible in the overall impression of college life. The Newsletter of the Student Association, "Baunen", that was published from 1931, gives some opportunities to follow the gradual, general process of transformation that the college went through. It appears that the erasing of the former specialties of the training college as an evangelical training college for women was no convincing advantage to the women. It seems as if the female students now in many ways were subordinated the more dynamic and extrovert male students. At the same time there were positive aspects to the new position of the women, in as far as they were given opportunities to transcend some of the sexual stereotypes and ideals that had characterized the college in former days. The picture is by no means unequivocal.

Among our contemporary, retired women teachers (born 1900-1925) most have attended co-educational teacher training colleges. For these teachers it could be quite

Graduates and teachers at the co-educational Aarhus Teacher Training College, 1936. The male principal Jacob Høyer has placed himself in front in the the middle of the students. Olga Paulsen is still present, standing in the third row to the left, wearing round glasses. The graduates are now both men and women. The young women are of the modern type, wearing cheerful floral dresses with short sleeves. Most are short-haired.

a shock to be employed at an oldfashioned school system as the one in Aarhus, where the sex segregated school survived well into the 1950s. The contrast between the student years when the students worked together freely, and the reality they met as newly graduated male and female teachers at the municipal school system in Aarhus was experienced as both intense and significant. Many of this generation increasingly came to see the sex segregated school system as oldfashioned, inappropriate or downright harmful. Many of these young male and female teachers became active in the effort to do away with sex segregation, and the years just after the war were experienced as a period with "growth and innovation all around" (Else Byrith, 1988: 41). The transition to co-education was a reform with far reaching consequences, also mentally. It was increasingly seen as old-fashioned and illegitimate when older women teachers defended the old sex segregated system. Today the retired teachers whom I have interviewed are almost all fierce supporters of a school system in which gender aspects are attempted neutralized or reduced.

The significance of the co-educational teacher training colleges has been to fix this attitude at an early stage in life. After this, it was no longer possible to turn back the clock, and in this way the training colleges became one among several factors to break down the sex segregated school and the sex segregated labor market.

What was lost were the unique values and the community which the training colleges for women represented. One of the young generation says about her attitude to the work as a teacher: "I don't believe I felt a calling; but I have always considered it valuable to work with children and education, and I have never regretted my choice" (Else Byrith, 1988: 38).

Conclusion

For a period during the first half of the century the women's culture that I have accounted for here was efficient as a tool for the interests of a particular group of women. As such, the women's culture was closely tied up with the women's move-ment in this period. But this women's culture had to be broken and dissolved. From the outside by the men, who felt threatened. But also from the inside by the young generation of women, because the women's culture had come to be seen as an old-fashioned solution to the problem of modern femininity.

As far as I can see, the women teachers in the 1940s and 1950s became aware of a kind of generational gap within their ranks. Both at the individual school and in the organizations of the teachers, there were signs that a gap and sometimes conflicts were experienced between older and younger women teachers. At the individual schools the younger teachers occasionally felt dominated by the older. The merger in 1965 of the Association for Women Teachers and the Association for Male Teachers can be inter-preted as a sign that the balance finally had tipped in favor of the young.

In an article Carroll Smith-Rosenberg describes the "new woman" as androgyne: it was a position that assumed woman's rights to existence beyond gender in the public world as an autonomous and powerful individual. The dilemma of the new woman was that she had to use a male language whereby she lost her old female identity and ended up being on her own (Smith-Rosenberg, 1985: 245-296). It would appear some-what exaggerated to describe the woman teacher in Aarhus in the 1940s as androgy-nous, but as an image attempting to catch the essence of the efforts of the new woman, I believe it can be useful.

I am less in agreement with Smith-Rosenberg on another point. Her explanation of the disintegration of the women's culture of the first generation relies heavily on a discussion of the way the medical profession constructed a new image of woman and simultaneously stamped friendships among women as lesbian and deviant. I shall not challenge the co-responsibility of the medical profession in the question of the creation of an image of the new woman on a general level. But I think that this explanation overlooks the specific behaviour and influence of the women themselves and the internal dynamics of the women's culture that contributed to its disintegration.

The disintegration of the women's culture reflects the changes in the conditions of women and the new hopes they nurtured. The teachers demanded the right to marry and have children, for instance. In these matters, too, they were pioneers in the labor market of the middle-class women. But as married women they had less time to spend and less use for the social space of the women's culture. In time the women teachers also demanded more space for individual development. Many, especially younger women, felt that the old culture was a straightjacket that did not allow divergent attitudes and interests in the individual woman. The culture of the women teachers was increasingly experienced as a restricted world. The new generations demanded access to all the opportunities that they saw belonging to men and married women.

I think that a good place to look for women's interests in the transformation of the women's culture is the ongoing process of individualization. The women of the first generation had caught on to some of the advantages of an individualized life-style, and this process was accentuated in the second generation. Women's growing individuality also epitomized their transition to modern life.

References

Archives and Interviews

The Archives of the Aarhus Teacher Training College. The Co-educational College in Aarhus and the Regional Archives in Viborg.

The Archives of the Municipal Schools in Aarhus. The Industrial Archives in Aarhus.

The Minute Books of the Aarhus Association for Women Teachers. The Aarhus Teachers' Association.

The Archives of the Danish Women's Society. The Women's History Archive, the State Library, Aarhus.

The Archives of Hulda Pedersen. The Women's History Archive, the State Library, Aarhus.

Interviews with Anna Mousten, Spring and Summer of 1989, Jensine Thomsen, August 4, 1989, Ellen Pind Olesen, October 16 and 23, 1989. In the possession of the author.

Literature

Andersen, Jørn Erslev et al. (1982) (eds.), *Ernst Bloch—en introduktion*, Århus: Modtryk.

Banks, Olive (1981), *Faces of Feminism. A Study of Feminism as a Social Movement*, Oxford: Martin Robertson.

Banks, Olive (1986), *Becoming a Feminist. The Social Origins of "First Wave" Feminism*, Brighton: Wheatsheaf Books.

Buur, Chr. (1930), *Aarhus Skolevæsen gennem 80 Aar*, Aarhus.

Byrith, Else (1988), "Hvordan var det? Skoleliv i Århus", *Ung i Århus*, Tredie Samling, Århus: Århus Byhistoriske Udvalg.

Corbin, Farge, Perrot et al. (1989), *Geschlecht und Geschichte. Ist eine weibliche Geschichtsschreibung möglich?*, Frankfurt am Main: S. Fischer Verlag.

Cott, Nancy F. (1975), "Young Women in the Second Great Awakening in New England, 1780-1835", *Feminist Studies*, vol. 3, no. 1/2.

Cott, Nancy F. (1977), *The Bonds of Womanhood. "Woman's Sphere" in New England, 1780-1835*, New Haven & London: Yale University Press.

Cott, Nancy F. (1987), *The Grounding of Modern Feminism*, New Haven & London: Yale University Press.

Dansk Skolestat (1933-34), vol. 1-4, København.

Davidoff, Leonore and Catherine Hall (1987), *Family Fortunes. Men and Women of the English Middle Class 1780-1850*, London: Hutchinson.

Dauphin et al. (1987), "Annales och kvinnohistoria", *Häften för kritiska studier*, no. 4, Stockholm.

Dubois, Ellen et al (1980), "Politics and Culture in Women's History: A Symposion", *Feminist Studies*, vol. 6, no. 1.

Dubois, Ellen and Nancy F. Cott (1989), "Comments on Karen Offen's "Defining Feminism: A Comparative Historical Approach"", *Signs*, vol. 15, no. 1.

Ehn, Billy and Orvar Löfgren (1986), *Kulturanalys. Ett etnologiskt perspektiv*, Stockholm: Liber Förlag.

Elgqvist-Saltzman, Inga et al. (1985-87), *Rostadprojektet*, Arbetsrapport no. 1-6, Kalmar & Umeå.

Florin, Christina (1987), *Kampen om katedern. Feminiserings- og professionaliseringsprocessen inom den svenska folkskolans lärarkår 1860-1906*, Acta Universitas Umensis, Umeå Studies in the Humanities 82, Stockholm: Umeå Universitet.

Freedman, Estelle (1979), "Separatism as Strategy: Female Institution Building and American Feminism, 1870-1930", *Feminist Studies*, vol. 5, no. 3.

Frykman, Jonas & Orvar Löfgren (1984), *Den kultiverade människan*, Stockholm: Liber Förlag.

Gejl, Ib (1978) (ed.), *Skoler og skolegang i Århus 1930-70*, Århus: Århus Byhistoriske Udvalg.

Hewitt, Nancy (1985), "Beyond the Search for Sisterhood: American Women's History in the 1980s", *Social History*, vol. 10, no. 3.

Hilden, Adda (1987), "Da kvinder lærte at lære", *Fortid og Nutid*, no. 2, København.

Hirdman, Yvonne (1986), "Särart—likhet: Kvinnorörelsens Scylla och Karybdis", Inge Frederiksen & Hilda Rømer (eds.), *Kvinder, mentalitet, arbejde. Kvindehistorisk Forskning i Norden*, Rapport fra det 2. nordiske kvindehistoriemøde 1985, Aarhus: Aarhus University Press.

Hunt, Felicity (1987) (ed.), *Lessons for Life. The Schooling of Girls and Women 1850-1950*, Oxford: Basil Blackwell.

Jensen, Bernard Eric (1990), "Kulturhistorie—et nyt og bedre helhedsbegreb", *Historisk Tidsskrift*, vol. 90, no. 1, København.

Kerber, Linda (1988), "Separate Spheres, Female Worlds, Woman's Place: The Rhetoric of Women's History", *The Journal of American History*, vol. 75, no. 1.

Koch, Lene (1984) (ed.), *Hendes egen verden. Kvindelighed og kvindefællesskaber i det viktorianske USA*, København: Tiderne Skifterne.

Kvinden og Samfundet 1885-, København: Dansk Kvindesamfund.

Lagemann, Ellen Condliffe (1979), *A Generation of Women. Education in the Lives of Progressive Reformers*, Cambridge, Mass.: Harvard University Press.

Lerner, Gerda (1979), *The Majority Finds Its Past. Placing Women in History*, Oxford: Oxford University Press.

Lützen, Karin (1986), *Hvad hjertet begærer. Kvinders kærlighed til kvinder 1825-1985*, København: Tiderne Skifter.

Meddelelser til Lærerindernes Missionsforbund 1910-, København.

Melby, Kari (1984), "Norges Lærerinneforbund og Norges Husmorforbund 1911/15-1940", Aura Korppi-Tommola (ed.), *Rapport från Nordiskt Kvinnohistoriskt Seminarium 1984*, Helsinki.

Melby, Kari (1990), "Kvinneideologisk mangfold", *Kvinnohistoria i teoretiskt perspektiv*, Konferensrapport från det tredje nordiska kvinnohistorikermötet 1989, Uppsala Papers in Economic History 8/1990, Uppsala: University of Uppsala.

Nielsen, Hanne Rimmen and Eva Lous (1986) (eds.), *Kvinder Undervejs. Dansk Kvindesamfund i Århus 1886-1986*, Aarhus: Aarhus University Press.

Nielsen, Hanne Rimmen (1987), "Arbejderpiger og arbejderdrenge i de århusianske skoler", *Årbog for arbejderbevægelsens historie*, Skolen og arbejderne, Aarhus.

Nielsen, Hanne Rimmen (1988), "Rejsen til Kina. Kvindemissionærer omkring århundredeskiftet", *Den jyske Historiker*, nr. 46, Rejsen i historien, Aarhus.

Nielsen, Hanne Rimmen (1989), "Kvindelighed og kundskaber. Pigers hverdag i århusianske kommuneskoler 1900-1950", Adda Hilden & Anne-Mette Kruse (eds.), *Pigernes skole*, Århus: Klim.

Nielsen, Hanne Rimmen (1990a), "Køn, kultur og historie", Henrik Horstbøll & Henrik Kaare Nielsen (eds.), *Delkulturer*, Aarhus: Aarhus University Press.

Nielsen, Hanne Rimmen (1990b), "Troende og dygtige Lærerinder". Lærerindeuddannelse og -fællesskab på Aarhus (Kvinde)Seminarium 1909-1950. En kvindekulturs rum og forestillinger, Aarhus: Unpublished Dissertation.

Nielsen, Hanne Rimmen (1990c), Mine Hvid, Samsø—Den første kvindelige førstelærer, Aarhus: Unpublished manuscript.

Offen, Karen (1988), "Defining Feminism: A Comparative Historical Approach", *Signs*, vol. 14, no. 1.

Paulsen, Olga (1920), *Hvordan kan L.M.F. blive til Velsignelse?*, København.

Rupp, Leila J. and Verta Taylor (1987), *Survival in the Doldrums. The American Women's Rights Movement, 1945 to the 1960s*, New York and Oxford: Oxford University Press.

Scott, Joan Wallach (1988), *Gender and the Politics of History*, New York: Columbia University Press.

Smith-Rosenberg, Carroll (1975), "The Female World of Love and Ritual: Relations between Women in Nineteenth-Century America", *Signs*, no. 1.

Smith-Rosenberg, Carroll (1985), *Disorderly Conduct. Visions of Gender in Victorian America*, New York: Alfred A. Knopf.

Ware, Susan (1981), *Beyond Suffrage. Women in the New Deal*, Cambridge, Mass. and London: Harvard University Press.

Verdier, Yvonne (1981), *Tvätterskan, sömmerskan, kokerskan. Livet i en fransk by genom tre kvinnoyrken*, Stockholm: Atlantis.

Vicinus, Martha (1985), *Independent Women. Work and Community for Single Women, 1850-1920*, London: Virago Press.

Aarhus Seminarium 1909-34, 1909-59, 1909-84 (The Anniversary Publications of the Training College).

Aarhus (Kvinde)Seminariums Elevforening 1931-34, Baunen 1935-73 (The Newsletter of the Student Association, from 1937 an annual publication).

Notes

1. In the second half of the nineteenth century there was a very strong evangelical innovation movement in Denmark. The movement made itself felt in church, education, and social matters. The denomination came to be called "Indre Mission" (Home Mission) emphasizing the internal perspective in contradistinction to "Ydre Mission" (Mission to Foreign Countries), which was an institution that was concerned with missionaries abroad. In this article, I shall maintain the term "evangelical" throughout, whether I am writing about the movement in general or the denomination in particular. A peculiarity about this denomination is that it exists within the established Church of Denmark.

2. Natalie Zahle (1827-1913) was a pioneer in the girls' schools and training colleges for women teachers in Denmark. She founded her secondary girls' school in 1851, a private school teacher training college for women that same year, a training college for elementary school teachers in 1860 and a school preparing mature students for O-levels in 1877. She has had an immense impact on the educational possibilities of women and indirectly on the women's movement.

3. Theodora Lang (1855-1935) founded her girls' school in 1882 in a small town called Silkeborg in Jutland, approximately 25 miles from Aarhus. Later she expanded her educational activities and set up a teacher training college for women (1896). She was one of the driving forces of the association of girls' schools called "The Danish Girls' School" (Den danske Pigeskole), which dates back to 1893.

4. Out of the 141 18 did not give their educational background (Dansk Skolestat, 1934, vol. 3).

5. Lützen, 1986: 74-80, shows the existence of similar ideas about the relationship between the female teachers and the students at N. Zahle's college.

6. When the Training College went co-educational in 1932, the inscription "Kvindeseminarium" ("Training College for Women Teachers") was removed. Kristine Nordby's words also refer to her (and many others') opposition to the college going co-educational.

7. Baunen, the Anniversary Publication of the Students' Association. Commemorating the 25th anniversary of the Aarhus Teacher Training College in 1934: 4-5.

8. Letter of October 11, 1917, from Astrid Blume to the College Board, the Archives of the Aarhus Teacher Training College, Box 3.

9. Letter of April 29, 1914, from Mr. Lambertsen, the Archives of the Aarhus Teacher Training College, Box 4. At this time Haslev Teacher Training College had gone co-educational, though it was still dominated by male students.

10. Danish women were enfranchised in 1915.

11. Olga Paulsen (1920), *Hvordan kan L.M.F. blive til Velsignelse? (How Can LMF Become a Blessing?)*, Pamphlet containing a lecture.

12. Non-synchronous is a translation of "usamtidig" (Danish) or "ungleichzeitig" (German) which is Ernst Bloch's famous concept of the phenomenon that individuals may live in the same chronological period, yet at the same time in very different time-bound cultural settings.

13. A list of the most common characteristics and expressions in the recommendations runs like this:

    Bright, conscientious, hard-working, kind, interested, dutiful, well-prepared,

    Good results in her classes,

    Is good at maintaining order and discipline (best if this is done by catching the attention of the children, i.e. without using punishment),

    Good with children, good at winning them over,

    Liked by her colleagues,

    Lively - serious (both are stated as positive characteristics),

    Cultivated, charming, from a good home.

14. For the women employed in village schools the reality looked different. They were cut off from a community with other women teachers. They could react to this, either by seeking integration in the local community or by seeking jobs in town. See Nielsen 1990c.

15. The Law of Teachers' Salaries of 1919 gave the same basic salary to female and male teachers.

16. I count both women teachers and students in this generation, even though there were actually two age groups. On the one hand there was a harmony in the experiences and ideal for the two groups, on the other, in my focus on the breaking up of the women's culture and the development of a new individualized way of living in the interwar period, I have found it more expedient to consider the two age groups one generation.

17. At one and the same time this is an oldfashioned and a quite modern attitude according to the interest in sex segregated schooling in parts of the new pedagogical women's research.

18. All names have been changed in the following.

19. Rigsdagstidende 1947-48, Appendix A, Column 4429-4432.

Spinsters and Families:
How Unmarried, Philantropic Women Taught the Working Class in Copenhagen to Live in Nuclear Families, 1877-1927

Karin Lützen

In the course of the past 10 to 20 years, research in homosexuality has undergone a shift of paradigms. American sociologists have described sexuality as a social construction, and they have pointed out that the forms of sexual behaviour have been dictated by social norms (Gagnon, 1973). British sociologists have described how "being homosexual" has been equated with learning a homosexual role (McIntosh, 1981), and they have expanded on this theory by showing how this role identification is constructed in a series of phases (Plummer, 1975). The French philosopher Michel Foucault has shown how sexuality—and homosexuality—are historical as well as social constructions, and he has described what he calls the discourse of sexuality at the end of the nineteenth century (Foucault, 1975).

Naturally, this constructivist view of (homo)sexuality has influenced research in lesbian history. If homosexuality is a category constructed as recently as the late nineteenth century, and if this marks the first experience of women and men lumped together as a third sex, the conditions for women who love women must have been different before then. In her article "The Female World of Love and Ritual" from 1975, the American historian Carroll Smith-Rosenberg demonstrated that loving and passionate relationships between bourgeois women were extremely common and accep- table in the nineteenth century (Smith-Rosenberg, 1979). Most likely these relationships did not include genital sexuality, and the American historian Nancy Cott has explained, why these bourgeois women preferred a loving heart to carnal pleasure (Cott, 1979). As possibilities for earning an income arose through the new female occupations in teaching and nursing, middle-class women in this period were given opportunities to avoid marriage and could instead settle down with another unmarried woman. This has been documented by Martha Vicinus (1985).

This Cockaigne for women's love disappeared abruptly at the end of the century, and the American literary historian Lillian Faderman in particular has claimed that this was due to the appearance of the category "homosexuality" in sexual science (Fader- man, 1981). She has presented a "theory of morbidification", which states that love between women was increasingly seen as a disease, because it became identified with homosexuality and was thus considered a perversion. As a result, romantic friends became worried about being considered sick homosexuals and preferred to stifle their love of women. This theory seems to me much too simple: sexual science becomes the culprit and romantic friends the victims of a historical development. I find this to be evidence of moral embitterment rather than of historical research. Nevertheless this is a theory that is adhered to by British women, in particular those who belong to the faction which is "against everything" so to speak: pornography, sado-masochism and butch-femme roles (Jeffreys, 1985).

Love between women was certainly considered as a perversion, when from now on it became identified with homosexuality, but is was also sexualized. Homosexual women were now considered to be women with sexual desires—and the power to satisfy these. Therefore other feminist researchers have seen the new female homosexual as a liberating potential, because it allowed women to be autonomous sexual beings (Newton, 1984; Lützen, 1986). It appears that behind this debate about who is guilty of causing the romantic friendships to die out, there is a hidden moral discussion about the nature of sexuality.

I find it important to trace the construction of "heterosexuality" as well as "homosexuality". If we only deconstruct homosexuality, the result may be that it will be pulverized to invisible atoms, whereas heterosexuality will remain fixed as a solid rock—as a symbol of its truth and universality.

Besides, in my opinion this single-minded focus on sexual science lands us in a cul-de-sac. It is true that its ideas were very persuasive, and it contributed to a new understanding of sexuality, but it had no effect on people's actions in the outside world.

Middle-Class Philanthropy

Private middle-class and Christian philanthropy was much more efficient. A large number of unmarried women worked in this context. Of course, married women supported philanthropic work with money, knitting or arranging bazaars, but because of their own family obligations they were seldom able to make as great a contribution as the spinsters. Philanthropy came, as it were, naturally to women—it was part and parcel of the middle-class woman's role to feel compassion, to devote herself to the service of others and to bring others up to live by middle-class norms. As piety was also part of the female role, many unmarried women felt an inevitable "calling" to dedicate their lives to philanthropic work. For some women this "calling" turned into a vocation thereby giving them an opportunity to support themselves and avoid marriage.

The mainstays of philanthropy were the class and gender norms of the philanthropists themselves. The qualities they had been taught to value—domesticity, responsibility, industriousness and piety—were also those which they now taught the lower class to value. Philanthropy was to save people from destitution—material as well as spiritual—with a view "to prepare a people that shall be fit for the Lord", as it said in Luke, Chapter 1, Verse 17. This was taken literally by many philanthropists.

The aim of philanthropy, then, was to teach the unfortunates the virtues of family life. The people at the receiving end of this philanthropic effort either had no understanding of family life because they had no knowledge of it from their social class (poor workers, intemperate workers, prisoners, prostitutes or fallen women), or they had no way of becoming part of a family (orphans, stray pets, tramps), or, due to their work, they were temporarily separated from their families (maids, sailors, soldiers, travelling artisans).

These people were to learn to cultivate a family life, learn that home is the best place on earth and that life at home is better than life on the streets or in the bars. But prior to their roping in by the philanthropists, they all lived in a manner which conflicted deeply with the middle-class norms of the philanthropists. No one, however, had sunk so low that they did not deserve salvation, and the philanthropists—unlike the public authorities—did not distinguish between the worthy and unworthy needy. All were seen as victims of their wretched circumstances, for they were "Objects of God's love and as such worthy of love", as the chorus sang.

Even though it could be said that, for example, prostitutes by their trade posed a threat to middle-class family life, this did not make them the unworthy needy. The only group of people who were not part of a family, and who were left completely to their own devices, were sodomites. In 1907, they had become famous in Denmark due to a major court case involving countless men. This could have qualified them for philanthropic help. But no philanthropist would touch them with a barge-pole, which shows that the men who *consciously* removed themselves from the family unit, would be left to stay out in the cold.

Heterosexuality as a Cultural Arrangement

Curiously enough the teachers of this education in family life were unmarried women—who were themselves able to avoid marriage because they supported themselves by socializing everyone else to marry. My thesis is that the dying-out of love relationships between unmarried women in our century is not only due to sexology developing the concept of "homosexuality" as a clinical term, but also of equal importance was the fact that "heterosexuality" as a cultural arrangement was introduced to all social classes—often with spinster-couples as energetic mid-wives. Perhaps the spinsters dug their own graves—but of course with the best of intentions. They worked so persistently to represent "father, mother and children in a nice comfortable home" as an ideal for everyone that they simultaneously turned their own way of life into a defective anachronism. Thus, "heterosexuality" came to equal normality and "homosexuality" equalled abnormality.

Traditionally, these two categories are seen as expressive of the "sexual instinct" wanting either the one thing or the other. But if sexuality is perceived as a social construction, it is possible to consider it more as a cultural product than as an anatomical/psychological product. The two categories can be studied as two cultural arrangements, the one, however, being more conspicuous than the other. That "homosexuality" involves conspicuous sub-cultural arrangements such as a bar culture, a deviant identity and role-playing, is usually explained by saying that those who saw themselves as homosexuals, arranged life around them to allow for the direction of their sexual instinct. Thus it becomes superfluous to examine the reason for the way in which "the normal ones" have arranged themselves.

"Heterosexuality" as a modern concept does not only mean that the sexual instinct is directed towards a person of the opposite sex. It also means that our culture is arranged like its sole purpose was to accommodate the normal direction of this sexual instinct. Culture is heterosexualized in such a way that everyone considers it normal to pair off with a person of the opposite sex in order to marry and have a family. Moreover, heterosexuality has defined a family life in which the husband and wife feel solidarity with one another and joint responsibility for their offspring. In the following I shall attempt to *deconstruct* heterosexuality by showing how it was *constructed* as a cultural arrangement.

Spinster Philanthropy

To illustrate my argument, I shall use examples from the philanthropic work undertaken by unmarried women in Copenhagen from 1877. This was a year in which many "Homes" were established and philanthropic "Homes" are a major hotbed of heterosexualization. "Magdalene Home" was inaugurated as a rescue home for young fallen women, with Miss Thora Esche as the matron. Miss Regitze Barner set up "Lindevangs Home" to receive young women on their release from prison. A few years earlier Miss Josephine Schneider and Miss Rosalie Petersen had each opened a children's home, Miss Henriette Beckman had founded a home for children and unemployed maid servants, and Miss Caroline Mathisen had opened a home for deaf-and-dumb children. The St. Joseph sisters built a hospital, as did the deaconesses in 1877—both had a "home" affiliated to the establishment.

The years that followed saw the opening of one "home" after the other, for every conceivable purpose. In 1878, Lady Thusnelda Moltke took the initiative to found "Talitha Kumi", a rescue home for young girls in danger of being drawn into a life of immorality; in 1884, Miss Athalia Rørbye started up a home for sailors, and in 1886 Miss Anna Sørensen established the settlement "Martha Home". In 1889, Miss Regitze Barner opened a second home—"Bethania"—a sheltered home where single girls could live while studying in Copenhagen and finally, in 1899, she founded an old people's home—"Vesterled"—for spinsters. Other homes were established by a variety of organisations such as the Salvation Army, the Church Army, the White Ribbon, the Association for Youth Welfare ... and yet more by private individuals.

All of these institutions were called "Home", accentuated in the name in order to underline the fact that they had little in common with the earlier type of institutions and asylums. Thus, the "Work Institutions for Deaf-and-Dumb Girls" which had been opened in 1869 changed its name in 1876 to "Work Home", the reason being

that this designation correctly emphasizes the double aim of the institutions, partly to educate deaf-and-dumb girls, partly to be a home in which they can take shelter when they need help and support, just as the establishment, also in accordance with its set of tasks, is a life-long home for the backward and partially disabled (*Arbejdshjemmet for døvstumme Piger*, 1919: 22).

It was not only the name of these "Homes" which differentiated them from earlier institutions and asylums; the way in which they were organized and run was also different. The asylums were large and barrack-like, with mixed ages and sexes, and run with a heavy hand by a man—sometimes a married couple. The "homes" were small, homely, grouped by age and gender and lovingly run by one or two spinsters. If a "home" was to be homely, it went without saying that it should be small, since the intimacy of family life was an important element in this socialization. Furthermore, a woman should be in charge as, according to middle-class norms, a house did not become a home until ruled by a woman.

Communities Based on Gender, Age and Type of Destitution

Yet another important ingredient was the separation of the different age groups and sexes. Philanthropy grew out of middle-class norms and the middle-class had, earlier in the century, divided men, women and children into their separate spheres. "Child-hood" was a new category that took care of the child(ish), and the gender specificity was allowed for in that which is now called "homo-sociality". The mystery of the opposite sex and the innocence of the younger generation were intensified by sepa-ration. The more the sexes were separated, the more improper intimacy between them seemed to be—that is, if they were not married to one another.

The lower classes had been stuffed into the same asylums irrespective of their gender or age. If the residents were also so-called abnormal, it seemed not in the least offensive—or remarkable—to put them with others. In the mental home of "Gammel Bakkehus" residents of both sexes from the age of 10 to 65 lived together in the same ward; this arrangement was not changed until 1882. In the public asylums no di-stinctions were made between gender, age or type of destitution, and orphans had been crammed together with old, blind men and young fallen women. The new private phil-anthropic efforts targeted people of the same kind, because this was considered more efficient. These new "homes" were therefore established for a specific sex, a specific age group and a specific type, so that the subjects of the philanthropist's work suddenly found themselves part of a family with people of the same sex, age and type. All philanthropists were fervent believers in homosociality, even such a heterosocial organization as the Salvation Army where "brothers" and "sisters" worked side by side in their rescue work.

It may seem paradoxical that the subjects could be socialized to family life amongst people of the same age and sex and in the same boat as themselves, but it all went splendidly, since all were given specific roles. Regardless of age, the needy were always "children", the matron was "mother" and the assistants were "sisters"—this also played its part in strengthening class divisions and maintaining the philanthropist's guardianship. That this was the case is suggested by a tribute paid to Miss Louise Bruun who, since 1910, had run a reformatory for intemperate women in the worst slums of Copenhagen. On her death in 1925, an assistant wrote that her memory was blessed among "the children" as

you called them, who you had the chance to help, among whom so many desperately needed to have someone they could call "mother" even though many of them had been wives and mothers for years (*Bud og Hilsen fra Sikem*, 1928-28: 67).

The Gender-Roles of the Spinsters

The spinsters, who worked so energetically to join the two sexes in a balanced family life, *themselves* kept to their own sex. They often lived together with another spinster, and the two ran the home jointly in that loving spirit, which was so important a part of philanthropic work. That they also cherished a love for one another, was merely considered an extra plus for the establishment.

Such was the case for the girls home "Talitha Kumi", which the Misses Anna Herreborg and Agnes Hansen had co-run since 1886. When they retired in 1926 they received a beautiful testimony.

They were both very gifted and in possession of rich, warm emotions. Faithful friends since youth, they complemented one another in an excellent way, the one being possibly the stronger, in the other gentleness being the predominant feature. Only such perfect harmony could allow for the total utilization of the mental and physical powers which their work came to demand.

That the spinsters were in harmony with one another simply resulted in a heightened ability to love the children, whose upbringing was in their hands.

The two women indulged in mothering with a mother's strong sense of duty and right. The aim, which they never abandoned, was to bind the children to each other, to the home and to their

The living room at the Home of Magdalene (Magdalenehjemmet), in Copenhagen, Denmark.

motherly friends with bonds equalled only by those tied by blood in the natural home (*Danske Opdragelseshjem i Billeder og Tekst*, 1926: 198).

Even though these philanthropic women never had children themselves, they experienced the mother role in relation to a large number of children or childlike adults. They lived out their lives in the Mother-role, that is if they did not, at a later stage, change gender role, as did Thora Esche. In 1908 she retired as matron of Magdalene Home, but did not move far away, for which her successor was grateful:

Although she was no longer Mother to the children, Miss Esche has been, as she herself says, like a father to our large family. A father one could safely approach when needing advice and guidance about the many serious and difficult incidents and experiences with which one is confronted (*Smaatræk fra det daglige liv*, 1909: 3).

A single room at the Home of Magdalene (Magdalene-hjemmet), in Copenhagen, Denmark.

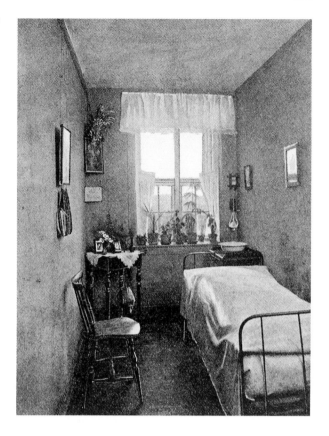

In her memoirs, Thora Esche wrote that in 1883 the church of God in Denmark sent her "the first believing woman, with whom I have lived a long, blessed life" (Esche, 1920: 181). But as she continued to be the absolute leader of the home, she had to take on the two gender roles successively. Other women, who ran homes, found a partner, who could take on one of the roles, as did Miss Caroline Mathisen. From 1887 she ran a home for deaf-and-dumb children together with Miss Anna Thorup, and when they retired in 1899, the journal of the deaf-and-dumb noted that

"Foster mother" and "Aunt Anna" knew how to make a true home for the children. Seldom have two women, each in her way, possessed such rich potential to be "Father and Mother" for deaf-and-dumb children as these two, but it is also seldom that two women in complete under-standing and agreement used their talents as they did.

Those who had visited the home over the years would be able to remember

when "Foster mother" as "father" of the house presided over the dinner table with all the little chicks sitting along both sides of the long table, whilst "Aunt Anna" made sure that everyone was fed (*Smaablade for Døvstumme*, 1899: 947).

In this way, everyone was also fed their gender role—in these homosocial homes the subjects of philanthropy were both socialized to the role which corresponded to their biological sex and to heterosexuality with an unknown partner. But when one of the spinster-mothers so obligingly took on the opposite sexual role, it became an object lesson in preparation for a future heterosexual family life.

Private Life—A Middle-Class Invention

All of these "homes" were not only home by name, but also of purpose: the sailor's home was a substitute for native soil, the old people's home was a half-way house on the road to the eternal, heavenly home and the rescue home was the subject's first experience of a homely home. Magdalene Home for young fallen women was one of the latter and when, in 1902, it celebrated its twentyfifth anniversary, Pastor Blume wrote:

It has not been an establishment or a barracks-like institution similar to those seen in many other countries, but a "Home" with the constant endeavour to ensure that the residents should lead a comfortable and warm life, as in a good home; an important factor in the attainment of this has been that every girl should have her own room (Blume, 1902: 4).

"Private life" was a new, middle-class invention which followed in the wake of "home life". The family formed a closed, intimate circle, but it should also afford the opportunity for individual family members to withdraw into a private room. This was possible in large middle-class houses, but in working-class one-room apartments with thin walls and loose windows, private life was an unrealizable luxury and maybe not even particularly desirable. When, therefore, these people went into a "home" they not only experienced membership of a family consisting of people of the same age, sex and type as themselves, they may also have had their own room. It is thought-provoking that it was the home for *fallen* women, which first introduced the separation of residents at night. Pastor Blume, however, had a very innocent explanation:

This little room is of enormous importance for the rehabilitation and salvation of the young girl; here she can, should she want to, without being mocked, go down on her knees and seek help where help is to be found; here she can fight her fights, and should she want to do harm, here she can injure only herself (Blume, 1902: 18).

A Room of One's Own

So a single room could be a sort of religious closet; the matron herself, Miss Thora Esche, had another innocent explanation at hand:

These small rooms were the sanctuaries that contributed to making the Home into a home for each of its residents (Esche, 1920: 79).

She also intimated that their function was not solely to do with religion or cosiness when telling how, in 1877, she had to persuade the board of governors that the residents should have single rooms as

the large dormitories would mean that everything that had been built up during the day, would be broken down at night (Esche, 1920: 76).

Thora Esche had acquainted herself with the world of prostitution before she began her work as matron, so it is not unlikely that she had got wind of tribadism among prostitutes. However, due to her religious background there was a limit to how far she could go in calling things by their actual name, whereas Rudolph Bergh, chief physician at the hospital for prostitutes, having had a scientific education, was used to being forthright. In the hospital's annual report for 1888 he wrote that according to a French study

this inclination is often acquired when in custody the girls are kept together; detention conditions in Copenhagen have hitherto frequently necessitated the keeping of 2-4 young girls together around the clock, probably with the same consequent depravation (*Beretning fra Vestre Hospital* 1888: 13 note).

It was religious philanthropy which first introduced single rooms in the homes whether the reason was that in this way the residents could be alone with God, that they would be socialized to middle-class private life, or that they should be prevented from having sexual intercourse with people of their own sex. The public authorities and philanthropy based on humanitarian principles either did not suspect any possible danger or did not consider it worth their while to lavish such a luxury on their clients. For some years to come, the residents in these homes slept together in dormitories with people of their own sex.

A Well-Trained People

In this homosocial—probably not homosexual—universe, the subjects were not only socialized to family life, but also to life in the community. Previously, when these people had been crowded together in huge institutions, they had been virtually buried alive; perhaps they were hired out to sweep the streets or made to stick bags together, so that they could contribute a little towards their keep. Religious philanthropy, on the other hand, wanted to teach them a trade so that they could support themselves and not be a permanent burden on society. Even though their stay in the home, with all its luxury, involved great expense, this was, in the long run, reimbursed when the residents, socialized, were sent out into the world again as responsible self-supporting people or able to support a family. The philanthropists stressed time and again that they did not hand out charity, but "help to those who help themselves".

But it cannot always have been easy, as is shown by, for example, the annual report of "The Society for the Rescue of Erring Girls", established in 1877. This differed from other philanthropic societies in that it did not have any "Homes", but sent girls to industrious Christian families where they were trained as maids. There were quite a few unfortunate experiences; in 1887, for example, a 16-year-old girl had been treated for venereal disease and then sent out to a farming family:

There have been complaints about her slovenliness and sauciness, and she is never likely to become a capable person, but her good nature makes the household tolerant towards her, so that they in faith are helping her get on and be of service to the world (*Aarsberetning fra Foreningen til forvildede unge Pigers Frelse* 1887: 10).

Even the so-called abnormal people who had previously been obliged to struggle on in institutions or to go begging, were taught a trade. Single mentally deficient people, cripples, the deaf and blind now learned to sew, weave, knit, make brooms etc. in order to be able to earn a living. And those who had married and had a family, but had still not come to terms with the responsibility which this entailed, learned about such matters in the homes. This kind of responsibility was especially directed at the large number of men who drank up their weekly pay without a thought to the effect this would have on their wives and children. They were now offered lodging in the Homes for Inebriates where they were not only cured of their dependence on alcohol, but could practise getting up in the morning and being conscientious about going to work.

A Heterosexual People

The Lord—and capitalist society—was hereby rendered a people prepared for him. But it was also a heterosexual people, as the subjects were not only to enter the labour market—but also marriage. When women supported themselves by prostitution, they posed a threat to marriage as an institution and were also proof that this institution was a little frayed at the edges. If they could be prevented from living immorally, many a marriage would be protected, and if they could also manage to become respectfully married themselves, a good many birds would be killed with one stone.

According to religious philanthropy, an immoral past was in no way an obstacle for a woman's marriage prospects, just as long as she had un-learned her immorality. Even better if she had been "converted"; then she was a dearly-earned child, won for the Lord, as was the case with many of the women from Magdalene Home.

Many of these are saved for eternity, others only rescued socially to live a moral life. A not insignificant number of them are married; many, both married and unmarried, continue a warm relationship with the home, a connection which leads to many visits on both sides, in that both the women who have left, sometimes with husband and children, pay visits to the home; and the matron, on various occasions such as weddings and christenings, visits them in their new homes (Blume, 1902: 29-30).

By attending such heterosexual ceremonies, the spinster-mothers showed their approval of what was to themselves an alien life style.

That sexology made "Heterosexuality" a normality was possible, because it concerned itself with making sexual behaviour scientific and with putting deviant behaviour into a filing system. It satisfied its scientific curiosity in a way for which it had been qualified. But the socialization to "Heterosexuality" undertaken by the philanthropists had quite different motives.

During this period, Copenhagen was overrun by people seeking happiness in the big city, but they went to rot, because they did not find it. They saturated themselves with alcohol; they had illegitimate children and could not cope with looking after them, so the children turned to crime; they had difficulty in supporting themselves, because they had not learned city trades; they lived in wretched accomodation, because they could not afford anything better, and in the slums their only companions were those in the same sinking boat. In the eyes of the philanthropists this development would lead to mass death if someone did not intervene.

The cheapest course of rescue work was "help to those who help themselves". If the men could be cured of their excessive drinking habits, they could invest their wages in their families; if the women learned domesticity, they could manage the men's wages thriftily, and if they learned motherliness, they could keep their children from a life of crime—and in the bargain the Capital got a sober and conscientious workforce. The most obvious framework for this help-to-those-who-help-themselves was the nuclear family, and if a sentimental enough picture of family life was painted, it also became desirable.

The possibility that the fallen women were crazy about running around with men, that intemperate men possibly valued their constant drunken state in the company of their mates, and that delinquent children might actually like the freedom of street life, was quite inconceivable for the philanthropists. What was ideal for them, must be an ideal for everyone else. And by their efforts, so it became.

That the working class in Copenhagen was heterosexualized around the turn of the century is perhaps not only due to sexology's definition of this concept as proof of the natural drive of "sexual instinct", but equally due to the fact that this social class was only able to survive materially as heterosexual.

References

Article presented at the Conference on Sexuality and (Post)Modernity, Copenhagen, December 11, 1989.

Sources

Arbejdshjemmet for døvstumme Piger, 1919.
Beretning fra Vestre Hospital 1888.
Blume, P.E., *Magdalenehjemmet i femogtyve Aar*, 1902.
Bud og Hilsen fra Sikem, 1921-28.
Danske Opdragelseshjem i Billeder og Tekst, 1926.
Esche, Thora, *Erindringer fra mit Liv og min Gerning*, 1920.
Smaablade for Døvstumme, 1899.
Smaatræk fra det daglige Liv, 1909.

Aarsberetning fra Foreningen til forvildede unge Pigers Frelse 1887.

Literature

Cott, Nancy F. (1978), "Passionlessness - An Interpretation of Victorian Sexual Ideology 1790-1850", *Signs*, vol. 4, no. 2, 1978.
Faderman, Lillian (1981), *Surpassing the Love of Men - Romantic Friendship and Love between Women from the Renaissance to the Present*, London: Junction Books.
Foucault, Michel (1976) *La volonté de savoir*, Paris: Gallimard.
Gagnon, John and William Simon (1973), *Sexual Conduct - The Social Sources of Human Sexuality*, Chicago: Aldine.
Jeffreys, Sheila (1985), *The Spinster and Her Enemies - Feminism and Sexuality 1880-1930*, London: Pandora.
Lützen, Karin (1986), *Hvad Hjertet begærer - Kvinders Kærlighed til kvinder 1825-1985*, København: Tiderne Skifter.
McIntosh, Mary (1968), "The Homosexual Role", *Social Problems*, vol. 16, no. 2.
Newton, Esther (1984), "The Mythic Mannish Lesbian - Radclyffe Hall and the New Woman", *Signs*, vol. 9, no. 4.
Plummer, Kenneth (1975), *Sexual Stigma - an Interactionist Account*, London: Routledge & Kegan Paul.
Smith-Rosenberg, Carroll (1975), "The Female World of Love and Ritual - Relations between

Women in Nineteenth-Century America", *Signs - A Journal of Women in Culture and Society*, vol. 1, no. 1.

Vicinus, Martha (1985), *Independent Women - Work and Community for Single Women 1850-1920*, London: Virago Press.

Weeks, Jeffrey (1975), *Sex, Politics and Society - The Regulation of Sexuality since 1800*, London: Routledge and Kegan Paul.

Women's Ideology: Difference, Equality or a New Femininity
Women Teachers and Nurses in Norway 1912-1940

Kari Melby

Ten years ago, *Feminist Studies* published a debate about the women's movement with contributions from Ellen DuBois, Temma Kaplan, Gerda Lerner and Caroll Smith-Rosenberg and others (DuBois, 1980). The debate clarified the existence of the dichotomy of women's politics and women's culture. It raised questions such as: Which segments of the women's movement are important enough to be analyzed? And what phenomena can be understood as female protest? Later, Jane Rendall referred to this debate when she wrote that one must also look at the less politically defined part of the women's movement in order to grasp the breadth of women's political activity (Rendall, 1987: 4). Bearing in mind Jane Rendall's point, I have chosen to focus on the organizations of housewives, women teachers and nurses.[1]

In my study, I approach these organizations as parts of the women's movement. Thus, I consider the women's movement to be a broad movement comprising organizations based on gender[2] (Cott, 1987; Bock, 1989 and forthcoming). These organizations provided various fora in which women could have a public voice. They all defined themselves within a women's communality of interest; they were affiliated with the umbrella organization The Norwegian Council of Women (Norske Kvinners Nasjonalråd). They were created to safeguard certain interests in the home, in nursing, in school. At the same time, these organizations contributed to the construction of femininity. They gave active expression to what they believed to be women's qualities and their duties and were therefore instrumental in shaping the ideology of womanhood and the ideals of the relationship between the sexes. In this context I find it important to understand how these organizations actively contributed to women's construction of femininity and of secondary importance, only, to extend the definition of the women's movement.

The idea of gender as historically determined provides an opening for the identification of various interests within the construction process and of the different arenas where this construction takes place. Organizations are such arenas. When gender is seen as historically determined, it is also possible to point out that the construction of gender took different turns at different times. For example, Ida Blom characterizes the time between 1890 and 1920 as a period of struggle and crises concerning the construction of a new gender identity (Blom, 1990). On the other hand, one can certainly claim that a continuing conflict over gender is a characteristic shared by all modern societies. In my examinations of organizations, I have concerned myself with the efforts to define womanhood in the interwar period. This was a period of ambiguities and paradoxes. The social debate hinged on questions of the type: What ought to be women's contribution to the new industrialized society? This was a period in which women had achieved formal equality in important areas, where demographic changes seriously influences women's lives, and where paid employment outside the home opened up new employment possibilities for women.

One way of approaching this question is to analyze how "society", i.e. the foremost ideology producers, developed women's ideology. It is this point of view that Elisabeth Fox-Genovese adopts, when she concludes that "the society was to advance an ideology of separate spheres to justify separate and unequal education for women, and the exclusion of women from the emerging professions and political life" (1987: 542). Meanwhile, I shall here concern myself with the question of how women themselves formed women's ideology. With reference to Martha Vicinus, who points out that "women are never passive participants in the larger culture but actively transform and redefine their external constraints" (Vicinus, 1985: 7) attention is directed towards the ways in which women teachers and nurses contributed to creating femininity through the shaping of occupational ideals.

I shall examine the women's ideals that were forwarded. Was it the case that women adapted their contemporary paid employment to a domestic ideology, complementary to the employment ideals of men, or were men's employment ideals also models for women? More precisely, the question is, how and to what extent women employees created employment ideals, which were clearly different from male models. Did women attribute another meaning to paid employment? Did they see women as another type of workforce, compared to men? I shall discuss the question as to what degree gender provided a basis for organizational strategies. Finally, I shall discuss which concepts can be used to characterize women's movements.

Women's Ideals: Difference and Equality

Both women teachers and nurses gave meaning to their work by emphasizing the connections between unpaid domestic work and contemporary paid employment. They also emphasized the special female responsibility for these areas. Analysis of *The Norwegian Association of Women Teachers* (Norges Lærerinneforbund) and *The Norwegian Nurses Association* (Norsk Sykepleierskeforbund) points to the fact that both organizations saw domestic work as a woman's primary duty. Anna Sethne, a leader of women teachers, claimed that women ought to consider their work as school teachers an activity that could be added to their work in the home and second only to that work. Women teachers saw it as one of their future domestic duties. The home was considered the most stable, the most valuable employment arena for women and also the one which gave the greatest satisfaction. Anna Sethne said that she wanted to show women the way back to the home and declared: "Women serve life, most perfectly and irreplaceably, through the upbringing of and caring for the new generations, serve society best by preparing themselves as well as possible for the working duties of the home ... " (Sethne, 1920: 27f).

Parallel to this, Bergliot Larsson, leader of the nurses, appealed to her members to be "thankful for having been given the next best place in the world—when we do not become wives and mothers and are able to make a home—then to be able to utilize the talents and capacities inherent in every woman in the wonderful calling of nursing" (*Sykepleien*, 1919: 48). These statements reveal that in addition to domestic work at home they also considered the teaching and nursing professions suited as occupational areas for women. School and hospital were literally considered next best; almost as good as domestic work in one's own home and better than other employment possibilities.

Notwithstanding the fact that their membership consisted of women who earned their keep through paid employment and who were mostly unmarried, they maintained that domesticity was the most important thing for a woman. Subsequently they put forward no competitive alternative to domesticity. Other scholars, e.g. Martha Vicinus and Sara Delamont, have pointed out similar attitudes among women in an early phase of paid employment (Vicinus, 1985; Delamont et al., 1978: 178-84). This can be interpreted as an expression of responsibility for home and family, but also that they sought acceptance for paid employment for women as an extension of the duties of the home. Women teachers and nurses were in a nursing position to relate their work to the domestic framework; teaching and nursing represented more traditional areas of female responsibility and competence.

Domesticity constituted an ideological basis for the creation of employment roles among both women teachers and nurses. Women teachers drew explicit parallels between home and school, mother and teacher, "Women teachers in the schools (must) fill out a mother's place as well as they can" it was claimed. Further, "At any rate, women have special talents and capacities and therefore also special duties. And among all the special social duties there are hardly any greater than the one of being surrogate mothers at school" (*Lærerinnernes Blad*, 1912: 7). In a similar fashion, nurses built their work activities on an ideological basis with reference to feminine qualities and domestic ideals. They emphasized women's talent for self-sacrificing care and self-effacement. Employment as a nurse in a private home was declared the best way to develop character. The conclusion is that both women teachers and nurses supported an ideology which we may call social motherhood. They gave credo to their roles in the labour market by emphasizing these as extensions of their domestic role.

All the same, domesticity constituted only one ideological basis for these women. Women teachers did not only show how women differed from men, but they also claimed similarities between men and women teachers. Women's work had the same value as men's, their economic needs were just as great. Equal pay became an important demand. (See among other things Landsmøteprotokoll NLF 1913 and 1916, and *Vor Skole* 1921: 78, 120 and 1930: 377). During the economic crisis of the '20s and '30s, married women's employment opportunities were threatened. Women teachers armed themselves for defence and availed themselves of a double strategy. They fought for paid employment for married women teachers by claiming human rights and fairness and by emphasizing married women's unique maternal experiences as an important resource for school.

As a conclusion one can claim that the women teachers in The Norwegian Association of Women Teachers (Norges Lærerinneforbund) exhibited a plurality of ideologies between the Wars. They demanded equal rights and equality between the sexes in the labor force at the same time as adhering to the idea of difference between the sexes. Demands for paid employment went hand in hand with a praise of the home as a woman's real arena. Women teachers wanted to be mothers of society but also to have the same rights as male employees.

Women nurses also went beyond social motherhood. They were not only and not primarily mothers of society. The nurses aimed at consolidating their profession, and this was incompatible with being mothers. At the same time as seeing domesticity as women's primary calling and nursing only second to this, they looked to the male professions for a model for professional employment. More specifically, it was the doctors who provided the pattern for the consolidation of the women's profession (Melby, 1990).[3] The nurses emphasized their willingness to fulfill traditional professional demands so that they could be equal to other professional groups. At the same time they accepted inequality in wages, unregulated work hours and lack of own accomodation. This lasted well into the post-war period. Even though the nurses did not themselves use such words as equality or equal rights, we can see the struggle for professions by and large as a struggle for equality. The nurses would strengthen their position in relation to the doctors by consolidating their profession.

The nurses wanted professional consolidation on the one hand and were searching for a femininity of social motherhood on the other. On the one hand they pressed forward in a conscious effort to make a place for themselves among the emerging professions, and on the other they prided themselves on being reserved and self-effacing. They wish to consolidate their professional interests at the same time as they praised the home.

But there was an obvious incongruence here. Partly, one may say that the nurses were instrumental in creating a new femininity through constructing professional ideals which combined male professionalism with ideas about women's professional qualities and tasks. But what is more remarkable is that the nurses repressed gender in the struggle for their profession.

Gender as Strategy

The nurses looked upon nursing as a particularly feminine area of work. They did not question the division of labor by gender, but saw it as a matter of course that medical treatment and nursing were two different tasks divided according to gender. Their political strategy was professionalization without reference to gender. This left them no room for stressing particular feminine contributions or for associating their struggle to other women's struggle for a place in the emerging professions.

The Norwegian Association of Women Teachers (Norges Lærerinneforbund), however, saw the light of day because the women teachers wished to emphasize their difference from men teachers. When women teachers, primarily in urban and densely populated areas, broke away from the organization, they shared with their male colleagues, they pointed to their difference. "Men and women teachers represent, as men and women, in accordance with their natural and other relationships, different views, understandings and interests" (Historical document on the founding of Norges Lærerinneforbund 1912). This view was expounded by women teachers throughout the whole period between the wars. Femininity was their most important argument and not only in times of economic crisis. In general, the struggle for feminization of elementary education, which in times of crisis became a defence for maintaining women's position in schools was maintained with reference to particular feminine qualities and to a concept of gender differences. It was claimed that the woman teacher, because she was a woman, had special characteristics and potential which could not be replicated by a man, independent of how qualified he might be (Lærerinnernes Blad, 1912: 6; Vor Skole, 1930: 149ff., 378). Therefore women represented another type of labor force than men, precisely because of "what they have received at birth, that (...) fine instinct, that rich emotional life" (Sethne, 1913). The distinction between women teachers and men teachers became their most important strategic resource.

Jane Rendall has pointed out how differences in gender are given new meanings within new areas (Rendall, 1987). From women teachers' point of view it would appear that they wished to be the mothers of society but with the same rights as men. The teaching profession was defined and demarcated as a profession. It was more professionalized than nursing. For women teachers, the challenge was not to create a profession but to make it a female profession. Nursing was, as opposed to teaching, synonymous with being a woman. The challenge of women nurses was not to make nursing feminine but to make it a profession. Nurses did not wish to appear ostentatious as mothers of society but as professionals. These differing positions and projects had consequences for the meaning given to gender and gender differences within the two organizations.

This will be my point of departure for reflections on how not only gender, but also other "intersecting circles of experience"[4] (Kessler-Harris, 1989) determine organizational strategies. There were similarities between these two groups. They shared an ideological base and defined themselves within the idea of social motherhood. They were women, most of them unmarried. Their occupations represented paid employment within traditional areas of feminine competence. What the organizations wished to achieve was more or less the same; to expand women's possibilities for paid employment, to achieve acceptance as women professionals, to improve working conditions and to raise the quality of schools and hospitals. In spite of what brought them together, they used very different strategies. While in the interwar period women teachers based their strategy on a concept of gender and femininity, the strategy of women nurses was rather to repress gender.

Why Different Strategies? Gender, Class, and Culture

The comparison between two occupational groups gives us the opportunity to discuss what determines the different strategies of the organizations. Why did women teachers and nurses choose different ways to attribute meaning to their struggles? Their diverging strategies cannot be understood with reference to the sex of the professionals, nor alone with reference to the gender ideology they supported. The question will be raised: when does gender constitute a strategic resource? As a point of departure, I would suggest at least three factors of importance in understanding women's diverging strategies: social position (in some way this is related to the level of professionaliza-tion), cultural association, and gender relations specifically related to their work experience.

At the turn of the century, women teachers were safely rooted in the middle class. They were recruited from the upper middle class and normally had a more privileged social background than male teachers. With regard to social class, they had an edge on male colleagues. Women teachers were already professionalized in the sense that they belonged to a defined occupation. During the late nineteenth century women teachers gained greater employment opportunities and the feminization process in elementary education began. Education of women teachers was formalized and in principle equivalent to men's. It is my suggestion that the social position and professional status of women teachers was a necessary condition for their genderized occupational strategy.

At this time nurses had a very different social position. They were recruited from various social classes. Nursing and caring for others mostly involved working-class women. Formalized training was in its infancy. Those who performed the tasks of nursing had received varying and quite often insignificant formal education. The professionalization strategy adopted by the nurses can be understood as a strategy of upward social mobility. By creating a consolidated occupational group with a certain level of knowledge, certain ethical guidelines and bourgeois educational ideals, and by demarcating the distinctions between the trained and untrained nurses, a basis was laid for social consolidation and mobility. Upward social mobility presupposed a clearly defined distance to nurses from the working class. In other words, nurses had to struggle against other women to create their own well-defined occupation. In the first half of this century, their social position was an obstacle to a productive use of gender as an occupational strategy. The nurses' project of upward social mobility implicitly focused on that, which divided women from one another, and there was no room to consider what brought them together as a gender. Bearing this in mind, it is the question whether gender cannot comprise a fruitful occupational strategy for women when the struggle for upward social mobility has high priority. Is there, in other words, a mutually exclusive relationship between women's social aspirations and an emphasis on gender as a resource? Does this imply that there is a socially determined dichotomy between being a woman and becoming professionalized?

The different strategies of women teachers and nurses can also be related to their different work experiences in relation to men. Women teachers struggled for feminization. They wanted to gain a footing in an area of work traditionally dominated by men. This process gained momentum at the turn of the century. The process of urbanization represented more opportunities for women teachers. Women teachers dominated the urban elementary schools and here in particular teaching at the lower levels, while men teachers predominated in the country schools and were over-represented within the higher educational levels. But women teachers also wished to compete with men in male-dominated areas. They argued for a monopoly in the education of girls as well as for access to male-dominated areas. Their relationship with male teachers bore the stamp of competition. In this competition it seemed as if they had two strategic possibilities; they could appeal for justice, general human rights, and equality, *and* they could make the most of their special feminine resources. Women teachers used both strategies but concentrated on the latter. This can be understood in the following way: what they strove for was more than equality; they wanted to maintain their dominant position in the teaching of girls and younger children, but in addition they claimed access to male-dominated areas. Emphasis on their feminine qualities was the strategy used in the competition against male colleagues.

In contrast, nurses had no male colleagues to compete with. Their work was defined as women's work. Relationship to men in the workplace was strictly hierarchical. Nurses struggled for social change in a hospital system where they were subordinated male doctors. The challenge they faced was to go along with the male doctors. This was neither an equal match nor a possible struggle for equality. Women nurses had to accept a position beneath the male doctors in the same way as nursing and care for patients had to find its place below and as a part of medical treatment. Their strategy was to attempt to create a profession, to consolidate an occupation, principally with male professionalization as a model. Nurses had to cooperate with doctors, but the relationship was characterized by the subordination of the women. In my view, the existing hierarchical relationship between nurses and doctors, and between women and men in hospitals, represented an obstacle to using gender as an occupational strategy. Femininity represented no resource in a situation where the nurses wished to become more like the doctors, i.e. professionalized. Instead, gender became something to be passed over in silence.

We might expect diverging cultural traditions to play a role as well. Women teachers were affiliated with the equal rights movement. This movement had developed a gendered ideology emphasizing the positive potential of feminine characteristics within the emancipation of women. It appears that women teachers in towns and cities were quite familiar with claims of women's equality and with emphasizing the differences between men and women as well. Women teachers were familiar with contemporary urban culture of which the movement for the emancipation of women was one part.

These kinds of thoughts were unfamiliar to most nurses. They were not recruited from the social and geographical environments most strongly represented within the equal rights movement. We may say that if they had had the same economic, educational and urban background as women teachers, they would have tended to choose teaching rather than nursing as a living.

A comparison between women teachers and nurses provides a starting point for a discussion of how occupational identity and occupational strategy is decided by gender and by other factors. These two groups were similar in so many ways. All the same, they chose to present themselves so very differently. How groups choose to put forward their views and their struggle is decided within a very specific historical context, which is not the same for different occupational groups. Different experiences and different positions led women teachers and nurses to emerge in different fashions. We can say that there was a set of "intersecting circles of experience" which affected the way they emerged. It is important, though, to try and understand how these circles of understanding interact with one another. For example, it was social position, level of professionalization, and cultural traditions were not independent of gender. In the same way, gendered experiences and gender consciousness were not external to nor independent of these women's experiences of their social position or their efforts to gain social mobility. To understand how women teachers acted with such self-confidence on leaving the association they had shared with their male colleagues and using arguments that pointed out particular feminine characteristics and interests, we must take into account these women's superior experiences in relation to their class. I would suggest that they had a gendered class consciousness or a "classed" gender consciousness. When nurses developed an awareness of their uncertain social status and made concerted efforts to raise their social status through traditional professionalization, this was related to their gender experiences of being subordinated to male doctors within the health service. Their class experiences cannot be separated from their work experiences or from the gender relationships within hospitals.

The Norwegian Association of Women Teachers emphasized domestic work as a woman's primary duty. The women teachers saw it as one of their most important contributions to educate girls in elementary school for their future domestic duties. The photo shows girls learning needlework under the supervision of the woman teacher in the city of Trondheim about 1915.

Categories for Describing Women's Ideology

If we now turn to the question of the kind of femininity these two occupational groups created, it is difficult to draw any clear and consistent conclusion. The question that was posed initially was to what extent they had male occupational ideals as a model or defined their occupational tasks within a domestic ideology. This was a question that came out of the dichotomy between occupation and home, between the male and the female. Neither the nurses nor the women teachers looked upon the home and occupation, private and public, or differences and similarities as binary oppositions (Offen, 1990). Both groups defined their occupational tasks as part of an ideology of social motherhood. But it is important to note that they did this in different ways. Women teachers emerged explicitly as representatives of a new femininity. They wanted the same rights and opportunities as men but wanted, at the same time, to be a female labor force; i.e. a different and also a better labor force. A labor force that represented more feeling, greater insights and courage. Nurses, on the other hand, outwardly put forward the image of a neutral (male?) occupation, characterized by the struggle for professionalization. They wanted first and foremost to be a *professional* labor force. Inwardly, they adhered to feminine ideals such as reserve and self-effacement. Implicitly there was a preconception of nursing as something particularly suited to women as an occupational activity.

These results give an opportunity to reflect on the concepts we use to characterize and categorize women's ideology and women's movements. Scholars who study organizations have developed conceptual models for characterizing these organizations and systematizing the organizational field. Conceptual pairs such as organization on the basis of interests vs. organization on the basis of idealism are well-known (see amongst others Raaum, 1988: 239)[5] and were criticized early on, e.g. women's research (Hernes, 1982). Among women scholars, there are an increasing number offering theoretical contributions to characterize differences in what we call female identity, female consciousness or also women's ideology. This is linked with the attempted systematization within the field of women's movements and discussion of the question of who could be called feminists. One such systematization relates ideologies in relation to their origin, such as for instance Olive Banks' distinction between egalitarian, evangelical and socialist feminism (Banks, 1981).

Others have tried to identify ideas which characterize certain movements via conceptual pairs such as the dichotomy between similarity and difference (see for example Hirdman, 1986), which has been much used, but also much criticized the last few years (see for example Scott, 1988). The American historian Karen Offen (1988) has presented another theoretical contribution through the concepts of relational vs. individualist which refers to "analytically divergent ways of thinking about women and men and their respective places in human social organization". Are they concepts that can bring to the fore important differences within the women's movement, between organizations?

Karen Offen suggests that relational and individualist arguments represent "two distinct modes of historical argumentation" (Offen, 1988: 134). Even if she takes into consideration that these approaches could represent just another instance of much criticized binary logic, she strongly defends her two categories (Offen, 1988: 137, 150). The relational arguments are thus categorized by a gender-based but egalitarian vision of social organization, the male-female couple is seen as the basic unit in society. Relational feminism emphasizes *women's rights as women*, defined primarily by the child-bearing/ nurturing capacities, and women's distinctive contributions are insisted upon. Both biological and cultural distinctions between the sexes are included. Relational feminism is marked by gendered division of labor, ideas of complementarity and the mother-child dyad (Offen, 1988: 135f., 139). In a very recent article Offen has confirmed that the family, the mother-child dyad, society's interests, and not those of the individual are in focus in what is labelled relational feminism (Offen, 1990). Concomitantly with relational feminism Offen proposes an individualist feminism, distinguished by individual arguments. Here, the individual, independent of sex, constitutes the basic unit. The more abstract concepts of individual human rights are emphasized, socially defined roles and gender-linked contributions to society are played down. Special feminine qualities are not pointed out, neither does individual feminism refer to groups or to society (Offen, 1988: 136; Offen, 1990). This distinction between relational and individual arguments reflects the division of self—other in western thought (Offen, 1988: 137). It is important to note that Offen appears to move from a defintion of two types of *arguments* towards a characterization of two types of women's *movements*.

Returning to the Norwegian women teachers between 1912 and 1940 and keeping Offen's two argumentational models in mind, we may ask whether they represented the one or the other type of feminism. The female teachers claimed women's rights as women and used as arguments the interests of others: girls, pupils of both sexes, school, when they aimed for leading positions in schools and generally defended their position within the labor market. But at the same time, they fought for women's rights as human rights. They defended the right to paid employment for married women teachers during the years of crisis, and they fought for equal pay with arguments of general justice, human rights and equality between the sexes. They suggested woman/child as a basic unit in society and as a dyad, when they struggled for further feminization within the educational system, and when they aimed at special education for girls to meet the needs of future domestic tasks to be executed by women at home. At the same time, they installed the individual as a basic unit (though not as a gender-neutral individual) when they applied for equal pay and for equal retirement age in relation to male colleagues.

I would claim that women teachers argued both in a relational and an individualist manner, but that they placed most emphasis on the relational argumentation. We need to ask, why these ways of arguing are suitable for a characterization of analytically distinctive movements and for describing the differences between women, when they so obviously were used interchangeably. I sympathize with Karen Offen when she tries to show that too much emphasis has been placed upon the individualist tradition within feminism. This I believe has been the case in Norway too. Within the equal rights tradition in our country a mixture of ideas and arguments seems to have been the most distinctive characteristic (Agerholt, 1973; Moksnes, 1984). It is difficult to find arguments for equal rights which do not also make a point of women's particular contributions as necessary for society.

But it would appear to create problems when one defines individualist and relational feminism as two separate and different types of feminism. The doubt is fed by what Karen Offen herself writes when she acknowledges that the relational feminists also aimed at equal political rights, the right to equal education, women's right to work outside the household, and their right to participate in all professions. She also expresses the need to explore how these two modes of argumentation intertwine and interplay (Offen, 1988: 139). It is the intertwining and interplay which

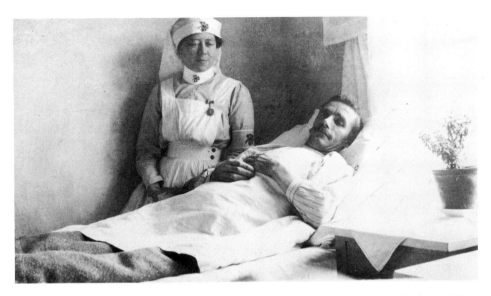

The nurses learned to be thankful for having been given the next best place in the world; to be able to utilize the talents and capabilities inherent in every woman in the wonderful vocation of nursing. The photo shows a nurse tending a patient suffering from tuberculosis at Orkdal hospital, Norway in the 1920s.

emerge as the characteristic elements of women's movements. It is not immediately obvious what the core of relational feminism should be, since it is also associated with demands for, and arguments for, equal rights. It would appear more correct to look upon these concepts as ideas and prototypes and a starting point for analysis, and not as blueprints for women's actual way of arguing and acting, or the basis on which they organized themselves.

It would appear that Offen's concepts have not previously met with this kind of criticism. She has been criticized for her way of interpreting her empiric facts, in order to make them fit into her categories. It seems, however, that both Ellen Du Bois and Nancy Cott accept the division between individualist and relational feminism (Cott, 1989). The explanation for this could be that either I am mistaken or this distinction is better suited to characterize the North American women's movement than the Northern European.

There is reason to question whether the conceptual dyad of individual-relational is used to describe the same phenomena. Is it analytical, conceptual polarity which spans mutually exclusive poles, and which is suited to characterize important differences between women's movements? Or is it the case that the relational and the individual are used in different areas, about different things, at the same time? Offen herself mentions that individualist arguments are used in connection with demands for equal intellectual opportunities for women and men, whilst the relational arguments have to do with which kind of social function the two genders shall fulfill. Such a distinction also emerges from my own material. Ideals of equality are put forward when it is *women's equal rights as employees* that are on the agenda: equal pay, equal pension age. While the complementary, relational is geared towards what *kinds of social tasks* women (and men) ought to have. It would appear in fact that individualist and relational arguments are used about qualitatively different things. While the former has to do with rights the latter is related to social tasks. But as a result, this conceptual apparatus is not suitable for coming to grips with qualitative differences between women's movements either. It does not characterize women's differing views on the same questions.

Another problem in relation to the categorization and understanding of women's movements becomes clear through the use of the concepts of *arguments vs. interests*. If we are to understand the movements, understand which kind of feminism they represented, we cannot be satisfied with only analyzing the movements alone. We have to look at a larger context. We have to take into consideration not only how women argued, but also what they actually did, and what goals they set themselves. Argumentation must be interpreted and understood in the light of the goals women had. Furthermore, the strategies employed by the participants are important for our understanding. The strategy they chose was related to the ways in which women could achieve legitimacy. Our ambition as historians ought to go further than a characterization of the explicit political level, if we are to be able to understand the women's movements in the past. We must study only the political texts but also the actual social practice (Rendall, 1987).

It is easy for us to find examples of women teachers, who argued "relationally" by referring to the woman/child dyad and by emphasizing the interests of other and more highly estimated social groups, while they were obviously defending individual interests as well. The struggle for feminization in the educational system is one example. This struggle was loaded with arguments emphasizing how girls, co-ed groups, and society at large would benefit from women teachers with feminine qualities. But at the same time it is evident that the female teachers, with this relational argument, struggles to improve their employment opportunities. Obviously, the women teachers were concerned with their own interests in the labor market as well as with the interests of others. It appears that relational arguments were one strategy used by women to support their own interests. This assumes that it is difficult for women to get support for their own interests, and therefore they can advance their view better by resorting to altruistic argumentation (Hernes, 1982). There is another example to illustrate this point. Women teachers made efforts to provide the young girls with special education in home economics. They primarily based their arguments for this by referring to the future domestic tasks facing young women in their homes and by referring to the interests of society (Protocoll The Norwegian Council of Women (NKN), 1916: 313; *Vor Skole*, 1922: 317 and 1926: 106). But we could equally well see this fight for an education specifically related to women as a strategy for expanding employment opportunities for women teachers, a strategy they could not be straightforward about in that period, which was characterized by economic crisis and unemployment. This was, however, part of their way of thinking, and part of their "feminism".

The nurses' struggle for professionalism was also followed by arguments about a consideration for patients. But this does not mean that we should interpret their organization purely as an unselfish movement for better quality within the health service. It is the task of the scholar to investigate how the actions of this group can also be understood as a struggle for the preservation of own individual interests. Nurses drew up clear demarcations in relation to their own occupation, demarcations first and foremost in relation to other women. The argument they used was one of consideration for the quality of nursing, but the driving interest was also the desire to create a well demarcated and exclusive profession (Melby, 1990).

If we only focus on their expressed arguments, we cannot fully begin to understand and interpret women's ideology and feminism. One can speculate as to whether or not women tended to propose mother-child, man-woman and nurse-patient as dyads exclusively because this was how they felt and thought. Obviously, the arguments and the language, they used, arose out of women's experiences (Rendall, 1987: 5), but, at the same time, this must be understood in the light of the dominant order of gender and of the political and cultural context. Those who wanted change, who wished to achieve something, also needed to make strategic decisions. Such an acknowledgement leads us to the conclusion that we cannot directly equate argumentation and feminism. The argumentation was an expression not only of what women thought and wanted, but also of what political context they found themselves in and what kinds of strategic possibilities they had. To make a too literal interpretation of the argumentation would appear to lead to an overrating of relational attitudes and an underrating of individual interests.

Who Were Feminists? What Is Protest?

The debate about which kinds of concepts we use to characterize the differences between women's movements is closely coupled with the question of who the feminists were. This was the key-point in the debate in *Feminist Studies*, to which I referred at the beginning of this article.

I have tested the conceptual dyad of relational and individualist constructed to categorize different types of feminism in the past, in relation to groups which possibly cannot be defined as feminists.[6] Nonetheless I believe that these concepts can be tried out on a wider selection of women's movements. The question of who the feminists were must be the result of an analysis, not the starting point.

In the discussion of who the feminists were, at least two directions have crystallized. Nancy Cott places definitive emphasis upon how women characterized themselves in the past. She reserves the word feminism for those who defined themselves as feminists (Cott, 1987). She criticizes Karen Offen for pressing everything into the concept of feminism, while she maintains that the core must consist of a criticism of male dominance and an acknowledgement of the gender order as socially constructed and changeable. Cott would like a more restricted definition of feminism, but wishes to visualize variation among women and acknowledge women's efforts in the past without necessarily giving them a place within the concept of feminism. This debate becomes complicated, when it emerges that those equal rights campaigners, Cott wishes to define as feminists, turn out to be those whom Karen Offen accuses of reflecting an abstract male way of thinking. Offen, in turn, places a lot of emphasis on defending a wide concept of feminism which includes most women (Offen, 1989).

What is important in this debate is probably not what kind of label we use for women's movements in the past but rather what we understand by women's resistance, rebellion, and their tearing down of barriers. We can concede that nurses by and large maintained gender stereotypes through creating a profession that presupposed a division of labor on the basis of gender, and by describing nursing as a female occupation which was partly based upon conceptualizations of what was naturally feminine. But at the same time we can contend that nurses, given the limitations in women's occupations, acted to emancipate women from men's control. They laid the foundations for a development of professionalism, which might have been a prerequisite for nurses to be able to defend their interests in relation to a male professional group with great authority within the health service. And when women teachers argued apparently conventionally for feminine qualities in order to gain leading positions in schools, is it then possible to say that this does not also imply a rebellion against male dominance and men's control of women?

References

Sources

Historical document on the founding of Norges Lærerinneforbund 1912 Landsmøteprotokoll NLF (1913, 1916).
Lærerinnernes Blad (1912-17).
Protocol from a meeting of the Norwegian Council of Women (NKN) (1916), NKN archive 3600, 25.
Sykepleien (1912-40).
Sethne, Anna (1913), "De overordnete stillinger i folkeskolen", *Lecture at LNF's 1st Meeting 1913*, Kristiania.
Sethne, Anna (1920), "Den kvindelige ungdoms utdannelse", *Skole og samfund*.
    Vor skole (1918-40).

Literature

Agerholt, Anna Caspari (1973), (1. Publ. 1937) *Den norske kvinnebevegelsens historie*, Oslo: Gyldendal Norsk Forlag.

Banks, Olive (1981), *Faces of Feminism. A Study of Feminism as a Social Movement*, Oxford: Martin Robertson.

Blom, Ida (1990), "Changing Gender Identities in an Industrializing Society: The Case of Norway c. 1870 - c. 1914", *Gender and History*, vol. 2, no. 2.

Bock, Gisela (1989), "Women's History and Gender History: Aspects of an International Debate", *Gender and History I*, vol. 1, no. 1.

Bock, Gisela (forthcoming), "Challenging Dichotomies. Perspectives on Women's History", to be printed in Karen Offen et al. (eds.), *Writing Women's History*.

Cott, Nancy F. (1987), *The Grounding of Modern Feminism*, New Haven and London: Yale University Press.

Cott, Nancy F. and Ellen Dubois (1989), "Comments on Karen Offen's Article "Defining Feminism: A Comparative Historical Approach"", *Signs*, vol. 15, no. 1.

Delamont, Sara and L. Duffin (eds.) (1978), *The 19th Century Woman, Her Cultural and Physical World*.

Dubois, Ellen et al. (1980), "Politics and Culture in Women's History. A Symposium", *Feminist Studies 6*.

Fox-Genovese, Elisabeth (1987), "Culture and Consciousness in the Intellectual History of European Women", *Signs*, vol. 12, no. 3.

Hernes, Helga Maria (1982), *Staten - kvinner ingen adgang*, Oslo-Bergen-Tromsø.

Hirdmann, Yvonne (1986), "Særart-likhet. Kvinnerörelsens scylla och karybdis?, Inge Frederiksen & Hilda Rømer (eds.), *Kvinder, mentalitet, arbejde, Kvindehistorisk Forskning i Norden*, Rapport fra det 2. nordiske kvindehistoriemøde 1985, Århus: Aarhus Universitetsforlag.

Kessler-Harris, Alice (1989), "Gender Ideology in Historical Reconstruction. A Case Study from the 1930s, *Gender and History*, vol. 1, no. 1.

Melby, Kari (1990), *Kall og kamp. Norsk Sykepleierforbunds historie*, Oslo: J.W. Cappelen.

Melby, Kari (unpublished), *Kvinners organiserte aktivitet: Norges Lærerinneforbund og Norges Husmoderforbund 1911/15-1940*.

Moksnes, Aslaug (1984), *Likestilling eller særstilling? Norsk Kvinnesaksforening 1884-1913*, Oslo: Gyldendal Norsk Forlag.

Offen, Karen (1988), "Defining Feminism. A Comparative Historical Approach", *Signs*, vol. 14, no. 1.

Offen, Karen (1989), "Reply to Cott", *Signs*, vol. 15, no. 1.

Offen, Karen (1990), "Feminism and Sexual Difference in Historical Perspective", D.L. Rhode (ed.), *Theoretical Perspectives on Sexual Difference*, New Haven and London: Yale University Press.

Raaum, Johan (1988), Norges Offentlige Utredninger 1988: 17 "Frivillige organisationer".

Rendall, Jane (1987) (ed.), *Equal or Different? Women's Politics 1800-1914*, Oxford: Basil Blackwell.

Scott, Joan Wallach (1988), *Gender and the Politics of History*, New York: Columbia University Press.

Vicinus, Martha (1985), *Independent Women. Work and Community for Single Women 1850-1920*, London: Virago Press.

Notes

1. The article is based on two larger works. One is Kari Melby. *Kall og kamp. Norsk Sykepleierforbunds historie.* 1990. The other is an unfinished manuscript with a working title "Kvinners organiserte aktivitet: Norges Lærerinneforbund og Norges Husmorforbund 1911/15-1940.

2. Amongst other things, this view of gender as a social construction is influenced by the Anglo-American use of concepts, which distinguish between *gender* as the label for the socially created, and *sex* which refers to the biological. This reflects a distinction between culture (gender) and nature (sex). Norwegian language has only one word, i.e. kjønn, which include both social and biological gender. Recently however, there has been some criticism of this type of conceptual division, which implies a division between what is changeable and unchangeable.

3. The Norwegian women nurses also took their inspiration from abroad. International women nurses' organisation provided a model.

4. Alice Kessler-Harris uses this expression to emphasize that not only gender, but also other factors decide individual identity. The reason for this is that she perceives that too much emphasis is put on the influence of an ideology of domesticity on the understanding of women's paid employment.

5. Johan Raaum defines the concept of voluntary organizations based on two dichotomies; the public interest vs. special interests, and idealistic vs. personal interests.

6. Among other things, Karen Offen has claimed that the Norwegian nurses, as I portray them, were not feminists, and women teachers only to a certain degree, c.f. discussion.

Women in the New Peace Movement in Denmark: Empowerment and Political Identity

Ann-Dorte Christensen

Throughout this century, women have been active in the peace movements. Either in organizations together with men or in independent women's organizations. As early as 1915—the year in which Danish women were granted the suffrage—the first women's peace organization was set up. This was Women's International League for Peace and Freedom. The League gave voice to women's protest against World War I, and it is still in existence.

The establishment of Women for Peace in 1980, as a part of the new peace movement, renews the historical tradition in which some women prefer to form independent women's organizations to deal with the peace issue. This makes it right and relevant to talk about a women's peace movement.

The peace movement has developed in waves, as have other social movements. Some periods have seen busy activity, a broad-based support, and many organizations. In other periods the movement has been more passive, and there have been only few organizations.

The 1980s saw a new vigorous period in the peace movement—old organizations awoke from their torpor, and new ones saw the light of day. This can be attributed to the fact that the NATO Double Decision of December 1979 meant that beginning in 1982 572 tactical nuclear missiles were to be set up in Europe, unless the disarmaments negotiations should prove this unnecessary.

The new peace movement has—as have other new social movements—been characterized by democratic and non-hierarchical organizations and by equality in number of male and female participants. But contrary to other social movements, the peace movement has been less of a middle-class phenomenon. In terms of its members' age and social background it has rested on a broader base. The new peace movement was a mass protest movement. The following will illustrate just how broad based was the women's mobilization.

Scenario

We shall go back almost 10 years and encounter people busily preparing for one of the huge Easter demonstrations. We see a vigorous peace movement where many activities are unfolding. There are many women. We will take a closer look at some of them.

First we meet Bodil, who is close to fifty. Bodil has three grown-up children. She joined Women for Peace a couple of months ago. Together with others, Bodil is creating a banner with the words "Millions for Food, not Weapons!". The banner is for tomorrow's Easter March. In Women for Peace Bodil has met a lot of other women, who want to work for a better future in the same way that she does. She feels that the peace movement has given her a chance of turning the fear of the future that she has had for many years to activity.

Then we meet Hanne. She is in her early twenties and studies Danish literature at the university. Hanne is on her way to a meeting in No to Nuclear Weapons. They are to discuss a suggestion for a resolution to be sent to the Danish Parliament (Folke-tinget) after the demonstration tomorrow. In the resolution they have presented a series of arguments in favor of a Danish No to NATO's plans for nuclear missiles in Europe. Hanne is a former activist of the environmental movement and she is currently engaged in the Student Union—besides the peace movement.

Finally we meet Lajla—she is dressed as a punk and has dyed her hair green to fit the occasion. Together with a group of women Lajla has travelled from a peace camp in central Jutland in order to join the Easter demonstration. She and other women are planning a non-violent action at a local airstrip after the main demonstra-tion. The originators want many women to participate, but they do not want to take non-violent action together with men. Lajla is seventeen. She has left school and spent a couple of months in the Women's Peace Camp at Greenham Common in England, before the Danish peace camp started. The women's community is a prerequisite for her work in the peace movement.

These three women illustrate the variety of women that participated in the peace movement in the 1980s. The women joined different organizations, networks, and social structures in their peace efforts. This reflects the marked difference in their everyday life and experience.

Empowerment, Social Movements and Political Identity

This article focuses on the active women in the new peace movement. It deals with those participants who were the moving force of the political and organizational work. In other words, I shall not concern myself with the broad base of the peace movement, but with what I call the core activists. The aim is to identify the essential differences between the women involved and the way they were mobilized.

With a theoretical starting point in the terms empowerment, organizing, and political identity, I shall analyze the connection between the women's experience and values in everyday life and the demands, aims and strategies that they formulate in the peace movement of the '80s. The article demonstrates the deep differences between the various organizations of the peace movement and the groups of women in it. Besides evidence points to the fact that there are no major differences between men and women, when they are organized together.

The differences will be discussed in relation to women's empowerment, ways of organizing and of shaping their political identities. I shall argue in favor of the necessity for building political strategies that will accomodate the multiplicity in women's political practice today.

By the word *empowerment* I refer to the strength and ability of individuals and groups to join in a process of change and preservation (Christensen et al., 1990). The classical understanding of power is expanded in the theory of empowerment. The term also encompasses the efforts of the acting subjects to change fundamental conditions at the micro- and macro-levels. This means that the understanding of power is not narrowly associated with social institutions and hierarchies, but also with social relations in everyday life.

Feminists in the peace movement have dealt with the question of power, especially in connection with a rethinking of Gandhi's philosophy of non-violence. Non-violence can be seen as an exemplary model for empowerment aimed at changing the foundations of social power from below (Ikkevold, 1984). For instance, Wheeler and Chinn (1984) specify the difference between a patriarchal and a feminist understanding of power. They argue in favor of a patriarchal understanding of power that focuses on power as results (I don't care how you do it, just get the job done), while a feminist understanding stresses the aspects of process and collectivism. It is the connection of ends and means of the philosophy of non-violence that are referred to in Wheeler and Chinn's understanding of power.

Jane Meyerding (1982) also argues that the integration of feminism and non-violence can form the basis for women's empowerment.

Feminism stresses the vital connection between private and political, and non-violence points to the way in which mobilizing can lead to radical change.

Both Wheeler, Chinn, and Meyerding emphasize individual and personal "power" as a decisive starting point for women's collective processes of empowerment. On the other hand they neglect the importance for women of relating to political institutions and social hierarchies.

The point is that empowerment is an expansion of the term "power". It encompasses "power from above" (the formal social hierarchical and political institutions) and "power from below" (social networks and communities in everyday life). This distinction must be treated as a major typology. It contains a risk of landing in an unfortunate dualism. In order to avoid this, it is important to develop a dynamic term for power that will integrate the two understandings at different levels (Christensen et al., 1990).

Social movements are understood as a pattern of collective actions, carried out by (different) organized groups with the aim of changing and preserving.

The activities of the social movements should be seen as a coherent whole working for change. They have a series of interrelated points of departure and values that together make up a shared project for social change (Gundelach, 1988). With the new social movements I refer to the movements that grew out of the '60s, '70s, and '80s.

In this article I focus on the movement's level, not on the effect of the movement or of its significance in the general and social processes. Instead I shall analyze the organizations of the movements as a framework for women's empowerment and the shaping of their political identities.

Just like other social movements the peace movement has rested on several—more or less autonomous—organizations. The anti-hierarchical and decentralized organizational structure is an important characteristic, distinguishing social movements and their organizations from other political forms of participation. According to Peter Gundelach, a Danish sociologist, the organizational structure is not just a formal framework but an expression of a learning process in which "those that wish to organize try to do so in a way that will express the values of the group" (Gundelach, 1988: 297). This makes the organizational structure an expression of the values, norms and attitudes that the members of the organization wish to promote.

The American feminist, Jo Freeman, has characterized the organizations of the social movements in the following way:
-   every organization has its own life cycle
-   there is a connection between personal and structural processes of change in the organizations (Freeman, 1983).

These characteristics are connected with the absence of an institutionalized organizational apparatus. Instead, Freeman emphasizes the activities of the members as the quintessential driving force of the organizations.

A similar approach is to be found in Gerlach and Hine (1970), who define a social movement in the following way:

A group of people who are organized for, ideologically motivated by, and committed to a purpose which implements some form of personal or social change; who are actively engaged in the recruitment of others; and whose influence is spreading in opposition to the established order within which it originated (Gerlach and Hine, 1970: XVI).

Gerlach and Hine's understanding of the new social movements emerge from the specific analytical model that they have set up: the SPN model, in which S means segmenting, P means polycephalous ("many-headed"/decentralized leadership) and N means network.

The term *political identity* first of all refers to the mobilization—i.e. how and why women become active politically. Secondly, it refers to the development of the political understanding of the participants through their mobilizing practice.

This gives to the forms of political identity a material base, which is embedded in the socially structured position of women. But they are also related to a biographical perspective, to experience and the understanding of self (Peterson, 1988 and Christensen, 1989a).

The collective political identity contains a variety of forms of identity. For example, Abby Peterson (1985), the Swedish sociologist and feminist, demonstrates how women's engagement in the peace movement can come about because of an identity as feminist, as wage-earner, as mother/housewife, as lesbian, or as citizen.

Through the term political identity, the transformation from everyday life to political organization and practice becomes central. This indicates that women's life cycles, their experiences and values, e.g. in the family, are significant in relation to their political mobilization as well as the development they undergo in the experience of their political practice.

I use everyday life as a broad term that encompasses the totality, the connections, and the patterns of significance in the lives and life cycles of individuals and groups (Christensen, 1989b and Jørgensen, 1988). Everyday life is a terminological approach to the understanding and systematizing of the totality and complexity of "the ordinary" and "the daily routines". I emphasize the coupling of social structures (e.g. the sexual division of labor, the social inequalities and ways of living) and the values and activities of individuals and groups (what people think, believe and do).

Empirical Point of Departure

In this article, I shall analyze two peace organization: Women for Peace and No to Nuclear Weapons. The organizations are national and both are part of Scandinavian and European sister organizations. Women for Peace is a women only organization, while No to Nuclear Weapons have male and female activists. The empirical data are collected in Aalborg (in Northern Jutland, the fourth city in Denmark in terms of size).

I also analyse the political and cultural processes of the Women's Peace Camp at Ravnstrup (a village in Central Jutland). Inspired by Greenham Common, a group of women set up the peace camp in 1984-85 as a protest against the construction of a NATO-site in the area. The analysis focuses on the feminist practice in relation to the everyday life of the activists, to their life cycles, their political motivation and socialization. Besides, I shall look at the process of empowerment in relation to civil disobedience and non-violence.

The empirical evidence is first and foremost based on qualitative interviews with the activists. In addition to this I have collected historical documentation from the movements and the peace camp (leaflets, letters, reports, diaries, newscuttings, etc.). Finally, I refer to a quantitative analysis based on a questionnaire answered by the activists of Women for Peace and No to Nuclear Weapons.[1]

Profile of the Activists in Women for Peace and No to Nuclear Weapons

The activists of Women for Peace average 45 years of age, while the activists of No to Nuclear Weapons average 34 years. This average age difference of approximately 10 years becomes more interesting if it is related to the generations and their life cycles.

Percentage of Activists by Life Cycle

	Women for Peace	No to Nuclear Weapons (F)	No to Nuclear Weapons (M)
The youth generation (17-28 years)	12%	33%	50%
The adult generation (29-45 years)	38%	53%	32%
The "parent" generation (above 45 years)	48%	14%	18%
Unknown	2%	-	-
Total	100%	100%	100%

Source: Christensen, 1990: 55.

Above, you will see that there are significant differences between the two movements when you look at the age and phase in the life cycles of the activists. The majority of Women for Peace (48 per cent) belong to the generation of "parents", while only 12 per cent belong to the youth generation and the majority or the women in No to Nuclear Weapons belong to the adult generation, while only 18 per cent and 14 per cent respectively belong to the "parents" generation.

Generational differences imply fundamentally different everyday lives, not least in the areas of work and family life. In Women for Peace there is a relatively high number of women who hold part-time jobs or are full-time homemakers (29 per cent), just as 86 per cent of the activists have one child or more. Only 9 per cent of the activists in Women for Peace are students. Contrary to this the activists of No to Nuclear Weapons are typically fully employed (approximately 45 per cent) or students (approximately 35 per cent). 22 per cent of the No to Nuclear Weapons group have children.

The activists of both movements are well-educated but with an important difference. While the activists of No to Nuclear Weapons hold higher educations, primarily with university degrees, or are university students, half of the activists of Women for Peace are women with the educational level of nurses, teachers, nursery school teachers, etc. (53 per cent of the activists who have finished their education) (Christensen, 1990).

The two organisations show major differences in terms of life cycles and everyday life. The activists in Women for Peace are closely connected to the areas of reproduction, both in terms of the relatively high priority given to their own families and in terms of the way they relate to the reproductive areas of employment. Contrary to this the activists of No to Nuclear Weapons are typically students with much less involvement in a family of their own.

Political Profiles of Women for Peace and No to Nuclear Weapons

Even though Women for Peace and No to Nuclear Weapons have existed side by side and have cooperated on many issues in the peace movement, there are major differences in the political profiles of the movements.

Bodil Graae, the Danish journalist who participated in the initial organization of Women for Peace, wrote the following in a feature article, which had a major function in mobilizing women for Women for Peace in the early days of the movement:

We are three women sitting around a blue kitchen table. Depressed on a heavy day in January. We look at the headlines. Afghanistan. Iran. Increased modernization, new deadly weapons. In the hour that passes before we begin to act in despair the Danish Defense has spent 720,000 DKK (...) How will this end? What about the children we gave birth to, and the children that they in turn will give birth to or that will be born in the future? All around us self-important men take action. Starting wars (always to defend themselves). And, full of awareness of their own importance, they act. (...) This counts for our own husbands and sons, too. They are glued to the TV set watching soccer matches. Intensely involved in the game and the competition. They play cops and robbers, too, while their wives take care of the children, the cleaning, the Sunday dinner (...). What would happen if we turned our powerlessness to strength..." (Bodil Graae, 1980).

The activists in Women for Peace have taken action because of their connection to reproduction and motherhood. For instance, the movement demands that the large resources that are spent on rearmament be spent on aid to developing countries. The movement appeals to a specific female responsibility for life and the preservation of this earth, and it sees women's traditional experiences and areas of responsibility (life and nurturing) as a political asset—the point where powerlessness can be transformed to strength. *Humanitarian, ethical and moral arguments* in a strategy for political action are expressed as a demand for *redistribution* and a demand for *democratic control* of military decision-making.

The basis of Women for Peace in the traditional female areas of experience emerge in the symbolic and cultural forms of expression in the movement. For instance, it was Women for Peace that generated the ideal of a so-called "laundry ceremony" at the Women's Conference, Nordic Forum 88 in Oslo. Many colorful "clothes banners" have been made with women's symbols and women's crafts. The national newsletter is called "The Kitchen Roll", and the local newsletter in Aalborg "The Potholder". Interviews in the Aalborg division of Women for Peace shows that the generation of mothers greatly appreciate these symbolic references to the old women's culture. However, the few women of the youth generation, who are active in Women for Peace, find it difficult to identify with these names. One of the young women says that a condition for recruiting more young women is that these names are changed. She feels that they are embarrassing and prefers to put the newsletters aside, when her friends visit.

While Women for Peace has concentrated on the attempt to point to injustices and the moral outrage of the current use of social resources as well as the lack of control with military decision-making, No to Nuclear Weapons has been much more oriented towards *influencing the current political decision-making processes*, partly through national and international movements of mass protest, and partly by entering into a dialogue with political and military authorities. The political pressure has been aimed at the Social Democratic Party in particular. The movement has attempted to influence the party through dialogue and by training the general public in Denmark to be more specific in its demands to the Danish Social Democratic Party.

The aim of No to Nuclear Weapons to set up a dialogue with the politicians has meant a political pragmatism as well as a demand for technical and political insight among the activists. The movement has tried to build a progressive and alternative expertise that as a minimum requirement matches that of the politicians. This expertise has appealed to specific groups and demanded specific qualifications. Obviously it is not by chance that so many active in No to Nuclear Weapons are students. The educational system has been a good basis for professional and technical insights. Parallel to this the movement has arranged an educational course for new activists.

Whereas Women for Peace was oriented towards ethical and moral issues, the key words in the work of No to Nuclear Weapons are *professional and technical-progressive expertise*. Furthermore, No to Nuclear Weapons is characterized by the fact that the movement is far more oriented towards the technical aspects of the peace issue.

If we see it in relation to the understanding of power promoted by Wheeler and Chinn (1984), the No to Nuclear Weapons uphold a more patriarchal and traditional strategy for empowerment than Women for Peace. For the No to Nuclear Weapons people the results are of greater importance than the processes.

In this connection, it is interesting that in No to Nuclear Weapons there is an agreement among men and women about the political goals and strategies. However, the women want more expressive and creative elements, but as supplements and not at the cost of the existing priorities in the movement.

Questioned about whether the women in No to Nuclear Weapons feel oppressed and dominated by the men in the movement, it is significant that the women answer that they do not think this is the case in the Aalborg chapter.

Organizational Profiles in Women for Peace and No to Nuclear Weapons

In the terminological discussion I pointed out that the organizational structure in the new social movements is an expression of the values, norms and attitudes of the activists. Let us look at the organizational structure and at the processes of decision-making in Women for Peace and No to Nuclear Weapons.

Women for Peace has a more democratic, more decentralized and segmented structure than No to Nuclear Weapons. In the case of Women for Peace, the national jobs are limited to the co-ordinating function of a letter-opener, and this job rotates among the local groups. There is no national office, and at the annual meetings no decisions are made to conform the work of the local groups. Locally, the organization consists of small, autonomous groups. These "kitchen groups", as they are called, decide for themselves what to do and how they might want to join other groups in joint ventures.

Even though No to Nuclear Weapons has a non-hierarchical structure, too, the national office in Copenhagen is of major importance. Many different functions are here coordinated and passed on. Some of the people are employed, and the office has set office hours, etc. Every year a national convention sets up the political guidelines for the work in the local groups.

In the analysis of Women for Peace and No to Nuclear Weapons in Aalborg *the attitude towards democracy and decion-making processes among the activists* has been described. In relation to the above-mentioned organizational differences it is interesting to note that the activists of Women for Peace are less inclined to see themselves as having a direct impact and the power to exert influence on decisions, than are the activists of No to Nuclear Weapons.

This can be owing to the more formalized structure in No to Nuclear Weapons which increases the awareness of the activist that they must secure for themselves a real democratic influence. But other forces can be at work, too. Among them, that the non-hierarchical structure of Women for Peace really breeds "stronger" informal leaders, and that due to the broader social and political background there are greater differences in political resources. It is obvious that Women for Peace in Aalborg to a large extent has been shaped by a few individual women with political/organizational experience and a high level of activity. The informal leadership of these women has been fully accepted by the other activists.

Peace March in the Soviet Union in 1982 arranged by Women for Peace

The Women's Peace Movement

The Norwegian Birgit Brock-Utne, who works in peace research, has analyzed the historical development of the women's peace movement and has set up three characteristics in women's empowerment in the peace movement:
- it rests on the care of other people, primarily children;
- it employs a series of non-violent strategies;
- it is a political coalition, and often its aims are to reach women of the opposite camp (Birgit Brock-Utne, 1981: 136).

It is in the women's peace movement that the connection between the women's movement and the peace movement is most obvious. A Swedish analysis had demonstrated how former activists in the new women's movement in Sweden today are active in the peace movement, and how the feminist perspectives are carried on in new organizations with new political goals (Peterson, 1985). In Denmark it is impossible to trace a similar identity of activists in the two movements. The picture here is rather that different groups of women join the women's peace movement with different political goals.

The formation of Women for Peace in 1980 has obviously influenced the development in the women's peace movement, because Women for Peace has recruited a large group of women, for whom it is their first experience of political action. Even though only women participate in Women for Peace, the points of contact between this organization and the women's movement are limited. The activists have not been recruited on a feminist platform, but—as we have seen above—on a platform, whose ideology belongs to the early women's movement. Central are women's traditional spheres and values. The analysis of Women for Peace in Aalborg shows that the activists find it important to point out that they are not Women's Lib'ers, i.e. that they do not agree with the feminist attitudes expressed by the Women's Liberation Movement in Denmark. Instead they stress that they see it as women's rights and duties to act according to their own situations and values. The independent women's organization is not conceived of as a goal in itself, but more as a means to allow women a space in which they can act politically without being dominated by men. Today Women for Peace is one of the main groups within the women's peace movement. The group is—as we have seen above—mobilized for peace work on the basis of a *humanitarian ethical and moral argument*.

The other important group within the women's peace movement consists of young women in particular, who have been recruited as *radical feminists*. These women identify with the new women's movement, but were attracted to the peace movement, which was the social movement most visible and with the broadest base. The radical feminists rally around a feminist perspective, which they integrate in their political practice in the women's peace movement. This group sees the violence and oppression of the military as closely linked with men's individual and social power and control over women. Similarly, they see peace and freedom as inseparable from the issue of an end to women's oppression and male hegemony. Contrary to Women for Peace the radical feminists consider the independent women's organization as a goal in itself—as a liberated space in which an alternative women's culture can flourish.

The differences within the women's peace movement were brought together in a shared political practice at the *Women's Peace Camp at Ravnstrup* (1984-85). Here women set up a tepee camp and took non-violent actions against the construction of a NATO shelter.

Women's Peace Camp and Non-Violence

At the Women's Peace Camp the different groups of women agreed to the political demands, the goals and strategies. However, there was a major disagreement about the connection between women's politics and peace politics. This was particularly obvious in the attitude to the women's community: to what effect the peace camp should serve as a space for a feminist culture, or as a frame around more limited political activities for peace in order to attract a larger group of women. As the young radical feminists

In one of the actions at the Women's Peace Camp at Ravnstrup, the women moved a tepee into the military area.

formed the core group of women living in the camp, they came to dominate it. This resulted in a strengthening and expansion of the radical feminist culture. This in turn meant a shift in the social and political balance in the camp to the effect that the last stage in the life of the camp became a radical feminist one (Christensen, 1989a).

Considering the great differences between the women, it is not the polarization that is of interest in this case, but the fact that these differences could be overcome for more than a year in the close atmosphere of the camp and the radical actions.

An important explanation for this is that the women in the Danish peace camp—just like at Greenham Common—employed a strategy of non-violence. Gandhi developed this strategy when struggling for an independent India against British Empirialism in 1947. Though there are difficulties in transferring a strategy from a previous historical epoque, a different culture and a different religion, the political practice in the peace movement demonstrates that non-violence can be of use in a Western world and in a strategy for feminist empowerment (McAllister, 1982).

The philosophy of non-violence rests on four basic tenets:

- knowing your own limits and creating a sense of security and comfort in small groups;
- non-hierarchical forms of organization and decision-making processes;
- the self-respect of the individual;
- the close connection between ends and means (Gandhi, 1983).

If one considers the political practice of the Women's Peace Camp at Ravnstrup, it becomes clear that the first three tenets of the philosophy of non-violence is one of the reasons for the containment of the differences between the women. It serves to stress the necessity of creating a space in which individual needs and limits can be maintained in a collective process. The tenets also underline democracy in decision-making to the effect that minorities cannot be forced to follow the majority. This means that actions must be organized to accomodate for a varied participation.

The philosophy of non-violence rests on the close connection between ends and means. It was maintained in the Peace Camp as long as the activists agreed that the main objective was peace work—the united protest against NATO's construction of a shelter in the area. But because of the shift in the political process towards an identification of peace and feminism, a differentiation entered the objective and created division in the opinion of which means would best serve the end. For instance, a disagreement arose as to the significance of the women's community and everyday life in the camp. Was the camp and the community a means in the peace work, or was it an end in itself? Here the groups differed. In other words the counterculture lost its coherence—the connection with the original political foundation of the camp.

Empowerment and Political Identities

The analysis shows that women in the new peace movement set up different organizations with different political identities. The difference can be located to women's everyday lives as well as to the political practices.

The results seem to point in the direction of the post-feminist stand, that "there are more differences between women than similarities" (Haugaard, undated). This is an argument to the effect that the feminist platform is outdated. Gender does not count. Sex and gender undergo continuous transformations—it neither can be nor should be thematized. Do the different political identities among women in the peace movement in the '80s not show exactly that gender as a constitutive category must be rejected, also in this case concerned with women's empowerment?

In this discussion it is a question of the scientific significance of gender as a category. I think that the conception of the differences between women voiced by, among others, Lis Haugaard, is highly criticizable. The post-feminists base their argument on value relativism. They refuse to talk about the result of the differences, the goals aimed at, or the perspectives of the discourse. It is not clear whether they are talking about psychological, cultural or structural differences (Christensen, 1989b).

Instead I agree with the Danish literary historian Lise Busk Jensen, who writes that if the interest in the differences among women in feminist scholarship is to avoid having a negative terminological effect, "it has to apply itself to the differences in what is shared, i.e. to the scope of possibilities within femininity" (Busk Jensen, 1990).

My point of departure in this article has been the *collective* mobilization of women in the new peace movement. The differences have been illuminated by the isolation of different kinds of political identity. These are neither purely normative categories nor personally chosen identities. The political identities of the peace women are closely connected to the social organization and the social reality of gender differences. They are an expression of the fact that a theory of women's mobilization has to build on a historical materialist foundation, which will contain the development in femininity/masculinity in its understanding of the relations between the sexes. The identities develop in the interplay between the everyday life/life cycle of the individual and the political and social focal points and values. This implies that the differences in empowerment is an argument against the notion of one essentialist femininity and one determined relationship of gender dominance.

In the following I shall evolve further the perspectives of the women's recruitment to the new peace movement. The table on the next page shows the relationship of the three central political identities[2] with respect to the organizational structure of the movements and to women's political objectives.

Organizational Structure and Objective

As can be seen from the above analysis, there are major differences in the degree of democracy in the non-hierarchical structures. Similarly, the activists differ in their assessment of the signification of the organizations and networks. Most distinctive is the fact that the part of the women's peace movement that has rallied around a radical feminist platform understands the organization and the social community as an end in itself. This does not count for No to Nuclear Weapons or Women for Peace, where the activists conceive of the organizations as means in the work for peace. This means that the choice to not organize with men but in independent women's organizations within the peace movement relies on different goals. Whereas the radical feminists find creating a space for an autonomous women's community part of the political objective, the activists in Women for Peace understand their organization as a means in peace work; a means that is to create a "space" for many women to be active on their own premises.

It is important to note that there is no possibility of an automatic equation of decentralized organization and democratic influence on decision-making. Even though Women for Peace has the most democratic organizational structure, it is in this organization that informal authorities and leaders have been most prominent. Here, too the activists reveal a rather poor knowledge of decisions made. This proves that factors

Women in the New Peace Movement

Political identity	Organizational structure	Women's political objective
A. **Humanitarian, morally oriented women**. Predominantly organized around issues concerning family and motherhood. Has its roots in the early women's culture. Wishes to create a space for the mobilization of a wide variety of women.	**Women for Peace.** Independent women's organization. Non-hierarchical organizational structure with autonomous groups. Very weak national co-ordination. The organization as a means in peace work.	**Equal worth.** Women and men are different but equal. No competitive relation or opposition to men. No aiming at changing the basic relations between the sexes, but rather give a higher priority to women's traditional areas of responsibility and experience.
B. Women, who like men, are committed to **influencing political decision-making**. Via an alternative, progressive expertise the group wishes to influence the general public in its attitudes and dialogue with the politicians.	**No to Nuclear Weapons.** Women and men organized together. Partly a non-hierarchical organizational structure. Local groups in the larger cities. Relatively high degree of national co-ordination, e.g. in the form of political guidelines agreed upon at a national level. The organization as a means in peace work.	**Equal rights.** Women and men are to have the same rights. Barriers must be broken down in order that women can obtain the same opportunities as men in the labor force and in political life.
C. Women who rally around issues of **radical feminism**. Peace and freedom are closely connected to the elimination of sexual dominance. Ideological connection to the new women's movement. In the '80s, the dominant political practice in the peace movement.	Parts of the **women's peace movement.** Part of the Network for Non-Violence, with its independent organizations. Builds on the philosophy of non-violence as a principle for action and community. The organizational a goal in the creation of a feminist counter-culture.	**Emancipation.** Focus on women's oppression and the relationship of power between the sexes. Patriarchy must be destroyed and society changed. For some, liberation must further femininity, for others it must change both men and women.

such as political experience and a high level of activity plays a major role. But it also bears witness to the fact that some groups—in the new social movements, too—apparently wish for and are attracted to charismatic leaders who, as figures of importance, become the political and organizational motive power. Perhaps the feeling of security that is shared by many of the women in Women for Peace is due to their ability to put forward some very active and politically experienced women.

In the perspective of empowerment, the ideal of participation in the decision-making process and direct democracy must be maintained as a way to stress the connection between ends and means in the new social movements. But at the same time this ideal has to be adapted and differentiated to the specific practice according to the resources, needs and divisions of labor to be found in the individual organizations.[3]

The Goals of Politics Concerning Women

The forms of identification are also related to the three classical goals in the policies concerning women: equal worth, equal rights and liberation. These goals have given rise to many a debate in the women's movement in the course of the past 100 years. But why consider these goals from the women's movement and feminist struggle here, where we are concerned with women in the peace movement?

First of all, because the peace women of the '80s show that the goals of policies concerning women are of importance to the form and content of the mobilization of women, and this in spite of the fact that it is not directly tied up with the women's movement/feminist struggle. In other words, this is a sign that the feminist struggle has spread out to a wider social context. Besides focusing on women's situation and inequalities, the feminist struggle today is an important part of a wider struggle for peace, a balanced environment, and global solidarity (Christensen et al., 1990). Women are active in these areas, but in addition the gender issue is an integrated aspect of the progressive attitudes inherent in the wider social struggles.

The examples of the peace women show that the many different attitudes in policies concerning women can be contained in one social movement. Here is probably an explanation why Bodil, Hanne and Lajla, whom we met in the opening scenario, were heading for the same demonstration.

But don't the differences mean anything? I shall deal with that question in relation to the debate in the women's movement and feminist research about the three goals in women's politics: equal worth, equal rights, and liberation.

The Women's Liberation Movement organized around the issue of liberation as a feminist strategy. The critique of patriarchy and capitalism as systems inherent in the liberationist struggle results in a rejection of both equal worth and equal rights as satisfactory solutions to women's oppression. But they can be incorporated as partial strategies (Gulli, 1982). The question of the importance of these partial goals has—together with the idea of femininity/masculinity—often resulted in disagreement among feminists in the Women's Liberation Movement.

This article testifies to the importance of the goal of emancipation in the shaping of a political identity among some of the peace women. But among other things, the stress on openness and respect towards differences of the philosophy of non-violence has meant that the radical feminists in the peace movement have shown a great readiness to co-operate on a political practice with women, who have other opinions about women's politics. This was not the case in a large part of the new women's movement.

But the attachment of the radical feminists to the liberationist perspective—including its critique of both patriarchy and capitalism—is vital when it comes to maintaining the perspective of radical change, in spite of the fact that this perspective will have shifted somewhat.

The early women's organizations in Denmark that came into existence at the end of the 19th century rallied around the issues of equal worth and equal rights. Analyses of the history of the women's movement have shown this contradiction to be a choice between differences and equality (Ravn, 1989).

The Danish feminist historian Anna-Birte Ravn argues that the contradiction between equality and difference is unnecessary, false and misleading.

Many women no doubt feel the choice between equality and equal worth, between sexual equality and difference to be painful and actually impossible. If we choose equality and avoid the differences, we create a false neutrality between the sexes. If we focus on the differences and avoid the similarities, we contribute to the stigmatization of women as different/deviant. Whether we focus on or refuse to see the differences, we risk calling them into existence (Ravn, 1988: 8).

This point is inspired by the American historian Joan Scott, who argues that difference is an integrated part of the demand for equality. The old feminists were conscious of this. In their political practice they managed to integrate the goals of equal worth and equality. Contemporary feminist scholars have created a false dichotomy, which has limited women's potential for action.

The analysis for women in the peace movement shows that the different objectives of the policies concerning women are important when it comes to shaping a political identity, especially in the recruitment phase. The various groups participate in a shared, collective practice, but it is clear that the basis for their mobilizing efforts is different. It appears that the women's objectives are vital factors. For the women in Women for Peace (equal worth) and No to Nuclear Weapons (equal rights) there is a close connection to their distinctive everyday lives and life cycles—the old and the new women's culture. The significance of and relationship to education/work and family/children plays a vital part in shaping the politics that will have a mobilizing effect on them.

The basis for mobilizing the radical feminists in the women's peace movement is not so tied to everyday life, but more to feminist analysis and practice in the Women's Liberation Movement.

The different objectives do not lead to conflict and division. Instead they have supplemented each other in the process of mass mobilization in the peace movement, where differences have been respected by the people involved.

Even though Women for Peace rallies around the goal of equal worth, this has not created a "false unity" amongst the women, which is one of the critical points raised by Ravn. She states that this tends to stigmatize women. Instead the equal worth agenda is an expression of the importance of women's everyday life and life cycles, when it comes to mobilizing women. It is not the same to be fifty years old, in part-time employment and with decades of responsibility for a family and children on the one hand, on the other to be twenty, still involved in the education and set on, as well as brought up to, expect a permanent relationship to the labor market alongside with men.

These generational differences influence women's political identities, and in practice they lead to differences in objectives, ways of organizing, and in political demands, goals and strategies.

A feminist strategy for empowerment must be open to the loosening up of the theories and practices in the strategies for equal worth, equal rights and liberation. The unfortunate dichotomy between equal worth and equal rights must be overcome. The perspectives for liberation must be maintained and developed in a constant dialogue with other policies concerning women and pivotal social issues. This process must be open to the real historical and generational differences between women.

References

Andersen, Johannes et al. (1989), Demokrati i udvikling—politisk styring, selvforvaltning og del-
    tagelse, unpublished paper from the Department of Economics, Politics and Management,
    Aalborg: The University Center of Aalborg.

Brock-Utne, Birgit (1985), *Educating for Peace. A Feminist Perspective*, Pergamon Press Inc.

Busk Jensen, Lise (1990), "Om, af, for og uden kvinder", *Newsletter: Kvindeforskning*, no. 4.

Christensen, Ann-Dorte (1989a), *Ulydige kvinders magt. Kvindefredslejren ved Ravnstrup som
    politisk proces*, Aalborg: The University Press of Aalborg.

Christensen, Ann-Dorte (1989b), "Forskelle blandt kvinder - og deres betydning for feministisk
    teori og praksis", Ulla Koch et al. (eds.), *Køn og videnskab*, Aalborg: The University Press
    of Aalborg.

Christensen, Ann-Dorte (1990), *Kvinder i fredsbevægelsen. Hverdagsliv og politisk organisering
    belyst gennem en undersøgelse af Kvinder for Fred og Nej til Atomvåben i Aalborg 1980-
    86*, Department of Social Development and Planning, Series no. 48, Aalborg: The Univer-
    sity Center of Aalborg.

Christensen, Ann-Dorte and Birte Siim (1990), "Køn, magt og demokrati - mod et dynamisk
    magtbegreb", Linda Andersen et al. (eds.), *Livsmagt. Nye perspektiver på kultur, magt og
    køn*, The Annual Publication of Women's Studies, Aarhus: Aarhus University Press.

Freeman, Jo (1983) (ed.), *Social Movement of the Sixties and Seventies*, New York: Longman.

Gerlach and Hine (1970), *People, Power, Change. Movements of Social Transformation*, New
    York: Bobbs-Merrill.

Gandhi, Mahatma (1983), *Om Mit liv* [All Men are Brothers, 1960], Viborg: Gyldendal.

Graae, Bodil (1980), "Kvinder for Fred", *Politiken*, February 2.

Gulli, Britta (1982), "Likeverd, likestilling, frigjøring", Harriet Holter (ed.), *Kvinner i fellesskab*, Oslo: Norwegian Universities Press.

Gundelach, Peter (1988), *Sociale bevægelser og samfundsændringer. Nye sociale grupperinger og deres organisationsformer ved overgangen til ændrede samfundstyper*, Aarhus: Politica.

Haugaard, Lis (undated), *Postfeminisme*, unpublished paper no. 1, Aarhus: Cekvina, Women's Research Center in Aarhus.

Ikkevold (1984), Tema: civil ulydighed, *Tidsskrift for antimilitarisme og fredsarbejde*, no. 5.

Jørgensen, Birte Bech (1988), "Hvorfor gør de ikke noget?", Charlotte Bloch et al., *Hverdagsliv, kultur og subjektivitet*, Kultursociologiske Skrifter, no. 25, Copenhagen: Akademisk Forlag.

McAllister, Pam (1982) (ed.), *Reweaving the Web of Life*, Philadelphia: New Society Publishers.

Meyerding, Jane (1982), "Reclaiming Non-Violence: Some Thoughts for Feminist Women Who Used to Be Non-Violent, and Vice Versa", Pam McAllister (ed.), *Reweaving the Web of Life*, Philadelphia: New Society Publishers.

Peterson, Abby (1985), "The New Women's Movement - Where Have All the Women Gone? Women and Peace Movement in Sweden", *Women's Studies International Forum*, 8 (6).

Peterson, Abby (1987), "Power and Authority in Feminist Theory and Practice", *Women in Political Movement*, Monograph from the Department of Sociology, Gothenburg: University of Gothenburg, no. 37.

Peterson, Abby (1988), "Women in Social Movements: A Theoretical Framework for Empirical Analysis", *Research in Inequality and Social Conflict*, Greenwood, Connecticut: JAI Press.

Ravn, Anna-Birte (1989), "Mål og midler i den gamle og den nye kvindebevægelse", *Forum for Kvindeforskning*, no. 3.

Wheeler, Charlene and Peggy Chinn (1984), *Peace and Power. A Handbook of Feminist Process*, New York: Margaretsdaughters Inc.

Notes

1. By activists I mean the participants in the two organizations who were or had been included in internal directories. In cooperation with the organizations the questionnaires were sent to the activists of the two organizations in Aalborg in the Fall of 1986. 186 members returned the questionnaires, 128 from Women for Peace (74 per cent) and 58 from No to Nuclear Weapons (36 women and 22 men) (91 per cent). In spite of the very high percentage there are relatively few questionnaires returned from No to Nuclear Weapons, and this means that the results must be taken with a grain of salt. The perspectives of comparing men and women are limited on such a small collection of data.

2. The table must be read as an overview of the *most important* political identities among women in the new peace movement. The table cannot be extended to cover other movement and arenas. E.g. the group of fully employed women with children has not been conspicuous in the peace movement. This group would no doubt rely heavily on the relation of work, family and state in the formation of political identity.

3. This is an issue particularly important to the debate about self-determination and
    decentralization. The decisive question is whether such initiatives actually create a greater
    polarization in society between the active and the passive. It is an issue central to the
    research project "Democracy in Development - Political Regulation, Self-Determination and
    Participation" (Andersen et al., 1989).

A Distaste of Dirty Hands:
Gender and Politics in Second-wave Feminism

Joyce Outshoorn

I think it is important to have more women who know how policy works and how to influence it. To overcome the aversion women have of policy. We should not just be concerned about ourselves and our immediate surroundings. We should move out into society. (Smit, 1979: 12).

Saying that I learned to distinguish between the personal and the political in my consciousness-raising group is too simple (...) Our discoveries gave me the feeling that it was possible to become politically active in a totally different way than I was used to in my left-wing group. (Meulenbelt, 1978: 35-36).

Two ways of conceiving politics, voiced by two leading Dutch feminists in the seventies.[1] Much writing on the women's movement has focused on the actions and dealings, the practices and projects of its members. In this article[2] I will focus on the history of its ideas, and examine the critical concept of politics as it was used in the new women's movement. Following the American political scientist William Connolly (1983), I think that in order to understand the movement, it will not do just to look at behaviour as students of collective behaviour have tended to do, as "actions and practices are constituted in part by the concepts and beliefs the participants themselves have". (1983: 36).

In this view concepts, and more particularly concepts of politics, are part of the political process, they give coherence and structure to political activity and function as "rules of the game".

Second-wave feminism contested the dominant meaning of politics, and tried to construct a new meaning. It is the fascination with the kind of politics that second-wave feminism evolved that led me to start this project. This article traces the idea of the political; it parallels two earlier analyses into second-wave thought on the concepts of power (Outshoorn, 1987) and autonomy (Outshoorn, 1991). It is also a reaction to two dominant approaches to social movements, the resource-mobilization approach and the "new social movement" approach. The first is strong on "how" questions: how do people organize around grievances and how do they set about fulfilling their demands? On ideas, or ideologies and how these create a collective identity, it is weak.[3] The second is strong on "why" questions: why did a strong wave of protest and a number of socio-political movements arise in the sixties in Western Europe? It is weaker on the "how" question and by lumping together all social movements it loses sight of the specific character of the women's movement. The specifics lie of course in the fact

that the movement organizes women on the basis of sex to fight against gender inequality, excluding men.

In standard accounts of the period of the seventies, the feminist critique of politics
in the Netherlands is usually seen as the heritage of Provo and the student movement
(Smit, 1978; De Vries, 1987). Its ideas are seen as influenced by the libertarian or
anarchist tradition. The "new social movement approach" (adepts for the Netherlands:
Van der Loo c.s. 1984; Kriesi, 1985) has tended to strengthen this view by its focus
on post-materialist values and political style. Their case (of seeing various movements
such as the peace, women's and ecological movements as a reaction to post-industrial
society) depends on it. Both views have in common that they view feminist ideas and
the women's movement as new phenomena, tending to see them in isolation of an
older feminist tradition (Outshoorn, 1989). Through participating in the women's movement in the seventies myself and in studying the politics of abortion in the
Netherlands (Outshoorn, 1986a; 1986b) it seemed to me (and others) that implicit ideas
about the "ideal woman" were also at play, drawn from a much older vein of thinking
about femininity, which defined women fundamentally as a-political, or politically "different". In retracing politics as a concept I hope to uncover this older thinking in the
second wave. In order to do so, the relationship between "gender" and the "political"
will be central. I shall be posing the following questions. What perspective did the
autonomous movement have on politics, and especially of "traditional" politics? What
did these conceptions include or exclude? What did these implicitly assume about
gender identity, not only about femininity but also about masculinity?

Second-wave feminism is of course a container-concept; every feminist is always
quick to point that there has always been various currents in feminism. This paper is
focusing on the current which used to be called the autonomous women's movement
in the Netherlands. In the seventies "autonomous" referred to an organisational
principle; meaning "separate from men" and from (party) political organisation
(Outshoorn, 1991). It was the key concept in legitimating organisation on the basis of
sex. The women's movement only started to call itself autonomous in the mid-seventies in order to distinguish itself from the revived women's groups in parties and the
like. Up to then what the women's movement was, was self-evident. In the early seventies consciousness-raising became the foundation of the new feminism; the small,
decentralised, non-hierarchical group became the basic practice of the new movement.
It is this autonomous feminist movement of the seventies, as part of second-wave
feminism, which redefined politics and politicised the "private"; in the wake of which
new demands were articulated.

For the purpose of this paper, I have selected one particular event in time: the
conference "Feminism and Political Power" in 1982. The early eighties are generally
seen as a rupture in the Dutch political landscape; the end of economic growth, the
beginning of cuts in the welfare state, a new right-wing coalition government which
was to last eight years. It can also be seen as a new stage in the women's movement.

For the autonomous women's movement it marked a new debate on "traditional politics", the term I choose to denote the democratic political arena, with its key-actors of parties, parliament, cabinets, committees and departments. The debates at this conference, in which practically all tendencies of the movement participated, highlight the tension between "old" and "new" politics, and therefore provide an excellent case for examining in detail the various conceptions of the political of the autonomous m-ovement. The topic merits a detailed analysis, which I shall give in: "Necessary but no Fun: Organizing for Power".

A word of warning is in order here. By focusing on the autonomous movement I do not want to replicate the common view (Smit, 1978; Van der Loo c.s., 1984; Ribberink, 1987) that the seventies form the period in which the women's movement turned away from "traditional politics". In this view the 1981-1982 period is seen as the one in which the movement came to its senses, re-entering the political arena. Small groups, consciousness-raising and feminist therapy may have been widespread and popular, but one should not forget that the seventies are also the period in which the women's movement is heavily involved in the traditional political arena because of the abortion issue (Outshoorn, 1986; 1986a). This was a campaign, in which wom-en from the autonomous movement took the lead and in which they employed the whole repertoire of political tactics, from influencing members of parliament to occupying buildings when the need arose. This experience was extremely pertinent in the debates around the turning-point of 1981-1982. In addition, many feminists were setting up women's groups within such institutions as political parties and trade-unio-ns from the mid-seventies on. These laid the foundations for the eighties, with its heavy emphasis on institutionalisation and state policy, accompanied by the emergence of "femocrats" and other feminist professionals. Things could not have taken off as they did after 1981 had this preliminary work not been done. Still, there is no point in denying that the dislike of "traditional politics" was part of autonomous feminism; it shows up in reminiscences of feminists active in the period, in writings of the time and in more serious and scholarly debate.

Earlier Views of Politics

Second-wave feminism took off in the Netherlands with the formation of MVM 1968 [Man-Vrouw-Maatschappij] (Men-Women-Society), an organization comparable to National Organization for Women (NOW) (founded 1966) in the US. It still held to a traditional concept of politics, setting itself up as a pressure group aiming to get a slice of the pie for women and setting out to obtain equal rights. Indicative are the views of its foremost founder and later spokeswoman, Joke Smit. Linking the politics of the new women's movement to feminine characteristics in her seminal article "Is the Second-wave of Feminism Doomed to Die?" (Smit, 1978) she points to what she saw as the failure of the movement: the failure of building a strong organisation for entering mainstream political life. According to her the legacy of the New Left reinforced the shortcomings of the traditional female role,[4] leading to a "a-political" and in the long run impotent movement, which would accomplish nothing more than the repeal of the abortion law. For Smit, who joined the Social Democratic Party very soon after setting up MVM, "politics" were unproblematical. In her view, traditional politics just needed to be expanded to encompass new issues. As Aerts (1986) has pointed out in her analysis of the work of Smit, women are the problem, they should become more equal to men by shredding the "handicaps of the female role". Then the ideal of an androgynous society can materialise. This position is, of course, very different to those feminists who see women having qualities which can reform the "public sphere",[5] precisely because they are different from men. It should be mentioned that women like Smit from MVM shared a gendered view of politics with other feminists. Smit coined the phrase "mannenland" for the political arena and her description of masculine behaviour in this arena has become a classic (Smit, 1971). Contrasting this to "womenland", she already sets up the opposition I shall discuss later.

MVM, the "older" branch of the movement (Freeman, 1975) was soon joined by Dolle Mina, very much the younger branch of the movement. Mainly recruiting from the student movement and also organising men (who played a dominant role until they were kicked out), Dolle Mina specialised in spectacular exemplary action. Their view of politics was refreshingly simple, although in their writings two lines of reasoning can be discerned. One is an orthodox Marxist analysis which saw the state as a bourgeois plot and political democracy as a sham. For "traditional politics" there is no place: politics is then almost naturally reduced to industrial action (where few women were located in the Netherlands at the time). The other stand is the New Left idea of the oppressive "system"; tactics challenging the system to reveal its "true face" were called for. In practice Dolle Mina did just that: action at the local or neighbourhood level aiming at attracting publicity and influencing public opinion was the dominant style of politics. The only demand directed explicitly at the state was the repeal of the abortion law. Both strands are part of the elitist view on politics; but the consequences of this for thinking about gender never became clear in the texts of the Dolle Mina period. This is in contrast to the public image which was about young sexy women living out the sexual revolution with no associations of bluestockings or outdated feminists.

Consciousness-raising started around 1971; Dutch practice not being different from that in similar movements in other countries, also in exploring that the "personal is political". For the first time women started to call themselves feminists, a label Dolle Mina had been anxious to avoid. From the groups the realisation grew that to change women's position, much more had to be transformed than the sort of demands, which fitted into the socialist or liberal paradigm of politics. Marriage, sexuality, childbearing and caring, relations among women, culture were all implicated, and not all of these were translatable into the social-economic discourse dominating traditional politics. This feminism, with its roots in consciousness-raising, managed to politicise new areas and became the source of inspiration for setting up the institutions for a feminist culture and feminist service sector. Women's houses and cafe's, festivals, exhibitions, publishers, magazines flourished. Battered women's refuges were founded, rape crisis centres set up, women's adult education developed. I stress this, to counter the idea that women's groups were engaged in "navel-gazing"; many initiatives were profoundly practical but soon finding traditional politics on its way. Consciousness-raising gave way to radical feminist therapy; a thriving feminist "consciousness-industry" as it became more professionalized.

At the end of the seventies the original autonomous feminist position was dissolving into three tendencies. One took the idea of the "personal is political" to the letter, which meant that in the long run one could do away with the niceties of conceptualising a realm of traditional politics. Found in radical therapy and encounter groups it took the form that in order to improve the world, one should start with oneself. Any activity as long as it involved women only was deemed political. This led to a kind of pan-politicism which could justify almost any practice. According to an anarchist feminist writing, being political is combining politics and emotions and acting on this directly: "For example, the pornshop we often pass we paint with slogans or pour glue into the lock; when we need a house we start a new squat; when we encounter sexism in the squatters' movement we start a women's group". (Anarca-feministes, 1982: 17). "The state chooses for those who already have it good, and is in their service (...) excluding political equality which is disguised by parliamentary democracy". (Anarca-feministes, 1982: 19). "Fighting in its structures costs negative energy". (Anarca-feministes, 1982: 21).

Another tendency of feminism, who had been radical feminists earlier on, switched to revolutionary feminism at the end of the seventies. It drew its ideas from "revolutionary socialism", opposing reformism and working in (male) institutions. Their conception of politics ran parallel. The state is seen as a patriarchal institution; trying to work in the traditional political arena not effective. Political action should focus on bringing about a revolution. This meant direct action like strikes in order to open women's eyes, and consciousness-raising as conversion as political strategies. As the two leading women of this tendency remarked at the conference of 1982:

At first we thought that women, once they realised how unjust everything is organised, would throw the towel in the ring, stop trusting men and rise in mass against all male bulwarks and develop alternatives. (Van Baalen et al., 1982: 27).

This view of politics has its roots in the elitist conception of politics, and these feminists shared the vanguardism inherent in this position, the elect who have access to truth challenging the false consciousness of the followers. The monolithic view of the state also implied that no attempt was made to differentiate state-institutions. Interestingly, these feminists jettisoned the idea of the personal being political and started a crusade against feminist therapy; political activity in their view became direct action. When their optimism about women's revolutionary potential abated, they blamed the "feminist movement establishment" (Van Baalen et al., 1982: 27) for deluding women by propagating a new femininity around biological issues.

A third tendency, many autonomous feminists, especially the ones working in feminist service projects (De Vries, 1981) encountering the opportunity of governm- ent subsidies, rediscovered reformism and reconsidered political activity. As many non- aligned socialist feminists preferred the same course of action, this pragmatism became the dominant mode in a surprisingly short time after the turn of 1981.[6] As one remarked at the conference:

The time for protest banners is over (...) we have shown how inferior women's position is and developed ideas about tactics and strategy around the way of organising. That had a function. But there are still women yelling angrily that it is a shame. It irritates me, because that's now pointless. You can't keep shouting that women are oppressed (...) at some point you should roll up your sleeves and make some move. (Sax, 1982: 133-134).

The Turning Point of 1981-1982

For the purpose of showing how autonomous feminists constructed their idea of politics in relation to gender, I will now focus on the 1982 conference about the "strategy" of the women's movement", aptly named "Feminism and Political Power". As mentioned, a broad range of women's groups participated; position papers and conference debates were published afterwards (Bleich et al., 1982). The conference organisers, mainly non- aligned socialist feminists with an old-left background, were quite clear about the purpose of this conference, and about their idea of politics, which was about power in the traditional political arena; "how can political power be achieved?" (Bleich et al., 1982: 184).

If the autonomous women's movement is conceived of all activities developed by movement women, there is indeed a powerful movement. If, however, one defines it as a political move- ment aimed at obtaining social and political power, a movement with issues and a strategy, there is hardly an autonomous movement worth speaking of. (Bleich et al., 1982: 187).

The participants came along with their own agendas. For some feminists, this was the "necessity of organising in the public sphere" and undertaking the long march through the institutions, for others (mainly the revolutionary radical feminists) it was seen as the last chance to stop women undertaking this march and being coopted into "malestream politics" (Van Baalen et al., 1979).

"Necessary but no Fun": Organising for Power

Probably the most informative document is the contribution of a longstanding and respected feminist (Francis van Soest) who had been active in both the socialist and radical feminist movements in the period in which this distinction had not yet hardened into opposing factions. She spoke their common language; it is in her essay (Van Soest, 1982) that the dichotomies and ambivalences about politics, and by implication about gender, are best illustrated.

The title is already revealing of this ambivalence. "Struggle in the Public Sphere: Necessary, but no Fun" it is called. A split is constructed between necessity and pleasure. Her article is a plea to feminists to undertake action in the traditional political arena, in which no part of the political action repertoire is to be eschewed: working on public opinion, lobbying, direct action such as disrupting meetings and even violence are all methods entertained. But this public sphere itself appears as rather undifferentiated. From the outset it is constructed as an opposition: the public sphere is "outside" (Van Soest, 1982: 79), with the women's movement being "inside". The description of "outside" shifts in the course of the article. At first it consists of "legislators, institutions and corporate life" (Van Soest, 1982: 75). Later "outside" is split into a "social level" and a "government level" (idem: 77). Finally "outside" is held to consist of: "government, political parties, social institutions, corporate level etc." (Van Soest, 1982: 77). The "etc." at the end of the sentence is indicative of the lack of preciseness in defining the public sphere.

The author then turns to the "inside". She maintains that the women's movement has been operating in its own circuit, "among ourselves" for too long (Van Soest, 1982: 79), therefore "we" now should move out "into the public sphere" (Van Soest: 78). She is well aware that this message may not be a popular one among her audience: the "repugnance against fighting in the institutions is quite easily accounted for": one has to leave the safe womb of the autonomous women's group and confront "male bulwarks" (Van Soest, 1982: 79) governed by "male rules of behaviour", "things which are diametrically opposed to the rules of behaviour of which feminist women approve and use among themselves". As she notes, it is not that the women's movement does not undertake action or demonstrate, but these manifestations

seldom necessitate a confrontation with the public sphere, the male world. You may risk some booing by onlookers, at worst a night in the local police station. You remain among women—amongst ourselves ("met vrouwen onder elkaar"). Warmth, solidarity, conviviality, encouragement, tolerance in case of failure (Van Soest, 1982: 79).

In these quotes the public sphere, the world outside is directly construed in opposition to the women's movement. Maleness is tied to the public sphere, which then by implication is diametrically opposed to feminist women. (Van Soest does not go into the implicit distinction of "feminist women" and "women"). It is "us", women, inside against them, out there; "out there" designated as a series of big institutions. And this world is definitely different: it is by implication cold, self-interested, business-like, discouraging, and intolerant in case of failure.

When describing the sort of actions needed to operate in the public sphere the author makes it quite clear this work is no sinecure, no cushy job. It means moving public opinion, lobbying, reading policy documents (which she dubbs "paper bother"):

When writing this down all my desire immediately starts to dwindle. This sort of fight is no fun, not short and intense, but heavy going, asking for stamina and dedication. (Van Soest, 1982: 79).

You have to throw yourself into

extremely boring work without immediate result, demanding strategic insight, alertness, decisive and goal-oriented action, expertise (...) The opponent is well-trained, well-informed and ready to fight to get you on your weak points (...) it is a tug-o'-war. The fight asks for courage, guts, without the support of the women's group (...) confronting male behaviour which we precisely reject. (Van Soest, 1982: 80).

By implication again: women do not behave like that, at least, feminist women do not want to behave like that. The opposition created by this discourse sounds more like the catalogue of lady-like behaviour still taught to young girls up to the late sixties, the girls who became the feminists of the seventies: women should not be strategic planners, decisive, expert, gutsy, courageous, and not venture outside the safe family-circle. At various points the author stresses that writing all this arouses her disgust: "I prefer to sit behind my typewriter (...)" (Van Soest, 1982: 80). The idea of having to fight with "a trade-union sexist" fills her with loathing. But in this very same paragraph she also mentions that the same feeling creeps up when she thinks about the reactions of the movement to her advocating all these tactics. Apparently, the movement is not quite the safe place that she makes it out to be at other points in her story; she says she is afraid of "accusations of lust for power and unfeminist behaviour" (Van Soest, 1982: 80). From that point on point she gives a very clear exposition, in the style of Smit (1987) of the barriers impeding the women's movement to "struggle in the public sphere"; its diversity, its norms, the primacy given to emotions, its distrust of leaders and spokeswomen and of expertise. What fighting in this sphere means

is being confronted with many kinds of male behaviour which fill us with loathing (cocksureness, paternalism, endless and abstract talk, sexist jokes (...) (it nearly makes me sick). (Van Soest, 1982: 83-84).

What it takes is "assertiveness, debating technique, being able to quarrel, being firm, chopping off others, taking the initiative, behaviour we identify with "men". (Van Soest, 1982: 84). To summarize, what is being constructed here are the following dichotomies:

Women's movement	*Public sphere*
inside	outside (= legislators, parties, corporate life, institutions)
fun	necessity
pleasure	work
feminine traits	masculine traits

So the female world is reconstructured as opposed to the male world. Looking at gender, for the author of the text the solution for change is that women should learn "masculine" qualities in order to reach their objectives. But she is very ambivalent about it. At the root of this is the paradox, Cott (1987) has analysed so well; in order to enter traditional politics, women have to change and become more like men. But if they do so, they not only forego their claim but also their capability of reforming the polity. Looking at politics, in the text the focus of political activity is still not sharply delineated: the public sphere, though less like a container than in earlier movement thought, still appears as a conglomerate of rather monolithic institutions staffed by tough men. These men are also undifferentiated, eliminating considerations of alliances across sex-lines.

Conclusion

This blurred vision of traditional politics has as consequence that the debate around the "strategy of the movement", to use the favorite phrase of the period, still operated in a void. Many feminists started calling for unity, more organization and for the setting of priorities, especially in the socio-economic field. The debates of 1981-1982 marked a turning point, but also a point of return. For the first time since 1974, two new broad alliances of feminist and traditional women's organizations were formed on a platform around economic independence issues. Having no analysis of the political arena, they have more or less operated in a vacuum oscillating between lobbying and influencing public opinion. The point of return was that women again became the problem, and not the solution. Women, it was now said, had to adapt to the rigors and demands of the traditional political arena. At the same time the broader vision of politics, the idea that the personal is political, evolved in the consciousness-raising groups receded into the background, including the feminist critique of political style. The older idea of women reforming the public arena, so prominent in women's organizations of earlier periods seemed to have disappeared from feminism, resurfacing in the women's peace and ecological movements. The feminism of the eighties sounds like the regular social-democrat and liberal equal rights platform. It makes one curious about the nineties.

References

Aerts, M. (1986), "Het persoonlijke is politiek. Een poging tot herdenken", *Te Elfde Ure 39*, Nijmegen, pp. 78-108.

Anarca-feministes (1982), "Wij willen alle scheidingen in ons leven vermijden", A. Bleich et al. (eds.), *Feminisme en politieke Macht. Deel 1. Posities, problemen en strategieen*, Amsterdam: De Populier, pp. 17-26.

Baalen, A. van en M. Ekelschot (1980), "Hoe krijgen we ze er weer uit?", A. Bleich en A. Steenhuis (eds.), *Vrouwen in links mannenland*, Amsterdam: De Groene Amsterdammer, pp. 15-19.

Bleich, A. and A. Steenhuis (eds.) (1980), *Vrouwen in links mannenland*, Amsterdam: De Groene Amsterdammer.

Bleich, A. et al. (eds.) (1982), *Feminisme en Politieke Macht. Deel I: Posities, problemen en strategieen*, Amsterdam: De Populier.

Briet, M., B. Klandermans and F. Kroon (1987), "How Women Become Involved in the Women's Movement of the Netherlands", M.F. Katzenstein and C. McClurg Mueller (eds.), *The Women's Movements of the United States and Western Europe. Consciousness, Political Opportunity, and Public Policy*, Philadelphia: Temple University Press, pp. 44-64.

Connolly, W. (1983), *The Terms of Political Discourse*, Oxford (2nd edition): Martin Robertson.

Cott, N.F. (1987), *The Grounding of Modern Feminism*, New Haven/London: Yale.

Freeman, Jo (1975), *The Politics of Women's Liberation. A Case Study of an Emerging Social Movement and Its Relation to the Policy Process*, New York: David McKay.

Klandermans, B. (1989), *Current Research on Social Movements*. Lecture, Annual Conference of the Dutch Society for Political Psychology, Utrecht, December 1989.

Kriesi, H. (1985), *Nieuwe sociale bewegingen: op zoek naar hun gemeenschappelijke noemer*, Amsterdam: Universiteit van Amsterdam (oratie).

Loo, H. van der, E. Shnel en B. van Steenbergen (1984), *Een wenkend perspectrief? Nieuwe sociale bewegingen en culturele veranderingen*, Amersfoort: De Horstink.

Meulenbelt, A. (1978), "Terwijl wij praten over ons isolement heffen wij dat isolement op", reprinted in A. Meulenbelt, *Brood en Rozen. Artikelen 1975-1982*, Amsterdam: Sara 1983, pp. 23-44.

Outshoorn, J. (1986a), *De politieke strijd rondom de abortuswetgeving in Nederland*, Den Haag: VUGA.

Outshoorn, J. (1986b), "The Rules of the Game: Abortion Politics in the Netherlands", J. Lovenduski and J. Outshoorn (eds.), *The New Politics of Abortion.*, Beverly Hills/London: Sage, pp. 5-27,

Outshoorn, J. (1986c), "The Feminist Movement and Abortion Policy in the Netherlands", D. Dahlerup (ed.), *The New Women's Movement. Feminism and Political Power in Europe and the USA*, London/Beverly Hills: Sage, pp. 64-85.

Outshoorn (1987), "Power as a Political and Theoretical Concept in "Second-Wave" Feminism", Leijenaar M. et al. (eds.), *The Gender of Power. A Symposium*, Leyden: Vakgroep Vrouwen-studies/Vena, pp. 25-34.

Outshoorn, J. (1989), "De vrouwenbeweging: gelijk of anders?", L.W. Huberts and W.J. van Noort, *Sociale bewegingen in de jaren negentig. Stand van zaken en vooruitblik*, Leiden: DSWO Press, pp. 61-75.

Outshoorn, J. (1991), *Autonomie als politieke categorie in het Nederlandse tweede golf feminisme*, H. Claessen, M. van den Engel en D. Plantenga, Het Kweekbed Ontbiemd, Leyden: Faculty of Social Science/Vena, pp. 189-198.

Ribberink, A. (1987), *Feminisme*, Leiden: Stichting Burgerschapskunde.

Sax, M. (1982), "De tijd van spandoeken is voorbij", A. Bleich et al. (eds.), *Feminisme en politieke macht. Deel I: Posities, problemen en strategieën*, Amsterdam: De Populier, pp. 133-138.

Smit, J. (1971), "Afscheid van de gemeenteraad", reprinted in J. Smit, *Er is een land waar vrouwen willen wonen. Teksten 1967-1981*, Amsterdam: Sara 1983, pp. 104-112.

Smit, J. (1978), "Is het feminisme ten dode opgeschreven?" reprinted in J. Smit, *Er is een land waar vrouwen willen wonen. Teksten 1967-1981*, Amsterdam: Sara 1983, pp. 292-327.

Smit, J. (1979), "Ik heb een heilig geloof in goede argumenten", reprinted in A. Bleich en A. Steenhuis (eds.), *Vrouwen in links mannenland*, Amsterdam: De Groene Amsterdammer, pp. 11-79.

Soest, F. van (1982), "Strijd in de openbaarheid: wel nodig, niet leuk", A. Bleich et al. (eds.), *Feminisme en politieke macht. Deel 1: Posities, problemen en strategieen*, Amsterdam: De Populier, pp. 75-87.

Vries, P. de (1981), "Feminism in the Netherlands", *Women's Studies International Quarterly*, IV, no. 4, pp. 389-409.

Vries, P. de (1987), "Het persoonlijke is politiek en het ontstaan van de tweede golf in Nederland 1968-1973", *Socialisties-Feministiese Teksten 10*, Baarn: Ambo, pp. 15-36.

Notes

1. For works in English on the Dutch movement: Briet c.s. 1987; Outshoorn, 1986b; 1986c; De Vries, 1981.

2. This article is a revised and elaborated version of a paper first presented at the Fourth Interdisciplinary Congress on Women, New York, June 1990.

3. Melucci. Quoted by: Klandermans, 1989.

4. Note that Smit ties these feminine characteristics to women's roles which they have strongly internalised. My project is not analyzing individuals' identity but the collective identity that women's movements produce in their writings and other practices.

5. But in the astute analysis of Aerts, politics itself remains a knot all tied. Focusing on gender, politics itself remains undifferentiated. The "political" is identified with the "public sphere", but there is no distinguishing its various and historically grown forms and institutions; these become conflated. This is of course in line with the marxist and new left habit of not recognising the particular and specific moment of the political. While acknowledging that feminism expanded the political to take account of phenomena like the family, and noting that it was also a critique of political style (Aerts, 1986: 81) the public sphere is rendered synonymous with "politics" or as "party politics" or it is used to denote the strategy of the women's movement, as in the phrase "a politics based on a feminine identity" (Aerts, 1986: 98). What is also not challenged is the designation of politics as "male" as opposed to "female".

6. What has happened to the autonomous movement in the eighties has not as yet been researched thoroughly. Some groups have disappeared; others seem to have undergone some kind of institutionalization. What has happened to the women in this part of the movement is not yet clear either.

The Gender System

Yvonne Hirdman

Introduction

In this article[1] I start with a critique of the unproblematic, often untheoretical (or a sex-role-based "explanation") approach in surveys or political descriptions of the situation of women in Sweden. In contrast, I develop the concept of gender system, with the aim to analyze how this system changed and how this change interfered and shaped basic structures in the Swedish welfare politics.

Critique of (implicit and explicit) sex role theories: Or: The Theoretical Obstacle which 1) causes us not to see the problems and creates assumptions about relations between the sexes that are full of systematic misinterpretations and 2) is (implicitly or explicitly) the basis for political action.

This theoretical foundation conceals power relationships and ignores the findings of women's research.

As a pedagogical example illustrating the usual way of describing relations between women and men, one could use a report entitled "Inequality in Sweden" (Ojämlikheten i Sverige) (Vogel et al., 1987, 316). Its authors have included in their report a chapter about equal status between the sexes. They write as follows:

What explanations can there be for the differences that in some cases exist between men's and women's living conditions? There is, of course, no general answer to this question. Instead it varies, depending on the area studied. Many differences can probably be explained by 'tradition'. But also lifestyle, interests, biological differences, division of labor, working environment, etc. are parts of a complex pattern that together influences how women and men live and choose to live their lives. From the old patriarchal agrarian society with its sex-bound division of labor and roles, many traditions still remain which explain much of the sexual segregation in today's labor market.

How does such an "explanation" work? In all its simple banality, it unfortunately has an oppressive effect and prevents changes in power relationships between the sexes, for the following reasons:

1. The differences between men and women in the labor market, political represen-

tation, economy, etc.—which the authors acknowledge—are (at least in some cases) described as being relatively trivial.

2. The authors reject general conclusions, i.e. the systematic pattern of differences between men and women reported by women's research ("there is, of course, no general answer").

3. When they describe differences between the sexes in terms of status and economic situation, jobs, etc., they do not speak in terms of inequities but of "differences". This choice of words is of strategic importance and implies that there is no power relationship here. Elsewhere in the report, the authors explicitly distinguish between difference and inequality, saying that the former is more positive and is attributable to a person's own life choices.

4. The explanation the authors provide for this "difference" between the sexes suffer from obvious circular reasoning: a "difference" arises because there is a "difference" in lifestyle, interests, division of labor and working environment. But embedded in these explanations is the "traditional" explanation: biology.

5. These arguments are supplemented by another common explanation: any inequality is attributable to traditions carried over from agrarian society, i.e. the "blame" is found in history, not in the present, which furthermore provides a "solution":

6. I.e. an implicit evolutionist assumption that a levelling of differences between the sexes will immediately and automatically occur.

This way of (not) describing the power relationship between the sexes can be supplemented at a higher level of sophistication by a general sociological theory of sex roles. In addition, the role metaphor is so deeply embedded in people's day-to-day, political and sometimes scholarly understanding of the world, that it is enormously difficult to replace this "comfortable" pattern of thinking with a more complex understanding. As part of the emergence of feminist knowledge, sex role theory has been subjected to harsh criticism, seemingly without disturbing the popularity of this concept.

Above all, women's researchers have pointed to the following theoretical weaknesses (and I am borrowing the outstanding systematization from the summary provided by R.W. Connell in the book Gender and Power (1987: 49ff.).

Such a role theory cannot explain social aspects, i.e. why people accept their roles. Connell believes that sex role theory simply uses assumptions and suppositions without theoretical validity, for example by saying that people "want" this situation. The result is therefore:

What happens in sex role theory is that the missing element of structure is covertly supplied by the biological category of sex ... The underlying image is an invariant biological base and malleable social superstructure. This is why discussion of sex roles constantly slides into discussion of sex differences.

In other words: although role theory speaks of roles as loosely pasted-on identities, it still rests on a biological, deterministic foundation. The entire power aspect, the unequal relationship between the sexes, is removed in a way that is not done in the case of other hereditary stratifications. The "innocence" of the role concept becomes even clearer when Connell reminds us that we do not speak of race roles or class roles (and, one might add, nationality roles). In these areas, sociologists accept and work with the power aspects.

Sex role theories avoid discussions of power—women's roles and men's roles are equal (though unequal) quantities.

With this simple dualism, men's roles, the complexity of relations between the sexes is reduced and simplified. All women are classified as part of the women's role and all men as part of the men's role.

These uniform roles create normative stereotypes that can then be used as national standards, to which "deviations" can be discovered.

Aside from criticizing this simplified harmony, Connell sees as the most serious shortcoming of sex role theory its inability to explain change:

The point is that sex role theory cannot grasp change as history, as transformation generated in the interplay of social practice and social structure. Structure is given to sex role theory in the form of biological dichotomy.

Connell summarizes in four points why sex role theory must be rejected:

1. Its voluntarism and inability to form theories concerning power relationships and social interests,
2. Its dependence on biological dichotomy and its consequent non-social perceptions of structure,
3. Its dependence on a normative stereotype and its systematic misinterpretation of resistance,
4. The fact that given such a theory, it is not possible to form other theories or understand changeability in history and in the future.

On Gender System Theories

Women's research has sought to develop new tools to escape from sex role concepts and deterministic theories almost of the "This is just the way things are" type (found, for example, in *En begrepsanalyse* from 1975)—in an attempt to combine an actor-oriented and structural perspective. (Or also to challenge this dichotomy). This is happening in the debate on gender theory that has become more widespread during the latter half of the 1980s. Some degree of consensus is beginning to emerge as to how the gender concept can be understood. Going back to Connell's above-mentioned

Gender rôles

critique of the sex rôle concept, one might say that by using gender theory, we are trying to create a category (or a school of thought) with the same status as class, nationality, race, i.e. far closer ties between a person and his or her surroundings, an understanding of cultural heredity and the role of social systems in human behavior. Gender (systems, structures, rules) should be regarded as a way of giving a name to the complicated process by which people are shaped to fit their gender, and the consequences this has in institutional, cultural and indeed even biological terms.[2]

This shaping of people to fit their gender implies the creation of differences and inequalities. Gender (system) theory therefore emphasizes the power relationship, both explicit and implicit, that exists between the sexes. Above all, it tries to understand the reproduction of female subordination. I have found it useful, (Hirdman 1988) to bear in mind two characteristic patterns—or logics—in the changeable picture of gender shaping that history demonstrates:

1. The logic of separation between the sexes.
2. The logic of the male norm.

But such a description of relationships between the sexes is too general and does not explain much. By concentrating more closely on the relationship between a man and a woman, however, the concept of "contracts" has begun to be used. Carole Pateman (1988) speaks of the underlying sexual contract that gives men sexual superiority (the male sex right). She regards this as the implicit precondition of the social contract. The concept of gender contracts, which I work with, is something I perceive as a broad concept. It should be regarded as a way of abstracting and analyzing the space (perhaps concreticized into the dependence) between men and women and the ideas, informal and formal rules and norms that this space generates or generated with regard to the places, tasks and qualities of men and women in a society. Consequently, these "contracts" between the sexes (or gender contracts) can be distinguished as more or less abstract phenomena at different levels. In all its changeability and variety, this relationship (or relationships) creates a system of the sexes, a gender system. What such a system does is that it creates a number of "irrefutabilities", i.e. a number of "obvious statements" about how things "are"; it soothes the worried brow by declaring that "things are just as they should be", but it also threatens those who challenge it, because the "irrefutable" systems of the sexes easily assumes the nature of a taboo.

It is also important to point out that particular gender contracts (i.e. a concretization of the gender system in different societies and periods) must provide the departure point for women's strategies and that the active, sometimes almost conspiratorial male resistance to such strategies also emanates from them. For the system has given them a number of privileges and has created male "homosociality", which is based on the subordination of women. Men must also fight—in individual cases even against their conscious desires—on behalf of a gender system that both segregates and creates a hierarchy between the sexes, because of (and in order to maintain) their positions in the homosocial order.

Another way of expressing this thought is that the gender system presupposes or creates different rationales of action for the two sexes.

The advantages of a gender concept compared with a sex role concept for purposes of research are numerous: 1). changeability—historicity, 2). variety—i.e. that we no longer speak of woman as in the 19th century, nor of women as in the 1970s, but of "women"—i.e. we are beginning to understand the differences between women (not necessarily related to class differences, but also to age, family status, etc.), and can hardly speak in terms of shared female "interests" in the same uncomplicated way as five years ago. 3). the relationship, i.e. not only "women" are in the spotlight, but the relationship between men and women, "maleness" and "femaleness" and the fact that this (gender shaping) relationship with its structurally given gender-differentiating rationale, plays a fundamental social, economic and political role.

The Growing Gender Conflict

With a gender system concept as an analytical tool for examining the past two hundred years of Western history, we see important features that are of decisive importance to our understanding of today's society.

We see that the breakthrough of modernity meant the development of strong sex-integreating impulses. "In principle" (i.e. built into its logics), the capitalist system did not care about earlier systems, but chose the cheapest labor. This might imply that it preferred female labor. Perhaps a more important sex-integrating "factor" was the democratic concept: ideas about the equality of human beings regardless of race, social position or sex. The consequence of this democratic concept, and its built-in tendency to continue expanding, were described by Ernst Wigforss, Sweden's minister of finance in the 1930s and 1940s:

"Those who have openly accepted a democratic principle of equality cannot arbitrarily limit its application to certain areas"—and we can add: or certain people.

Phrased in Marxist terms, both the base and the superstructure thus contain strong sex-integrating forces—or rules. The gender system's segregating and gender-hierarchizing rules thus worked against these. The outcome was that the emergence of modern society witnessed the lopsided development of male positions, tasks and "qualities", while the number of female positions shrank—both in comparative and absolute terms. Homes became "smaller". This did not merely happen; it was created through human acts. In particular, assumptions about conflicting dichotomies between the sexes began to play a fundamental (and legitimizing) role: for example the emergence of an understanding of the world as being divided into "productive" and "reproductive" economies, likewise a division into public and private spheres, where the public sphere was very clearly a male place, while the private sphere was assigned a subordinate and hidden role. The "productive" and "public" spheres became the "big world" or "big life" where a number of new salaried jobs and careers lopsidedly strengthened the democratization of men as a group and their conquest of social power. In addition, there was expansion both in spatial terms—colonization—and in the form of scientific advances. This expansion was again explicitly and consciously reserved for men. In contrast, the "little life" became a subordinate, unproblematized (forgotten) "prerequisite".

So, on this simplified, theoretical level, we might distinguish a triangle, where the integrative "forces" of capitalism/industrialism and of democratism constitute the two sides, and the segregative logics of the gender system constitute its base. And in the middle, as a result, one could almost see the built-in conflict between the sexes about issues of work, places and qualities: a gender conflict.

In other words, the distinguishing feature of modernity is a chronic conflict which, so to speak, insists upon the creation of new gender contracts, the basis for a modernized gender system, and which thereby obviously at the same time interactively helps shape society. We can also say that this gender conflict, becomes increasingly acute (also in the sense that it will affect more and more people) the more sex-integrated a society is. If we look more closely at this conflict, we see two forms of it:

1. The conflict occurs because women are moving into male-dominated areas, doing male jobs, demanding male rights (or, nota bene, they are expected to be able to do so)—i.e. the pattern of the gender system is being challenged, because integration means having both sexes in the same places, doing the same things and exhibiting the same personal characteristics. This threatens the rule of the male norm. The fundamental sameness of the sexes, i.e. the shared "humanness" of the species, becomes obvious de facto; this is the "conflict of sameness".

Stockholm in the 1930s.

2. But the level of conflict also escalates because integration of the sexes reveals their differences and makes them a subject of conflict: this is the "conflict of differences". The biological differences between men and women become a source of provocation because they so clearly illustrate that the various institutions of society are modeled on the male norm. Child-bearing is thereby transformed into an illness, a deviation and a punishment.

Formulated in this way, we see two characteristic features of women's relationship to modern societies:

1. They are forced into an insoluble, unfruitful definition of their own nature: are women primarily people and secondarily women, or vice versa? In other words, this conflict created an ideological dilemma of sameness vs. the separate nature of women.
2. We also see that women are the ones who are defined as the problem, i.e. the core

of the conflict. (And here we can hear Alva Myrdal's sarcastic(?) voice when she singled out women as the number 1 "problem children" of society). The fact that the conflict was defined as a women's problem, the "women's issue", admittedly implied a half-recognition, a half-solution. But the real problems nonetheless remained, calling for more firm solutions.

Using this theoretical blueprint on the understanding of the history of the Swedish Welfarestate, one will see, how the solutions to the two varoius types of the genderconflict operates. Despite the lack of research, we still have sufficient empirical data to be able to formulate the rather reasonable hypothesis, that conflicts between the sexes are automatically transformed into issues that the system "can handle". It is part of the very "nature" of the gender system that conflicts between the sexes "cannot" be formulated. Behind this formulation is also Harriet Holter's insightful observation, "But the main tendency is that the subordination of women is illegitimate, while the processes that it is built into possess economic and political legitimacy" (Holter, 1984).

In other words: "the women's issue", i.e. the structural conflict between the sexes, contains a revolutionary potential that must be defused. The conflict is therefore transformed from a power issue, a democracy issue, a superior-inferior issue, into manageable, unformulated issues that

1. fit into the rules of the system, and
2. benefit the system,

and thus issues that benefit one gender, i.e. strengthen the primacy of the male norm. One could even formulate the hypothesis that this conflict (which is defined as a women's problem), tends to be transformed into a fruitful male strategy where women are used in order to fulfill welfare goals that are more beneficial to the male group.

The result of this is an expansion of the political sphere, the labor market, the "public sphere". In these new positions, finally, room is created for new male and female positions, i.e. for new segregation.

Brief Historical Illustration

During the period 1930-1975, the crisis-ridden relationship between the sexes created two diametrically different gender contracts: the "housewife contract" during the period 1930-1960 and what we can call the "equality contract" from 1960 to 1975/80.

The Housewife Contract

This contract may be regarded as an answer to the acute economic crisis situation of the interwar period, when the male collective became increasingly democratized, while the female collective was "privatized", as both the conflicts of sameness and differences became evident. The articulation of the conflict involved the conflict of sameness, which focused particularly on the infected issue of whether married women should really be entitled to hold paid jobs. But it also concerned the conflict of differences, formulated as concern over the declining birth rate.

The conflict was transformed or reformulated into a progressive weapon for a modern social welfare policy (Hirdman 1989). The consequence was that the boundaries of public policy were dramatically expanded, that a new—or modern—social welfare policy was created, with the home and not the workplace as its focus. One can speak here of a "hidden historic compromise" between women and the state. The gains for the female collective were—nota bene—not so few: greater economic security because their pure dependence on men disappeared and the state took over some of this responsibility both in economic terms and in connection with childbirth and child welfare services, while an increase in material standards made their lives less exhausting. And not to be forgotten, a "female" view of sexuality became the accepted sexual ethics. The result was an institutionalization of womanhood into housewifehood, both in physical and institutional respects. In addition, a more modern and thereby legitimate form of segregation between the sexes was created: a continued division between the "small" and the "big" life in irreconcilable forms. (Where the "small life" was increasingly institutionalized and controlled). This, in turn, created the legitimate basis for a continued expansion of democracy among males.

Transitional Phase: The 1950s and 1960s

The post-war period witnessed a reinforcement of the pattern on which the housewife contract was based, but at the same time the level of conflict was stepped up. This occurred because of an expansion in female wage labor and increased democracy in Sweden, primarily because of the gender neutral coeducational school system. The conflict was even more clearly articulated as a monosexual (i.e. women's) problem, now with strong psychological overtones.

The period was marked by double segregation: between the "small" and the "big" life and within the big life, especially in the labor market, where previously clear patterns of segregation were reinforced. At the same time, the increased demand for women's labor meant that the needs of women were allowed to restructure the labor market within certain areas, for example part-time work. The principle of equal pay was also enacted, but nota bene: it was implemented in a labor market that was strictly divided by gender and not necessarily to the advantage of women. The "law" of segregation between the sexes was also reflected at the political level, where representation by women tended to stagnate and even decline. Speaking in terms of gains for each sex, women enjoyed greater material and consumer-related welfare. But nota bene: their status as MOTHERS was greatly strengthened (thus, for example, beginning in 1949 all children born out of wedlock were placed in the mother's custody; the newly created state child allowance was also disbursed to the mother) while the male sex's monopoly on democracy became stronger. This strengthening of male political dominance should also be seen in the light of the "universal" reforms that were being implemented in the labor market—mainly a compulsory, employer-financed, income-related supplementary pension system (*ATP*), which lopsidedly favored men. The mature Swedish welfare state democracy was thus a male democracy. Despite their right to vote and certain formal political rights, women's status as citizens still went via their husbands (was tied to the household, i.e. subordinate to the husband).

The Contract of Equality, 1965-1975/80

In 1971, the Social Democratic women's organization unveiled a long-term program which outlined a future, totally different from the previously accepted social welfare future: instead of segregation between the sexes, instead of the "housewife contract" that had prevailed during the preceding decades, it sketched a future of equality between the sexes. In other words, the conflict was defined more broadly than as a mere women's problem. Earlier solutions were rejected. The new ones were based on reducing or eliminating both the conflicts of differences and of sameness between the sexes with the help of radical political reforms and/or legislation. New future utopias were now born: the vision of a gender contract based on equal status, with a six-hour working day, with fair distribution between men and women of work and responsibility in the home, on the job and in politics. In 1970 the housewives' insurance system was changed into a home spouse insurance system. Joint taxation of spouses' incomes was changed to separate taxation. In 1973 the marriage code was amended so that the father was entitled to apply for custody of children. In 1975 mothers' insurance was changed to parental insurance, and in 1976 parents' legislation was changed to permit joint custody. Parallel with this, the public sector began building day care centers on a large scale, and political experiments were implemented with the aim of ending sexual segregation in the labor market by encouraging women to take male-dominated jobs. Women's right to paid jobs became a national (or at least Social Democratic) motto, and women's free right to abortion also had to be regarded as a reform aimed at giving women individual, autonomous status.

These gender-specific reforms had the explicit purpose of bringing the gender closer to each other and literally breaking the strongly sex-segregated gender contract of the preceding period. More important than these "utopian" reforms, however, was it that women began to partake of other "universal" reforms thanks to the gender-blindness of the educational system and because of the increasing number of women with paid employment. In other words, intentionally or not, the citizenship status of women increased—because their lives were becoming more similar to men's and because the "conflict of differences" was softening.

These solutions also meant that homes became more socially integrated in a growing number of "functions": school and work-day lunches were served outside the home (a revolutionary reform that helped free women for paid jobs), while child care, old age care and medical care became more institutionalized.

This was the direction in which solutions were generally sought: shifting over more and more responsibility to the public sector's social welfare system, (although proposals for government bordellos met with a cool response). Despite attempts, especially by the women active in public life during that period to make the conflict seem to be that of both sexes, the "gender-neutral" shape it assumed (parents instead of mothers and fathers, for example) was unintentionally deceptive and could, on the contrary, be used against women and to benefit men. This was because the solutions that were implemented de facto favored the rules of the prevailing system; they were based on the primacy of stereotypical wage labor and legitimized continued political expansion (the growth of the public sector). In other words, they satisfied and legitimized the expansionary tendencies that are the inherent necessity of the modern welfare state. In this way, the conflict between the sexes, revealed by the feminine dilemma of being both "the same" and "different" compared with men, could again be used for the expansion of political power.

As in the earlier housewife contract, however, women made major gains. Their choices increased drastically—above all, perhaps, their perception of what was possible. The new gender contracts was undeniably based on the individuality of men and women. In other words, women were set free from the household and family and were given the economic option of choosing independence—despite the conflict of differences, i.e. children. As for what women as a group were losing, reforms aimed at social leveling and based on the sameness of the sexes, which sought to draw the father into the family (in keeping with Alva Myrdal's vision from the 1930s), entailed the loss of absolute Motherhood. Men consequently gained a stronger sense of fatherhood, at the same time as their position in the labor market was not weakened. Meanwhile some competition began to make itself felt in the educational field (and perhaps in politics). The most notable male "loss" was a weakening of the male's self-evident dominance in the home. Instead the home has become (can become) an arena of negotiation. For both sexes the period of the contract of equality—i.e. of attempts to create an institutional, political and economic solution to the gender conflict—had the result of transforming the intimate relationship of couples into an area of conflict.

The Contract of Equal Status, 1975/80

The acute, real character of the conflict must be understood on the basis of the ever-increasing sociality of women—an irreversible social integration of the sexes, especially in the labor market, but also in other fields of public life such as politics, education, cultural life, etc. But this integration generates new segregation according to this simple formula: no women—no segregation; some women—a little segregation;

many women—great segregation. Segregation between the sexes has assumed new shapes. Segregation is becoming more subtle or sophisticated, for example within an integrated area, within different occupational groups, raising the theoretically important question of what we are actually talking about when we use the concepts of segregation and integration. Integration is perceived as incorporating, bringing together, adding, contributing. Demands for integration can nevertheless now be understood (with some justification) as demands for a transformation. The clumsiness of these concepts indicates that one of the more difficult modern problems of power is buried here. We can now distinguish the fact that it concerns two processes: the first is about integrating quantitatively, the second—which in no way necessarily has to follow, is qualitative integration. Despite (or because of) the new sophistication of the mechanisms of separation, the previous dramatic difference between a male and a female world has nevertheless ended, so that it is always possible (and almost inevitable) to compare female and male life chances, economic status, choices and freedom of movement. And given the often detailed statistical comparisons, the prevailing injustices are increasingly apparent. The gradual heated conflict of sameness (the problem of low-paid groups, the problem of political representation, the small percentage of women in the "corporate channel", the male-dominated structure of the business community, etc.) are followed by a reinforced conflict of differences (i.e. that only women give birth to children). The latter is increasingly obvious the further the integration (or socialization) of women progresses. Despite all the political reforms that have made women's lives in Sweden more reasonable compared with other countries, giving birth and caring for children is still punished today in economic and career terms.

Women are still defined as problems and become the bearers of the conflict. In concrete terms, this means a heavier physical burden on women during an intensive period of their lives, at an age when they are putting down roots in the labor market and/or beginning to build a career. To exaggerate a bit, we could speak of an Eastern Europeanization of women's lives—cross-pressures and double work burdens.

In other words: greater socialization of women creates greater problems, because the conflicts of sameness and differences between the sexes are becoming more pronounced. Or we could put it more paradoxically: the more successful the strategic reforms based on the similarities between the sexes, the more problematical the conflicts based on their dissimilarities.

But another characteristic of our contemporary gender crisis is that the chances that women themselves can solve the problem by dint of extra effort, are beginning to fade away. Such solutions have always occurred within the female collective. But today there is a shortage of unpaid labor and free time among women. Neither maids nor grandparents are easily available any more.

The social welfare solution, based on equal status between the sexes, which implied that the public sector would take over the duties of chambermaids and grandmothers (using low-paid female labor) has admittedly not been written off, but it has become one of the great dilemmas of the welfare state. There is a crisis in the public sector, too: a shortage of labor (women) and money.

What helps make the gender conflict so severe is that so far, we have not found any way to connect the problem of the sexes with a sociopolitical or labor market policy reform desired by "everyone"—i.e. a political solution that will rejuvenate, improve and expand the system.

On the contrary, expansion no longer seems to be a politically opportune method and thus finds it hard to gain economic sanction. Enlarging the public sector is portrayed instead as economically (and politically) impossible. Instead we see attempts to cut back subsidies and programs.

For the crisis of the welfare state is no mere economic crisis. It can perhaps be defined, above all, as a crisis of legitimacy: without trust from below, there can be no further welfare reforms based on a sense of social solidarity.

It is important to point out, however, that legitimacy is connected to the gender system. We then see that the source of the difficulties is that the requisite reforms will lopsidedly benefit women as a group. The monosexual solidarity of the "brotherhood" finds it hard to show solidarity with the "second sex" in ways that de facto imply that men will be deprived of fundamental privileges—above all, their position as Number One in the labor market. It is a crisis of legitimacy because there has to be a redistribution of resources from men to women. This goes directly against the grain of solidarity according to the Swedish Model, which is undoubtedly a national variation of homosocial behavior during a particular historical period when men as a group became increasingly homogeneous due to male-dominated democratization. This was made possible by the "housewife contract's" gender-based division of labor and segregation between the sexes.

This, in turn, can enhance the discussion underway today—employing different labels from right to left on the political spectrum—concerning the meaning of citizenship and future changes. It is important to analyze what lies behind this debate and what its participants are so worried about.

On the right end of the political spectrum it is a matter drawing lines between the "small" and "big life"; a return to earlier, unpoliticized homes where people decide for themselves how things ought to be. From the political left, it is a blurrier issue of new social (and economic?) rights that will broaden the concept of citizenship.

What does it all mean? It can be understood as a rightist reaction to previous solutions aimed at improving relations between the sexes, dating from the 1930s and later. Because these solutions have undeniably made the home into a place where social experiments have been carried out.

During the first period, that of the housewife contract, these "experiments" in homes involved a government-sponsored transformation of the small life by means of a modernization process aimed at radical change. But above all, it must be seen as a reaction to the radical shift that began during the period of the equality contract and later, i.e. the increasing socialization of the home. Today people say that the lines between the "small" and the "big" life have become blurred. There is said to be a need for greater clarity in the relationships between people (men? women?) and the "public sector", either a clear demarcation of limits or a clarification of what these relationships mean from a democratic perspective. From a leftist perspective, the somewhat unclear lines of thought should be regarded partly as a defense of the expanded home—inscribed in a ("neoconservative") democratic discourse—and partly also as an attempt at a new expansion, i.e. an attempt to create a new basis for the legitimacy of a stronger "common sector".

But the genuine gender conflict not only creates conflicts between the sexes; it also erects barriers between categories of women, sorting them into different pigeonholes. This is also due to women's growing sociality and reduced dependence on men for their social status. Women as a group were previously stratified exclusively on the basis of their relationships with men (fathers and husbands); the dividing line ran between married women, with their husbands's status being decisive (whom she married depended on her father's status), as well as between married and unmarried women i.e. between those with husbands and those with none.

Now women are ranked according to social hierarchies in the labor market. This creates confusion for the still-dominant, more or less Marxist-influenced class theories. Because how are women ranked and in relationship to what?

We have various indications that something is afoot that is turning our set of assumptions upside down. According to the latest survey of social status in Sweden, The Swedish Class Society (Det svenska klassamhället)—which employs traditional class categories—the people occupying the category "unskilled workers" are primarily women (709,000 women and 598,000 men). Women also dominate the category known as "low-level white collar employees" (430,000 women, compared with 212,000 men).

In other words, we might speak of the feminization of the working class. Our understanding would then be based on the fact that most of those in jobs at the bottom of the labor market hierarchy are women. By describing reality in such a way that women dominate the "working class"—a feminization of the working class"—we gain two advantages:

1. We disavow the concept of the "blue-collar worker" and take away its male status.
2. We focus attention on a power relationship.

But this may cause us to disregard the essential thing that creates this system: the fact that a power relationship between the sexes (i.e. the gender system) is operating here. For the women behind these figures act according to the rationale of the gender contract, i.e. they prioritize male superiority in the home and organize their lives in keeping with its unwritten laws. This rationale, in turn, is exploited in a labor market where male rationales govern. (On the other hand, saying that women are forced to live on male terms in the labor market is a misunderstanding of prevailing relationships: women are there on "female" terms). This "contract-determined" rationale is at its clearest among certain groups of immigrant women, who follow more patriarchal gender contracts. (See also below for a more detailed discussion of contracts).

The class concept thus conceals the radical transformation of society that has taken place in the past 20-30 years. It also conceals the fact that completely different types of work are found behind the categories "underskilled worker" and "low-level white collar employee" if they are performed by men and if they are performed by women. It conceals the most characteristic feature of the transformed labor market: the emergence of a new lower class that—all other considerations aside—we might call the service proletariat. Nor can it explain the dividing line that has already been noted running between the sexes in the labor market: the one between state/public sector employees, where women dominate, and employees in the private business sector, where men dominate.

On the one hand, women are found in the lowest-paid service proletariat occupations. On the other hand, we find more and more women in the looser category of "middle class". People even speak of its feminization. Behind this are statistical truths about the explosion of women's education, the feminization of the teaching profession, the growing stratum of women in public administration, etc. Again, it would be tempting to use the old class concept and substitute "female". But again, we would miss the structuring principle that has the effect of creating hierarchies between women in the labor market. For it is better to view the new female role in the "big life" as a modern variation of the old stratification of women that revolved around men, invisible or highly visible. Because the "housewife"—the woman now "married" (i.e. loyal) to central and local government—obviously still supervises and bosses around the "chambermaid", the "unskilled", publicly employed servant. This analogy has a point: it underscores the position of "middle-level women": as managers and instruments of the welfare state (local government) and in charge of subordinate women, whose loyalties are with the home rather than with the central or local government.

This stratification of women in working life could also possibly be understood on the basis of the new labor market of the service-oriented society on the one hand, and the "knowledge-oriented" society on the other. It is typical of large groups of women workers in both sectors, that their jobs involve service and support, that they are not independent and are (most often) supervised by men. We could thus add to the female service proletariat a feminized information proletariat.

The profound gender conflict is a daily experience. It can be described in different ways. For example, more equality between men and women has created a greater dependence in both sexes (or rather, greater interaction between them). Certain "self-evident" male rights have ceased de facto. We could interpret reports of increased violence against women as a reaction to this loss. In the home, there is bargaining about who will do what, but here the husband's symbiosis and roots in the "big" life still have an impact, giving him a number of self-evident rights, which in turn coincides with women's heavier work load, because they are the main representatives of the home (i.e. cooking, washing, cleaning, child-rearing). We see the effects of this simple division of labor in quantitative surveys that attempt to measure people's time budgets and interests.

We may call this description the "standard contract" of the couple. For both men and women this is carried over into their work lives. This is quite clear if we look at women: there are a number of "arenas" where consideration for husband and children comes first. Such a contract is reflected in for instance the choice of part-time work, which must be regarded as a rational female choice aimed at making the best of the situation.

There are, however, clear differences in this between women from different strata of society and different parts of the country. In Gerd Lindgren's study of a female-dominated workplace, she sees how women use different contractual solutions depending on what stratum they belong to, which in turn means that they can end up in conflict with each other (Lindgren, 1990). A good "contract" for one woman may seem like a threat to another woman. Nurses' aides and assistant nurses, for example, have similar contracts (home situations) with deep roots in the housewife contract of an earlier period, which was described above as a "standard contract". Other groups of women with a higher education such as registered nurses have other, more uncertain contracts. Greater variation, greater uncertainty, higher levels of conflict.

But men's behavior in workplaces (toward other men and toward women) should also be related to their respective contracts. Male homosociality is what unites them, which means that they are seeking the best contract in relation to women (i.e. a contract in which women get the worst of it, so to speak). In other words, what prevails here is brotherhood, male solidarity, which thus stands in direct conflict with women, who are increasingly divided. The often well-organized resistance to equality between the sexes, reflects and regenerates homosocial strategies.

The lack of clever system-favoring pseudosolutions (structurally prevented by the male homosocial strategy) means that the gender conflict threatens to become "pure" or revolutionary, and thus politically unmanageable. It is impossible to admit that the problem is as radical as it is, because an admission of the real nature of the crisis would imply an almost revolutionary transformation of society built upon a restructuring of resources between the sexes.

Going back to Harriet Holter (1984), in other words the "legitimate" base is threatened and is consequently being defended. Now we see the "structural dilemma"—"things just are this way"—in the fact that social institutions are built up around men as the norm of human behavior.

The Articulated Conflict

The interesting thing is that the conflict is now defined in two parts: as a problem specific to women, but (within an entirely different political discourse, as if the problems had nothing to do with each other) also as a profound economic welfare problem with a legitimacy, i.e. democratic, aspect.

"The First Problem"

Of course we can regard the act of delegating to women the task of handling the problem "specific to women" as a way of admitting the existence of the problem without being forced into an "impossible" political act. But we can also interpret it as a semi-acknowledgement of the gender problem. Government policy on equal status between the sexes *can* be understood in this way, not merely as the vehicle for harmonization of sex-rôles, but also as a theoretical paradigm.

The ghettoization (or segregation) of the problem does not only occur in (and because of) the government equal status bureaucracy. It also develops as a consequence of increased feminist awareness, for example the rapid expansion of women's research. Things have to be this way because the male collectives almost automatically starts resorting to exclusion or containment strategies.

What does this imply for attempts at problem-solving?

Female problem formulation paired with (male) political avoidance of the conflict due to its "impossibility" means that the solutions assume a distinctive rhetorical bias. An arena of words is created, where the conflict between the sexes is talked out. An eloquent example is the emphasis placed on "attitude changes" instead of quotas, for instance. This "confession" occurs both inside and outside the institutionalized forms of equality between the sexes. It is a solution that lies in the act of speaking.

It embodies a strong tendency to wallow in the conflict caused by the differences between the sexes and to legitimize a new philosophy of separate male and female natures. There may be reason to discuss this trend at greater length, because it is in the process of shaping tomorrow's political solutions and laying the foundations of a more modern gender system.

1. We can find the roots of this trend in the institutional system associated with government policy on equal status between the sexes, because its rules force the emergence of a parallelism of the sexes that quickly assumes institutional forms (for example, male crisis hotlines), which in turn pushes the rules further toward a belief in separate natures, etc.
2. The main effect of emphasizing conflicts rooted in the differences between the sexes is to distract attention from conflicts based on the sameness of the sexes with their implicit "impossible", i.e. redistributive solutions.

3. Because of the profound gender conflict, there is a market for "explanations" and new gender contracts everywhere in society, at different levels, not least between man and woman, where there is profound uncertainty about what is reasonable in the relationship between the sexes. More clearly than for 100 years, we now see active attempts to create new gender contracts, new gender assumptions, to define men and women again and indicate their respective areas, tasks and "natures".

4. This market requires apartness and distinctions. We can see this requirement as a reaction to the preceding period's excitement about the fundamental sameness of the sexes.

5. This need is exploited by media institutions. The trend toward emphasizing differences meshes well with the rules of the media themselves (media dramaturgy that works with opposites, black-and-white, simplification, etc.) and the internal segregation found there as in all institutions, generating segregation both in terms of form and content. So a new philosophy of the separate natures of the sexes is emerging, legitimized not least by certain womenscholars who analyze "differences" on the basis of "character traits". This creates a legitimate basis for separate treatment—a more modern form of sexual segregation. The old arguments for keeping women outside various spheres of power were based on "biology": i.e. women were believed unable to fulfill the requisites of power. The new arguments, on the other hand, are based—preferably backed by the findings of womenscholars—on the argument that women are not willing. But the trend toward emphasizing the differences between the sexes may also conceal the growing stratification among women as a group, as increasingly formalized sexbased institutions bargain about "men's" and "women's" "interests". In the new political climate, the parental insurance system (now expanded to 15 months)—which was in fact designed to distribute repsonsibility for children even-handedly between mother and father—has contributed to the trend toward emphasizing the separate natures of the sexes and creating differences between them. But it has also contributed to the process of stratification among women. Some women do not need to (and do not want to, because of enjoyable, well-paid jobs and attractive careers) use their full parental insurance benefits, while other women with low-paid, dull jobs prefer to stay at home and take advantage of their parental insurance payments for as long as they can (Åstrøm, 1990).

"The Second Problem"

The second problem was the interpretation of the gender conflict not as the problem concerned with men and women but as a crisis of the social expansion of the welfare state. One of the characteristics of the old Swedish Model was—as has been pointed out above—the political fruitful solutions by expanding the "social house", thus avoiding the core of the problem. So what can be expected now ? Let me close by presenting four possibilities:

1. No expansion, i.e. the "house" cannot be extended. Instead, it has to be renovated, and no redistribution of resources between the sexes will occur.

   This solution involves a "more efficient" and "more streamlined" public sector, at the same time as certain previously socialized "functions" are restored to the home, without built-in quotas between the sexes. Women will therefore be affected, both in the labor market and home in life.

   On the other hand, a restructuring and streamlining process can remove hierarchical barriers (in the medical care system, the costly and inefficient power of doctors in particular) and give women greater power, since they are obviously in a rather good bargaining position.

   However, either alternative may increase the differences between women, because improving the efficiency of this field will favor the female professionalization strategies now noticeable among registered nurses, for example, while jobs involving personal care will be further differentiated according to the unwritten law of the "modernization process".

   Streamlining, efficiency drives and cutbacks in the child-care and educational sector—day-care centers and schools—will most likely affect mainly women, both as mothers and as employees in this sector.

   Individual contract solutions between the sexes will, to a great extent, be influenced and controlled by new reforms that primarily restore child care (but also old age care) to the home. It will become harder for women to bargain their way to good contracts if they are not already well-assimilated in the labor market and have good, well-paid jobs.

   The Matthew principle, i.e. "he who already has shall be given", will automatically be reinforced.
2. No expansion, but a redistribution of resources between the sexes. A trade union policy advocating higher women's wages and more reasonable conditions for women in the labor market—such as a six-hour day. Quotas within the parental insurance system, for example. Is there anything that indicates such a trend is underway?
3. Expansion, but no redistribution—i.e. the creation of a new area, where both men and women will (temporarily) be favored, i.e. a "traditional" solution based on two slogans: full employment and increased growth.
4. An expansion and a redistribution. For the sake of consistency, this fourth (Utopian?) possibility must be introduced: i.e. a policy characterized both by growth and by ambitions for the success of a policy of redistribution, where sex rather than class is decisive.

The third alternative is perhaps the one we can see today—but perhaps probably the field of political solutions. And having said this, I will present what I would like to call: "The silent solution".

The lack of systematic political solutions and the segmentation of the problem into two parallel areas, have created what I call a "silent" solution, or solutions outside the political field. Something must be done, and it is being done by individuals, but especially by a rather attentive business sector. Something is happening in certain companies: they are establishing their own day-care centers, distributing perks in the form of window-washing, home cleaning services, etc. This represents a crossing or blurring of the lines separating "work" and "home"—which home can compete with Christmas parties sponsored by a cheerful company? We can regard this as a response—within a well-educated stratum (where women have incidentally bargained rather good "contracts") to compensate men for the loss of the "good cheer function" of the home by making companies/workplaces more homelike. In addition, there is a more aggressive solution: creating a separate market for home services.

But these silent solutions spread to the political levels, where ideas for privatization and for the "domestication" of institutions can be found. Some have argued (with particular force the Liberal Party) that women should be able to become "small-scale entrepreneurs" in their "own field"—start day-care centers, old age care centers, maternity wards, primary schools and what not.

Again, the solution would thus be for women to solve the crisis, but within entirely new limits, and with one initial gain perhaps—greater autonomy—but with a built-in "bomb": the creation of yet another women's labor market, i.e. a "base" of their own for democratic participation and for female citizenship.

To make a very brief summary:

1. Both the politically articulated (the equal status discourse) and the silent (market) solution seem to bring with them a form of segregation (which articulates the need for a deeper understanding of these concepts) and a more profound stratification among women.
2. The acceptance of a new "difference" between the sexes can be paired with the new general acceptance of "differentiation", "pluralism", "multiculturalism", etc.—the 1980s' version of inequality.
3. By focusing on the relationship between women and men we see how the fiction, the dichotomization of the world into a small and a big world, into a private life and a public life, maintains the male norm (= men's general rights both at home and at work, the patriarchal structure). But the dichotomy not only has an oppressive function, it also blocks our social understanding, because it maintains the fiction of two separate worlds without a given connection.

The "normal" gender contract between people of different sexes demonstrates something completely different: how the "small life" has a changing and restructuring effect on the "big life"—which in turn has effects on the "small life", etc.

During the respective periods of the three gender contracts, we consequently see the key political role of the home (private or "small life"): a). the modernization of the home creates a new social welfare policy and new political institutions, b). the socialization of the home constitutes the legitimacy and the fundamental prerequisite of the public sector and c). today's multifaceted movements, where certain portions of the previously socialized home are restored in changed form, at the same time that the "big life" is increasingly "domesticated" and takes over many of the former "good cheer functions" of the home, which creates a completely new kind of work arena, a completely new "big" life.

References

Connell, R.W. (1987), *Gender & Power. Society, the Person and Sexual Politics*, Stanford, California: Stanford University Press.

Hernes, Gudmund (1975), *Makt og avmakt. En begrepsanalyse*, Bergen Universitet.

Hirdman, Yvonne (1988), "Genussystemet - reflexioner kring kvinnors sociale underordning", *Kvinnovetenskaplig Tidskrift*, nr. 3.

Hirdman, Yvonne (1989), *Att lägga livet tilrätta - studier i svensk folkhemspolitik*, Helsingborg, Carlssons förlag.

Holter, Harriet (1984) (ed.), *Patriarchy in a Welfare Society*, Norge: Universitetsforlaget.

Lindgren, Gerd (1990), "I broderskapets skugga", *Kvinnovetenskaplig Tidskrift*, nr. 3-4.

Pateman, Carole (1988), *The Sexual Contract*, Cambridge: Polity Press.

Vogel, Joachim, Lary-G. Andersson, Uno Davidsson & Lars G. Hull (1987), *Öjamlikheten i Sverige. Utveckling och miljö. Levnadsförhållanden 1975-85*, Rapport 51. Statistiska Centralbyrån, Stockholm.

Åström, Gertrud (1990), "Föräldraförsäkring och vårnadsbidrag. Om förhållandet mellan ideologi och verklighet", *Kvinnovetenskaplig Tidskrift*, nr. 2.

Notes

1. For a more extended and detailed version, se my contribution to the head report of the Swedish Investigation on Power and Democracy, SOU 1990:44, chapter 3, Genussystemet.

2. In what follows, I try to use "sex" and "sexes" as the everyday word synonymous with real men and women, whereas gender is used as the "abstract sex".

Researching the Women's Movement. Considerations Arising out of a Comparative Study of the New Women's Movement in Finland and the Federal Republic of Germany

Solveig Bergman

In a critical review of American research on new social movements Carol Mueller (1983:1) claims that "because of the magnitude and diversity of the women's movement and because of several inadequacies in social movement theory, it is more likely at present that the movement will inform theory than the reverse". Moreover, Silvia Kontos' (1986) analysis of German research shows that an empirical study of the women's movement reveals the failures and weaknesses of the general theories on the new movements. These are, however, usually considered to have a general relevance for all social movements, including the women's movement.

Mueller and Kontos undoubtedly have an important point here. They show that the new women's movement cannot easily be subsumed into the heading of 'new social movements', because it both *is* and at the same time *is not* a new social movement. On the one hand, for example, peace, ecological and women's movements share many characteristics in their values, visions and strategies, as well as in their social recruitment basis. Social movement theory often sees the so-called 'new' movements as a reaction to the pathological aspects of the process of modernization. It is emphasized that these movements have emerged as a result of the clash between the economic-political-technocratic system and the 'Lebenswelt' (Habermas), or as a protest to the 'Modern Project' (Touraine). On the other hand, it is problematic to see all new social movements as representing similar and qualitatively new conflict lines in society or having grown out of the same ground. I myself sympathize with those who do not want to see the new women's movement merely as a by-product of the student radicalism of the 1960s or 1970s. As Petra de Vries puts it, "It is commonplace to say that 'feminism grew out from the left'... Feminism did not grow out from the left, it grew out of women's oppression!" (1981: 394). Women's collective protest and actions take shape in a diversity of times and places. Feminist research has been able to focus upon both important similarities and distinct differences between the 'old' and 'new' feminism (see e.g., Schenk, 1983; Clemens, 1985; Metz-Göckel, 1987). Such findings show the importance of a historical approach and challenge the often advanced thesis of the 'qualitatively new' aspect of today's social movements (cf. Raschke, 1985: 9).

Another theoretical problem is that we often fail to recognize the full extent of the substantial differences that exist between the women's movements and tend to generalize on a superficial level. Without any deeper analysis, we consider the women's movements, irrespective of geography, to have common ideological goals, strategies, actions, slogans and ways of organizing. There are, of course, a large number of important similarities between the new women's movements in all Western countries. This is partly due to the similar socio-economic, political and cultural structures in these countries, but it is also a result of international collective learning processes and the diffusion of ideas across national borders. At the same time, however, distinct differences exist between women's movements in different countries. Women's movements are embedded in specific historical, cultural and political settings. These national features have a deep impact on the development of the movements, their ideological visions and strategies as well as on the allies they choose and the ways in which social interaction occurs.

Unfortunately, very few comparative studies of the new women's movement exist (cf. Bouchier, 1983 and Chafetz et al., 1986; see also Dahlerup, 1986a). This is hardly surprising, since comparative studies often face major theoretical, methodological and empirical difficulties and research on the women's movement is a very recent endeavour. However, comparative studies could provide a more differentiated picture of the new social movements and contribute to our theoretical knowledge of social movements in general and feminism in particular. We could try to find out how specific socio-structural conditions, political culture and different 'opportunity structures' form social movements. In addition, comparative and cross-national studies help to reveal the impact and effects of the women's movement and enable us to differentiate between the 'national logic' and the 'inherent logic' of the movement as such (Katzenstein et al., 1987: 4). It is difficult, for example, to distinguish the direct effects of the movement from the social changes that would have taken place irrespective of the movement.

And—to speak about ourselves as academic researchers on women's movements as well as feminist activists—through learning from the experiences of women's movements in other countries, we might be able to avoid pitfalls and learn from each others' mistakes and successes. It is important to remember that we are not doing this research just because of an abstract research interest, but for the benefit of feminists and women in general.

The main purpose of my study is to analyze why and in what way the new women's movement develops national characteristics. This discussion is developed in more detail in my Ph.D. thesis "The New Women's Movement as a Social Movement" (Bergman, forthcoming). Simultaneously, I analyze whether concepts and 'general' movement theory can be adapted to a study of the new women's movement. My concrete research subject is the new women's movement in Finland and Germany (West). I consider the patterns of ideology, mobilization and organization, as well as strategies and actions of the two movements. Through a comparative approach and by

Women's Action Day for Disarmament in Helsinki, May 1982.

contrasting the two case studies against each other, I try to reach some general conclusions about the new women's movement as a social movement.

In this context, the following questions were of special interest to me: Firstly, why did the women's movement emerge later in Finland than in most other Western countries and why did it not fully begin to unfold until the 1980s? Why was the movement for a long time rather weak, reformist and integrated into the formal political structures? Was Finland a 'deviant case' simply because feminism here had a somewhat different way of expressing itself compared to many other Western countries? Furthermore, I wanted to break the 'Finnish paradox'. On the one hand, we have the image of a country that is in the forefront of gender equality: strong, emancipated women, who were the first in Europe to gain the vote, women with a high degree of political participation, full-time employment and a high educational level. On the other hand, on the basis of 'everyday experience', Finland is a country that in many ways appears more patriarchal and sexist than for instance, the other Nordic countries. I thought that comparing Finland with another capitalist, industrialized country with a welfare state structure, and at the same time a more active and radical feminist movement, would be a fruitful approach. For the purpose of comparison, I chose West Germany, partly for personal reasons, but also because I wanted to challenge the much cherished image of German women being tied to the 'three K's' (Kinder, Kirche, Küche).

Feminism and Diversity

Women's research has shown the great diversity of contemporary (as well as past) feminisms. For this reason, the concepts of 'feminism', 'women's movement' and 'new women's movement' are extremely problematic. 'Feminism' for example, is often defined in a broad way by scholars, especially by historians. Olive Banks (1981: 3) defines feminism as "all efforts to change women's position or prevailing images of women". This definition would include groups from the most militant and revolutionary feminists to more traditional or liberal-reformist women's organizations. This notion of feminism can also include both organizations and movements that see women as a social category and emphasize women's common interests, and those groups or organizations where the gender aspect interacts with class, race, etc. The definitions of feminism also vary over time and place: for example, during the last century the term was often used in relation to the middle-class based liberal feminists. In the United States, 'feminism' has often been used as a rather neutral collective name for several ideological orientations, i.e. more or less synonymously with 'women's movement' (cf. Ferree, 1987: 174). In Finland and Germany, especially in the 1970s, 'feminist' or 'feminism' were widely associated by the public with radical feminists and either seen as a synonym for 'man-haters' or as a glorification of biological and cultural womanhood. This has since partly changed and today 'feminist' has a somewhat broader meaning in both countries. I myself use a broad definition of 'feminism' in my study, and also use the concept of 'new feminism' to distinguish it from the 'old' feminism. I do so for analytical reasons and for reasons of clarification, although it is important for me to emphasize the continuity of women's protest.

Many Finnish and German researchers or authors on the new women's movement restrict their analysis to the 'autonomous' activists, projects, groups or organizations, i.e. to all those independent of political parties and other mixed-gender organizations (see e.g., Jallinoja, 1983; Juusola-Halonen, 1981; Schwarzer, 1981; Schenk, 1983). I prefer a broader conception that includes all forms of female movement activity that have contributed to the emergence of a new collective identity amongst women and a consciousness of the political relevance of gender (Jenson, 1985: 5-9). Thus, I also look at feminist activity within political parties and trade unions as well as on equality-orientated or reformist organizations outside the political parties. This is especially important in a country like Finland where women's political activity to a large extent was channelled through institutions and parties and where the traditional women's organizations have been fairly strong and independent (Dahlerup et al., 1985: 16ff., 32). If I left that out, much of Finnish feminism would remain invisible. Similarly in Germany, in spite of the fact that the 'autonomous' feminist movement was at the centre of the women's movement throughout the 1970s and 1980s, other fractions of the movement were also of importance. These included socialist-feminist and liberal-feminist groups both within and outside organizations or political parties (cf. Pausch,

1985; Pust et al.. 1983). The relations between the various women's organizations and groups were often divisive and antagonistic, but I think it is important to include all forms of feminism in a scholarly study of a social movement in all its heterogeneity and complexity.

For example, organized sex-role groups and organizations existed in both Finland and the Federal Republic of Germany in the 1960s, emphasizing issues like equal rights, day-care etc. In Finland, the sex-role debate had a strong impact on the state equality policy and the apparatus of 'state feminism' that was established during the 1970s and 1980s (cf. Bergman, 1989). A similar sex-role debate can be noted in the Federal Republic where several social-liberal action groups for emancipation and gender equality emerged towards the end of the 1960s (Schenk, 1983: 83, 86f.; Knafla et al., 1987: 93f.). Later, this activity was channelled either into the Social Democratic or the Liberal parties or into the autonomous feminist movement. The reason why many German researchers leave this kind of activity outside the scope of their study or treat it only as a 'primitive pre-stage' before the 'real thing' started in the 1970s, is probably that they view the new women's movement as both a part of and a critical reaction to the student movement. The activists in the gender equality or sex-role groups were not part of the student radicalism of the time. They were often somewhat older, employed or even professional women. This had an impact both on their political views and the strategies they used.

Empirical Studies of the Women's Movement

The empirical study of new social movements is a difficult task. Movements are seldom clearly defined social entities or already finished social processes. The women's movement is here with us now, in our minds and bodies. It is dynamic and constantly changing in structure and content. Even the choice of objects to study empirically is difficult, as social movements often lack formal organizations, lists of members, minutes of meetings, etc. Furthermore, the women's movement as an object of analysis is more than the sum of all organized women or women's organizations. Thus, the analysis should also include more 'diffuse' elements of the movement, like its cultural or ideological expressions in e.g. literature, art and research (Peterson, 1984; Dahlerup, 1986b: 6). Source material is not easy to obtain. You have to rely on press reports, the movement's own documentation (leaflets, newsletters, magazines etc.), interviews with activists, etc. It is, however, difficult to say whether a book, magazine, newsletter or a leaflet produced by the movement is 'representative' of the movement. Moreover, mass media presentation is extremely difficult to evaluate. Journalists often focus upon what they consider interesting for their audience, which is not necessarily representative of movement activists. Which period to study is another problem. Social movements experience ups and downs, expansion and stagnation. The goals and strategies of a movement might change over time, phases of self-reflexion and active, outwardgoing

Women's Peace March 1983.

spectacular actions take turns. The research methods used, the level of abstraction and the time-span of the analysis determine to a great extent which sides of the movement are made visible.

Another crucial question is whether it is possible, or even desirable, to study a social movement like the new women's movement, from inside academia and, in addition, to do so in a neutral, non-attached way. I attended a conference in Germany for scholars on the new social movements and there the question was posed as to why academic studies of the women's movement are so few in number. One movement activist (obviously not considering this to be a problem) replied: "Don't study the women's movement—be an activist instead!" When a movement starts to reflect on itself, it is in danger of ceasing to be a political movement. One could ask whether this is the reason for the present trend of founding archives for the new women's movement and setting up research projects? Are women's movement researchers the archeologists of the movement?

Moreover, I think that as researchers we should not separate our feminist commitment from the scholarly study of feminism as a social movement. To be able to study the women's movement you have to be familiar with that movement. You need your own experiences of the movement. You have to have shared both the joys and the sorrows of the movement. Traditional social scientists may say that you need emotional distance to study any social phenomenon. I think, especially in this case, that it is indeed a prerequisite for you as a researcher to have personal experience of the movement. Comparative studies are difficult also in this respect because you seldom are able to 'know' more than one or two countries or movements. In my case, I was fortunate in being able to benefit from a familiarity with both Finnish and German conditions. At the same time, the years I spent in Germany gave me much needed distance from my own country which I also consider necessary. Thus, thanks to my research visit to Germany I was able to look upon Finnish society with partially new eyes.

The closeness to the phenomenon studied and one's own activity should, however, be balanced with a critical distance and self-reflexion to the movement and to oneself as a feminist researcher (Becker-Schmidt, 1985, calls this 'Perspektivenwechsel'). Last but not least: no one can analyze all sides of feminism or interpret them in the 'one and only' way. One researcher, even if she is simultaneously a participant in the movement, can only give her personal contribution to the collective theoretical discussion and thereby, at best, combine an insider's and an outsider's view (Ferree et al., 1985: ix).

How to Study the Women's Movement—'cases' Finland / Germany

Broadly speaking, the women's movement can be studied in three different ways: firstly, you can focus on a structural-political analysis and theories of social change. In this case, you are interested in those macro-level structural phenomena which stimulate or produce the movement. You look upon the social conditions for the emergence of the movement and examine how the movement's goals, structure, strategies and relations to its social environment are affected by the wider structural processes and conditions.

Secondly, you can analyze the ideological discourses of the movement, for example through a qualitative contents analysis of the movement's bulletins, leaflets and magazines or through discussions with activists and participant observation (cf. Glennon, 1979).

The third approach concentrates on the internal dynamics of the movement. This approach has as its starting point the fact that although social movements emerge as expressions of structural conditions they are never a mere reflection of these conditions. Movements live a life of their own and have a dynamic of their own. The movement can be seen both as an individual and collective learning process. Thus, the internal changes and the interaction within the movement are analyzed as well as its various fractions and the motivation and consciousness of its activists (cf. Haukaa, 1982: 13f.; Holter, 1982: 35f.; Ryan, 1989).

In my research the emphasis is clearly on the discussion of the structural conditions of the movement. However, in addition to the focus upon socio-economic and political structures and an analysis of change in the social environment, I try to balance the study with qualitative data (interviews, discussions, reinterpretation of publications and above all, personal experiences and observations) which give valuable information about the motivation and consciousness of movement activists as well as about the changes in the ideological trends of the movement.

In many ways, throughout the 1970s and for a large part of the 1980s, the Finnish and the German women's movements have been complete contrasts. The Finnish movement has been relatively integrated into the fabric of the political system and the public apparatus and has represented a moderate and reformist ideology (cf. Jallinoja, 1986). Contrary to this, the German movement has advocated a markedly separatist strategy ('Autonomie') combined with a radical ideological orientation and a general mistrust of the state's ability and willingness to improve women's situation (cf. Brand et al., 1986: 118-154; Knafla et al., 1987).

The participation of women in the public sphere has long roots in Finland. The traditionally high level of women's political and labor market participation undoubtedly contributed to the late start of the new feminist movement in its autonomous form. Although the process of modernization started late in Finland, it changed Finnish society very dramatically and rapidly. The comparatively late starting point for the new social movements, including the feminist movement, depended in part on a major shift in the economy from an agriculturally-based to an industrially-based system of production in the 1960s and 1970s. Obviously, these factors had an impact on the ideological aims and strategies of the new Finnish women's movement which helps to explain why so-called 'state feminism' has distinguished that movement to such a large extent.

The change in the life-situation of German women in the 1960s and 1970s was more abrupt and fundamental than it was for Finnish women. In this period, middle-class women started entering the universities in larger groups than ever before and ceased considering employed work after marriage a completely impossible thought. The clash between the norms of traditional femininity and womanhood on the one hand and the demands and expectations created by the societal changes for middle-class women on the other hand led to the bursting out of feminism. Female employment amongst married women and mothers also rose steadily in Finland during the 1960s. However, Finnish women's early integration into the public sphere made the effects of those changes relatively weaker than in Germany.

In Germany, the anti-authoritarian New Left movement of the 1960s and the 'extra-parliamentary opposition' had a deep impact on the political culture and the emergence of broad sub- and countercultures of the 1970s and 1980s. This tradition is clearly to be seen in the German feminist movement with its strong anti-state orientation and its distrust of traditional politics and power structures. In Finland, on the contrary, the New Left and the anti-authoritarian student movement were shortlived and weak. Instead, the culturally orientated student movement of the 1960s (which included the sex-rôle movement) was rapidly incorporated into the political parties during the following decade. In addition, another feature of the time was the strong commitment amongst many Finnish students and intellectuals—including women—to the 'old left', and especially to the orthodox Moscow-orientated fraction of the Communist party. This was probably due to the fact that this group was seen as the sole representative of a radical opposition to the establishment. The party-politization of protest effectively suppressed and postponed the emergence of a feminist movement in a Western sense. As a consequence, the Finnish women's movement was, for a long time, relatively small, weak and more integrated into the public sphere and mainstream party politics than elsewhere. Typically, the new social movements in Finland are often tied to more traditional types of organisations. Loose and non-hierarchical organizations scarcely have roots in Finland. Direct action and civil disobedience have not been strong, neither in the feminist movements, nor in other "alternative" or new social movements (Parvikko 1990; Paastela 1987).

Finnish feminists have mainly channelled their political demands through the state. In this, they have considered the state equal policies as a conciliator and mediator of the gender conflict (Holli, 1990: 69). This form of Finnish 'state feminism' which started in the 1960s, is still a predominant trend in Finland, especially in the party-political women's organizations. A critical view of the state is new in Finland and has only been expressed very recently in the feminist movement and in feminist writing (cf. Parvikko, 1990).

Indeed, new feminism in the form we know it in many other countries, did not start to grow in Finland to any real extent until the end of the 1970s or the beginning of the 1980s. The first post-war collective feminist protests were channelled into the influential 'sex-role movement' of the 1960s. As such, those protests emerged at the same time as in many other parts of the Western world (i.e., in the late 1960s), but in those days Finnish protests were more reformist in character, emphasizing equal rights and obligations of both women and men. In Germany, the feminist movement arose out of a confrontation with men in the left-wing student movement. However, when the more radical feminist movement started to expand in Finland towards the end of the 1970s, the student movement already had lost much of its dynamic thrust.

An important catalyst for the Western feminist movements around the end of the 1960s and early 1970s was the issue of abortion and women's right to control their own bodies. The Finnish sex-role movement also demanded a reform of the law on abortion. Legislation on this issue was enacted in 1970 in the absence of strong feminist struggle. As a result, instead of being treated as a women's issue, abortion was either defined in medical terms or seen as a question of social and regional equality. For this reason, sexuality and 'body politics' were for a long time almost 'non-issues' in the Finnish movement. The situation was quite different in West Germany, where the feminist movement took shape in the early 1970s in the context of a massive struggle by women for abortion on demand. The strong emphasis of German feminism on autonomy, i.e. separatism from men and male-dominated institutions or organizations, may be seen as a result of German women's experiences of this struggle as well as of the sexism in the New Left movement.

In my study I also look at why and how the women's movements in both countries have changed in recent years. I argue that for several external and internal reasons (which cannot be developed here), some 'convergence' is now in evidence and thus, the picture given above should be treated cautiously. In this respect, the German movement has witnessed a development from autonomy to a higher degree of institutionalization and a partially new view of 'party politics' and the 'state' (Ferree, 1987: 184f.) while in Finland, the trend has been from integration to a more pluralistic system (Bergman et al. 1988). The core of Finnish feminism is still the old 'Union for Women's Rights' (originally founded in 1892 and 'radicalized' since the mid-1970s). At the same time, however, autonomous groups, projects and networks both within and outside institutions and organizations are more visible than before and many forms of feminism known in other Western countries since the 1970s have recently been established in Finland. A number of examples of women organizing without men and for each other exist today: women's centers, women's coffee-houses, crisis phone lines, women's publishers, etc. On the other hand, German women have started the 'long march through the institutions' entering male-dominated organizations and institutions in larger numbers. Currently, Germany has a growing 'gender equality industry' with equality officers and consultants in local councils, companies and organizations and feminists address their demands increasingly to public authorities or cooperate with them in issues concerning e.g., social welfare provisions and family policy.

Concluding Remarks

Because of the large number of similarities between the new women's movements in many Western countries, it is often too easy to overlook the full extent of the differences that also exist. I have tried to shed light on a number of features characteristic of the feminist movement in two countries in Europe, i.e. Finland and Germany, and the differences between these two movements, their ideologies, goals and strategies. I try to explain these differences by looking at the structural and institutional conditions for the emergence and development of the women's movements in these two countries. Clearly, women's movements take shape differently in different societies depending on socio-economic, political and cultural features, and the position attained by women within their prevailing society.

I also try to analyze in what way and to what extent the national political culture and specific 'protest traditions' have an impact on the strategies used by the social movements in the two countries. My starting-point is that social movements are, at one and the same time, tied to a society's political culture and values and, simultaneously, engaged in a struggle to change these. In addition, the strategies or counter-strategies used by the larger 'society' in the interaction with protest movements also differ. In Finland, radical movements have often been 'depoliticized' and 'disarmed' through a process of cooptation and institutionalization. In Germany, a more repressive attitude on the part of the state and the 'establishment' has increased the movement's hostility towards those in power. Thus, German feminists did not regard the state and the public authorities as an instrument for improving women's position in society.

Finnish women's deepseated trust in the state is reflected in women's researchers' analyses of the ideology and practices of the welfare state. The view of a 'women-friendly' welfare state (see e.g., Simonen, 1990) is thus common amongst feminist researchers in Finland. Together with the other Nordic countries, Finland is often considered to be in the forefront of gender equality and welfare provisions. The Finnish gender system and 'gender contract' as well as the cultural traditions and the political system differ in many respects from those in Germany. Finnish women enjoy a number of social rights that facilitate the role of women as both wage-earners and mothers. The cultural ideology of motherhood alongside the principles and the infrastructure of the welfare state (from e.g., parental rights and organized day-care to closing times for nurseries and schools or meal provision in schools) differ in the two countries. Different attitudes towards the organization of social reproduction and public responsibility for caring may also partly explain the differences in the goals and strategies of the women's movements.

The equality reforms introduced by the authorities in Finland have primarily focussed on the interests of employed women and mothers. The current 'policy of equality' is more concerned with social and family policies than with labor market policy. Reforms with a positive impact on the position of women in the labor market have mostly been of a symbolic character, as e.g. the law on gender equality. 'Affirmative action' and 'positive discrimination', for example quotas for women, the improvement of women's career prospects or the reintegration of women in the labor market after interruption because of family responsibilities have been non-issues in Finland. Unlike the situation in Germany, the official policy of equality in Finland builds on gender-neutral concepts, which do not explicitly favor women.

References

Banks, Olive (1981), *Faces of Feminism. A Study of Feminism as a Social Movement*. Oxford: Martin Robertson.

Becker-Schmidt, Regina (1985), "Probleme feministischer Theorie und Empirie in den Sozialwissenschaften". *Feministische Studien*, 4, no 2, pp. 93-104.

Bergman, Solveig & Vellamo Vehkakoski (1988), "Die Frauenbewegung in Finnland. Eine Ehe zwischen 'Staatsfeminismus' und Politik der Unterschiede". *Frauenbewegungen in der Welt*. Band 1, Westeuropa. Argument-Sonderband AS 150. Hg. von der Autonomen Frauenredaktion. Hamburg: Argument-Verlag, pp. 77-94.

Bergman, Solveig (1989), "Ein frauenfreundlicher Staat? Zum Verhältnis zwischen Frauen und dem finnischen Wohlfahrtsstaat". Ursula Müller & Hiltraud Schmidt-Waldherr (Hg.), *Frauen-*

SozialKunde. Wandel und Differenzierung von Lebensformen und Bewusstsein. Bielefeld: AJZ, pp. 82-101.

Bergman, Solveig (forthcoming), *Den nya kvinnorörelsen som social rörelse. En komparativ studie av nyfeminismen in Finland och Förbundsrepubliken Tyskland*, Ph.D. thesis, Finland, Åbo Akademi.

Bouchier, David (1983), *The Feminist Challenge. The Movement for Women's Liberation in Britain and the USA*. London: MacMillan.

Brand, Karl-Werner et al. (1986), *Aufbruch in eine andere Gesellschaft. Neue soziale Bewegungen in der Bundesrepublik*. Frankfurt/M: Campus.

Chafetz, Janet Salzman & Anthony Gary Dworkin (1986), *Female Revolt - Women's Movements in World and Historical Perspective*. Totova, N.J.: Rowman & Allanheld.

Clemens, Bärbel (1985), "Bürgerin im Staat oder Mutter in der Gemeinde? Zum Politik- und Staatsverständnis der bürgerlichen Frauenbewegung." *Beiträge zur feministischen Theorie und Praxis*, 8, no 13, pp. 49-57.

Dahlerup, Drude & Brita Gulli (1985), "Women's Organizations in the Nordic Countries: lack of force or counterforce?" Elina Haavio-Mannila et al. (ed.), *Unfinished Democracy. Women in the Nordic Politics*. Oxford: Pergamon Press, pp. 6-36.

Dahlerup, Drude (ed.) (1986a), *The New Women's Movement. Feminism and Political Power in Europe and the USA*. London: Sage.

Dahlerup, Drude (1986b), "Introduction". Drude Dahlerup (ed.), *The New Women's Movement. Feminism and Political Power in Europe and the USA*. London: Sage, pp. 1-25.

Ferree, Myra Marx & Beth B. Hess (1985), *Controversy and Coalition: The New Feminist Movement*. Boston, Mass.: Twayne Press.

Ferree, Myra Marx (1987), "Equality and Autonomy: Feminist Politics in the United States and West Germany". Mary Fainsod Katzenstein & Carol McClurg Mueller (eds.), *The Women's Movements of the United States and Western Europe*. Philadephia: Temple University Press, pp. 172-195.

Glennon, Lynda M (1979), *Women and Dualism. A Sociology of Knowledge Analysis*. New York: Longman.

Haukaa, Runa (1982), *Bak slagordene. Den nye kvinnebevegelsen i Norge*. Oslo: Pax.

Holli, Anne Maria (1990), "Why the State? Reflections on the Politics of the Finnish Equality Movement Association 9". Marja Keränen (ed.), *Finnish Undemocracy. Essays on Gender and Politics*, The Finnish Political Science Association, Jyväskylä: Gummerus, pp. 69-88.

Holter, Harriet (1982), "Kvinnevillkår og fellesskapsformer". Harriet Holter (red.), *Kvinner i fellesskap*. Oslo: Universitetsforlaget, pp. 15-41.

Jallinoja, Riitta (1983), *Suomalaisen naisasialiikkeen taistelukaudet* [The Campaign Periods of the Finnish Women's Movement]. Porvoo: WSOY.

Jallinoja, Riitta (1986), "Independence or Integration: The Women's Movement and Political Parties in Finland". Drude Dahlerup (ed.), *The New Women's Movement. Feminism and Political Power in Europe and the USA*. London: Sage, pp. 158-178.

Jenson, Jane (1985), "Struggling for Identity: The Women's Movement and the State in Western Europe". *West European Politics*, 8, no 4, pp. 5-18.

Juusola-Halonen, Elina (1981), "The Women's Liberation Movement in Finland". *Women's Studies International Quarterly*, 4, no. 4, pp. 453-460.

Katzenstein, Mary Fainsod & Carol McClurg Mueller (1987) (eds.), *The Women's Movements of the United States and Western Europe*. Philadelphia: Temple University Press.

Knafla, Leonore & Christine Kulke (1987), "15 Jahre neue Frauenbewegung". Roland Roth & Dieter Rucht (Hg.), *Neue soziale Bewegungen in der Bundesrepublik Deutschland. Schriftenreihe*, Band 252. Bonn: Bundeszentrale für politische Bildung, pp. 89-108.

Kontos, Silvia (1986), "Modernisierung der Subsumtionspolitik? Die Frauenbewegung in den Theorien neuer sozialen Bewegungen". *Feministische Studien*, 4, no 2, pp. 34-49.

Metz-Göckel, Sigrid (1987), "Die zwei (un)geliebten Schwestern. Zum Verhältnis von Frauenbewegung und Frauenforschung im Diskurs der neuen sozialen Bewegungen". Ursula Beer (Hg.), *Klasse-Geschlecht. Feministische Gesellschaftsanalyse und Wissenschaftskritik*. Bielefeld: AJZ, pp. 25-57.

Mueller, Carol (1983), *Women's Movement Success and the Success of Social Movement Theory*. Wellesley College. Center for Research on Women. Working Paper No. 110.

Paastela, Jukka (1987), *Finland's New Social Movements in a Frozen Political System*, Paper presented in the ECPR workshop "New Social Movements and the Political System", Amsterdam, 10-16 April, 1987.

Parvikko, Tuija (1990), "Conceptions of Gender Equality, Similarity and Difference", Marja Keränen (ed.), *Finnish Undemocracy. Essays on Gender and Politics*, The Finnish Political Science Association, Jyväskylä: Gummerus, pp. 89-111.

Pausch, Wolfgang (1985), *Die Entwicklung der sozialdemokratischen Frauenorganisationen*. Inauguraldisseration zur Erlangung des Grades eines Doktors der Philosophie im FB Gesellschaftswissenschaften der J.W.Goethe-Universität Frankfurt/M.

Peterson, Abby (1984), "Den nya kvinnorörelsens betydelse". *Kvinnovetenskaplig tidskrift*, 5, no 1, pp. 66-68.

Pust, Carola & Petra Reichert, Anne Wenzel u.a. (1983), *Frauen in der BRD. Beruf, Familie, Gewerkschaften, Frauenbewegung*. Hamburg: VSA.

Raschke, Joachim (1985), *Soziale Bewegungen*. Frankfurt/M.: Campus.

Ryan, Barbara E. (1989), "Ideological Purity and Feminism: The U.S. Women's Movement from 1966-1975". *Gender & Society*, 3, no 2, pp. 239-257.

Schenk, Herrad (1983), *Die feministische Herausforderung. 150 Jahre Frauenbewegung in Deutschland*. München: C.H. Beck.

Schwarzer Alice (1981), *So fing es an! 10 Jahre Frauenbewegung*. Köln: Emma-Verlag.

Simonen, Leila (1990), *Contradictions of the Welfare State, Women and Caring*, Acta Universitatis Tamperensis, ser. A, vol. 295, Tampere: University of Tampere.

Vries, Petra de (1981), "Feminism in the Netherlands". *Women's Studies International Quarterly*, 4, no 4, pp. 389-409.

Contributors

Solveig Bergman is a politics magister (MA, social sciences) and postgraduate researcher in sociology, Åbo Academy, Finland. She is Nordic Coordinator of Women's Studies 1991-93. She is the author of *Women and the Scientific Community* (1985) (in Swedish). Her publications also include articles on the new women's movement, e.g. *Die Frauenbewegung in Finnland* (1988) co-author with Vehkakoski. She has also published *Ein frauenfreundlicher Staat?* (1989), and *Post-War Feminism in Finland* (1989) (in English).

Ann-Dorte Christensen studied at the University Center of Aalborg, Denmark and holds a degree in social science. Her Ph.D. dissertation is on *Women in Social Movements—their Organisations, their Identities, their Power.* Currently, she is working for The Committee of Feminist Research as a Research Coordinator and holds a part time research grant with which she works on a project called "Political Culture, Counterculture and Women's Culture". This project is part of a larger research project on *The Changing Democracy—Political Participation, Autonomy and Self-Management.*

Yvonne Hirdman, professor of women's history, Department of History, University of Gothenburg, Sweden. Member of the Swedish Commission on the Study of Power and Democracy 1985-1990. Furthermore, she has been involved in the foundation "Forum för kvinnoforskning" in Stockholm since 1979. Works about the Women's League in the Swedish Social Democratic Party, the "hidden utopian agenda" of the welfare state and theoretical reflections on the gender system.

Karin Lützen studied folklore at the University of Copenhagen, Denmark. Her main topic is in history of sexuality, especially homosexuality. She held a fellowship at the Women's Studies Centre at the University of Copenhagen and did research in "Philanthropic Spinsters and the Creation of the Modern Family". She is author of *Hvad hjertet begærer* (1986), translated into Norwegian with an epilogue by Kari Melby and into German. She is also author of *At prøve lykken* (1988) (in Danish). Recently, she has written a volume of a broader work called "The History of Europe" (forthcoming). Her current research is "What is a Home without a Spinster?".

Kari Melby is a historian and the head of the Centre for Women's Research at the University of Trondheim, Norway. Her main theoretical topic is the deconstruction of the dichotomy of the ideological ideas of equality and difference. Her empirical field of work is Norwegian teachers, nurses and housewives and their organizations. In her research she has shown the presence and variations of the ideological ideas within different groups of women. She is the co-author of *Det kriminelle kjønn* (1980), and of *Oppe først og sist i seng. Husarbeid i Norge fra 1850 til idag* (1985), and author of *Kall og kamp. Norsk Sykepleierforbunds historie* (1990).

Hanne Rimmen Nielsen studied history and political science at the University of Aarhus, Denmark. She has held a scholarship at the History Department and the Women's Research Center in Aarhus (1987-89). Her Ph.D. dissertation is about *Christian and Competent Schoolmistresses. The Space and Ideas of Women's Culture* (in Danish). She has also published articles about the local Women's Movement and the Danish Women's Society in Aarhus. Currently, she holds a research grant from the Danish Committee of Feminist Research and works at a project called *Generations in the Women's Movement. A Historical Analysis of Two Generations in the Danish Women's Movement 1910-50*. She is a member of the umbrella project "The Women's Movements Project".

Joyce Outshoorn studied political science and contemporary history at the University of Amsterdam, Holland, where she was senior lecturer in political science. Since 1987, she has been professor of women's studies at The University of Leyden. Her current research is on women's movements, public policy and women, feminist theory.

Jane Rendall is a senior lecturer at the University of York, United Kingdom, teaching at the History Department and the Centre for Women's Studies there. She is also book review editor for *Gender and History*. Her publications include *Origins of Modern Feminism. Women in Britain, France and the United States, 1780-1860* (1985). *Equal or Different* (1987) (ed. with Susan Mendus), *Sexuality and Subordination* (1989). She is now researching women's writing in Britain in the period 1780-1840 and the gendered discourses of political theory in the same period.

Leila J. Rupp teaches women's history at Ohio State University, USA. She is the author of *Mobilizing Women for War: German and American Propaganda 1939-1945*, co-editor with Barbara Miller Lane of *Nazi Ideology Before 1933: A Documentation*, and co-author with Verta Taylor of *Survival in the Doldrums: The American Women's Rights Movement 1945 to the 1960s*. She is currently engaged in research on the history of the international women's movement.

Aino Saarinen, a sociologist and political scientist. She works as a junior fellow at the University of Tampere, Finland where she is completing a sociological dissertation *Feminist Research—an Intellectual Adventure?* She has published *Vapautta Naisille!* (1985) (Freedom of Women!) in Finnish and articles on feminist theory. In cooperation with Eva Hänninen-Salmelin and Marja Keränen (1987) she has edited *Kvinnor och makt. Kvinnoperspektiv på välfärdsstaten.* Currently, she is working on a research project *Women's Political Culture and the Struggle for Suffrage. A Study on Women's Mobilisation in Tampere, Finland.* She is a member of the umbrella projects: "Women's Tampere" and "The Gender System of the Welfare State".

Verta Taylor is a sociologist who teaches courses on women, gender, and social movements at Ohio State University, USA. She is co-author with Leila J. Rupp of *Survival in the Doldrums: The American Women's Rights Movement 1945 to the 1960s* and co-editor (with Laurel Richardson) of *Feminist Frontiers II: Rethinking Sex, Gender and Society.* In addition to her continuing research on the women's movement, she is currently writing a book on postpartum depression and the social control of mothering.

The Women's Movement Project

The Women's Movement Project was founded in 1989 as an interdisciplinary "umbrella" project. The main purpose of The Women's Movement Project is to be a forum for junior and senior scholars' research on the Vomen's Movement.

In this forum we discuss the empirical, theoretical and methodological approaches to the study of the Women's Movement and organizations. The project initiates activities such as conferences, the collection of archival material and interviews, production of bibliographies and a guide to the archives of women's history.

The Women's History Archive at The State Library i Aarhus, represented by Eva Lous, already holds archival material from different women's organizations, notably the archives of The Danish Women's Society since 1871. However, archival material from the new women's movements is still scarce. One of the aims of this project is to encourage the activists of the new women's movement to deposit material about the new women's movements in the collection.

The addresses of the participants in The Women's Movement Project are as follows:

CEKVINA - Center for Feminist Research and Gender Studies, University of Aarhus, Finlandsgade 26 B, DK-8200 Aarhus N, phone: 86 16 58 55

Tayo Andreasen, Tjelevej 1, DK-8240 Risskov, phone: 86 21 09 47

Anette Borchorst, Institute of Political Science, University of Aarhus, Universitetsparken, DK-8000 Aarhus C, phone: 86 13 01 11, fax: 86 13 98 39

Hilda Rømer Christensen, Ny Munkegade 70, DK-8000 Aarhus C, phone: 86 18 26 82

Hanne Marlene Dahl, Ingerslevs Boulevard 24, DK-8000 Aarhus C, phone: 86 18 43 10

Drude Dahlerup, Institute of Political Science, University of Aarhus, Universitetsparken, DK-8000 Aarhus C, phone: 86 13 01 11, fax: 86 13 98 39

Eva Lous, The Women's History Archive at the State Library in Aarhus, Universitetsparken, DK-8000 Aarhus C, phone: 86 12 20 22, fax: 86 13 27 04

Hanne Rimmen Nielsen, Montanagade 45 A, DK-8000 Aarhus C
phone 86 19 00 60